William H Eyre

Catholic Doctrine and Discipline

Simply Explained

William H Eyre

Catholic Doctrine and Discipline
Simply Explained

ISBN/EAN: 9783744649070

Printed in Europe, USA, Canada, Australia, Japan

Cover: Foto ©Lupo / pixelio.de

More available books at **www.hansebooks.com**

CATHOLIC DOCTRINE
AND DISCIPLINE

SIMPLY EXPLAINED

BY

PHILIP BOLD

REVISED, AND IN PART EDITED, BY
FATHER EYRE, S.J.

LONDON

KEGAN PAUL, TRENCH, TRÜBNER & CO., Ltd

1896

APPROBATION OF THE MOST REVEREND THE
ARCHBISHOP OF ALGIERS.

*Je suis heureux dejoindre mon approbation à celle de
l'Eminentissime Cardinal Vaughan.*

+ AUGUSTE ARCHEVÊQUE D'ALGER.

INTRODUCTION.

AMID the whirl of the manifold occupations and pleasures of life, religion—sterling religion, abiding in our heart, and showing itself in our actions,—too frequently comes to be forgotten. Yet if we have not known it as we ought, or if we have relinquished it for worldly pursuits, unaware of their worthlessness, religion awaits us ever, from our earliest wanderings, to give us hope and strength, and to bring our soul into harmony with all that is pure, consoling, and able to fit us for happiness eternal. It unfolds to us the secret of dwelling in peace with God, with ourselves, and with mankind; teaching us how we may live tranquilly in the consciousness of fulfilling our duty in this world, and of amassing infinite treasures for the world to come.

We, who now strive after transitory enjoyments and are occupied with ambitious schemes, could find with much ease, in the love and practice of our holy religion, the peace of our own conscience, as well as the temporal and eternal welfare of those nearest and dearest to us; whereas we too often make painful efforts to satisfy ourselves or others with fleeting pleasures or mere worldly advantages—a thankless task, indeed, proffering but a vain reward. For never was there a time since we became capable of feeling the sweet influence of religion, when it was not our duty to study and implant deeply in our mind and heart those truths and precepts regarding God, our neighbour, and ourselves, which are meant to direct our footsteps throughout life, and lead us onward to the bourne of perfected holiness in eternity.

Now, we cannot possess true faith without knowing and understanding what we are called upon to believe; and this knowledge must be gained, first and foremost, by the teaching of our parents and instructors. "Teach your children that they meditate on My words,"[1] said God, in the Old Law. And He enjoined His people to study His precepts, saying, "Lay up these My words in your hearts and minds, and hang them for a sign on your hands, and place them between your eyes."[2] Again, we must obtain this knowledge from the pastors of the Church, for our Lord commanded His Apostles, saying: "Teach ye all nations;"[3] and, "Preach the gospel to every creature. . . . He that believeth not shall be condemned."[4] We have, therefore, the twofold obligation of learning from those above us, and of teaching those dependent on us. Thus, while ample means are afforded us of knowing what is necessary for our salvation, we are answerable for the right employment of the talents entrusted to us, not for our own use only, but also for the benefit of others.

This reasoning applies, of course, to any enterprise in life. If we would become adepts in a calling suitable to our abilities, we must learn from some one possessing the knowledge we are desirous of obtaining, since, if we do not

[1] Deut. xi.   [2] Deut. xi. 18–20.
[3] Matt. xxviii. 19.   [4] Mark xvi. 15, 16.

profit by the opportunities placed within our reach, we lose the recompense of proficiency in the art we fain would cultivate. So is it with the knowledge of religion, which is a science to be learnt from those who have made it their pursuit, and whose vocation it is to expound Scripture and Tradition. Ignorance of religion, therefore, is sinful when voluntary, for if we wilfully neglect to instruct ourselves in God's laws and to make appeal to Him in prayer for the gift of understanding them, we do offence to Him and wrong to ourselves. Knowledge of religion communicates fuller power to withstand evil; it teaches us to show intelligent resistance to attacks made against the true faith; and to live in more complete accord with our fellow-creatures, while working for their salvation as well as our own, rendering thereby just service to God, to ourselves, and to mankind. We should also enshrine in our memory the truth that those among us who have most leisure very often stand in greater need of religion, because they who indulge in idleness are more liable to be assailed by temptations of various kinds. Consequently, we never ought to let precious moments slip by unheeded and beyond recovery, but should study, in whatever position we occupy, to make the most of our opportunities ; utilizing our time to the best advantage, and remembering that we have our mission to fulfil in the service of our Maker.

The simple explanations of Catholic Doctrine and Practice contained in this book are an humble attempt to make the one true Church of Christ more clearly apprehended, and more generally known.

CONTENTS.

CATHOLIC DOCTRINE AND DISCIPLINE

SIMPLY EXPLAINED.

———

CHAPTER I.

THE CHRISTIAN DOCTRINE AND CREED.

CHRISTIAN doctrine is divided into three parts. The first teaches the truths revealed to us by God, which we are required by Him to accept and believe : the substance of these is found in the Apostles' Creed. The second part explains our duties toward God, our neighbour, and ourselves : these are contained in the Commandments of God and of the Church. The third part treats of grace and the means of obtaining it, by prayer and participation in the holy Sacraments.

As far as actual words are concerned, a large number of those who " protested " against the faith and separated themselves from us, under the general appellation of Protestants, use the same Creed and the same Commandments of God as ourselves. Our different understanding of Christian doctrine is based on the fact, that Protestants admit of no infallible authority in doctrine or rule of faith other than the written word of God. We, in addition, believe in the authority of the Church established by our Lord and guarded by Him against error according to His promises, which to us,

Christian doctrine.

B

is sufficient justification for the sanction of those dogmas and practices assumed by Protestants to be deviations from what our Saviour instituted.

Apostles' Creed.

The Apostles' Creed is a profession of faith or declaration of religious belief; being a summary of dogmatic truths taught by our Redeemer to His Apostles for the whole Church. It is an expanded form of that used from the Apostles' time, the substance of which is by some supposed to have been by them compiled before they separated to preach the Gospel throughout the universe.

Nicene Creed.

The Nicene Creed, which was composed in the year 325 at the Council of Nicæa held against the Arian heresy, is a development simply of the Apostles' Creed. This declaratory form was afterwards added to, and is now recited at, Mass on Sundays and many other days.

Fundamental truths of the Creed.

The fundamental truths expressed in the Apostles' Creed, are—the existence of God, the chief mysteries of our faith, and the origin and end of man. These are obligatory for every Christian to know and understand. That is to say, belief in all these principal truths is indispensable, and some knowledge of them, greater or less, is requisite, according to the opportunities and capacity of each individual; any voluntary neglect in learning about them being, according to circumstances, more or less culpable.

Component parts of the Creed.

The Creed is divided into twelve articles, which may be subdivided into three parts. The first article treats of God the Father and the work of creation. From the second to the seventh article inclusive, our attention is directed towards God the Son and the work of Redemption. The remaining five articles speak of God the Holy Ghost and the work of sanctification.

CHAPTER II.

"I believe in God the Father Almighty, Creator of Heaven and earth."

In saying "I believe in God," we signify our belief in the existence of one God, perfect beyond all we can conceive :— a profession of faith that each must make individually; and therefore it is expressed in the singular, because not admitting of our making it for others. *Belief in the existence of God.*

We know by the Scriptures, that God manifested Himself to Adam and Eve, to Moses and the Prophets, as recounted, with other historical proofs, in so many books of the Old Testament. These writings were not only recognized as authentic by the Evangelists, who continually quoted from them, but by our Lord Himself. His references are repeated by the Apostles, and His birth, life, and death were predicted therein. *Existence of God proved by Scripture.*

Faith in God is inherent in humanity, springing from nature and reason. It makes us feel the necessity of believing that there must be a Divinity,—a supreme Will,— an Almighty Intelligence,—who has formed the heavens, the world, and all therein contained: for the effect cannot exist without the cause, and it is demonstrable that the world has not always existed. *Existence of God proved by reason.*

The harmony, order, and wonders of nature, and of the *Existence of*

God proved by nature.

human race refute any theory of spontaneous generation, and proclaim the existence of a primary and omnipotent Being, who, as the necessary and independent cause of all things, possesses infinite power and perfection, and is therefore God. He, by His own might and Divinity, is, and was, and ever will be, God through all eternity, and from Him emanates all that is good and beautiful and true.

God is a spirit, pure, immutable and entirely distinct from anything material, "and they that adore Him, must adore Him in spirit and in truth." [1]

Existence of God proved by conscience.

We have faith in God through our own consciences, giving us the moral sense to realize duty and guilt,—to distinguish right from wrong, and to acknowledge the just recompense or chastisement our actions deserve. It is a natural law engraven in our hearts by the hand of God,— coming as a whisper from the soul,—leading mankind to admit that there is a sensible difference between vice and virtue, wrong and right.

Existence of God proved by a natural aspiration of the soul.

The soul of man, spiritual and immortal as it is, has the faculty of spiritual intelligence as well as of feeling, elevating the whole being above all other living creatures, whose principle of life does not lift them so high. And as we can conceive it, so do we possess an unconquerable desire for perpetual happiness, that we cannot find in this transitory life,—a desire that teaches us there is a God from whom every blessing flows, and towards whom our most holy aspirations tend.

Existence of God proved by the universality of faith in God.

Faith in God is manifest in all nations and in all ages, for no country is without religion. "Cast your eyes over the face of the earth, you may there find cities without

[1] John iv. 24.

ramparts, without education, without magistrature ; people without fixed habitation, without property, without money ; but you will nowhere find a city where the knowledge of God does not obtain."[1]

In saying "the Father Almighty," we signify our belief that in God there is a first Person, called the Father, who is the principle or origin, from whom proceed the second and third Divine Persons.

First Person of God.

Faith teaches us, that there are, in one Divine nature, three distinct Persons, equal in perfection and omnipotence, immutability and indivisibility. This first mystery of the Catholic religion, from which the two other principal mysteries proceed, is called that of the Holy Trinity.

Belief in the mystery of the Holy Trinity.

The word "mystery" is used in the Christian doctrine to express the truths God has revealed and we must believe, albeit we cannot completely explain or comprehend. That a thing is not within the grasp of our intellect, is no reason why it should not exist ; for how numerous are the secrets of nature, inexplicable and in their own way even mysterious, and withal accepted as undoubted facts ! —It is fitting therefore we should believe, and that most firmly, mysteries of the Christian doctrine revealed to us by God, and which oblige us to recognize His almighty dominion over our intelligence. It is only reasonable that we should receive with faith the teachings of God, whose perfection and omnipotence are unlimited and infallible, instead of refusing to accept mysteries of the Christian religion simply because we cannot fathom them. Such refusal, in the case of many, even of the most highly gifted, arises undoubtedly from prejudice, insufficient knowledge,

Mysteries, and belief in them.

[1] Plutarch.

hasty conclusion, egotism, or personal motive in accepting what is contrary to the precepts of our holy religion.

Equality of Persons in the Holy Trinity.

In the Blessed Trinity—the mystery of one God in three Persons—the distinction of Persons in no way separates their unity of nature, Divinity, intelligence, power, and will. Though power and creation are more specially attributed to the Father; wisdom and redemption to the Son; and holiness and sanctification to the Holy Ghost;—all these qualities belong equally to the three Persons as being one God. Therefore, while we pray to the Father, to Jesus Christ, or to the Holy Spirit separately, we address all three Persons collectively. When we appeal, for example, to some one's intelligence, power, or feelings, which are three distinct qualities, we still appeal only to one individual: further, for the execution of any action, there are brought into play by one person three agencies,—namely: thought, will, and movement. An equilateral triangle is another illustration emblematic of the Trinity, in that there are three angles, perfectly distinct and equal, forming only one figure. Therefore, in speaking of the Father, or of the Son, or of the Holy Ghost, we mean one God: for what the Father is, that is the Son, and that also is the Holy Ghost.

Belief in God as Creator.

In saying "Creator of Heaven and earth," we signify our belief that God created Heaven and earth and all things spiritual and material, invisible and visible; producing from nothing all that is: "He spoke, and they were made: He commanded, and they were created."[1]

God as Creator proved by reason.

Creation is absolutely impossible to any one but God, as is proved by our own reason, because man, in whatever

[1] Ps. cxlviii. 5.

he may produce and contrive, is obliged to make use of something already existing, and which therefore was created by God.

In Genesis is written the order in which all things were made, the time given to the creation being six "days." But, although God could undoubtedly have created whatever He wished, within this period, it is equally possible that the six "days" referred to may have been indefinite spaces of time. Creation, its time and order.

The earth, far from being now what it was at the creation, has been subject to notable changes;—from the effect of God's wrath after the disobedience of Adam and Eve, by the deluge, and by natural transformations and revolutions, which have taken place during a lapse of time indeterminate. Furthermore the actual creation of the earth may have been anterior to the general order of nature, as God made it in the six days described in Genesis; which organization or creation is, by some, supposed to have taken place about four or five thousand years before the coming of our Lord; whereas others believe the world and man to be of far greater antiquity. Creation of the earth.

"In the beginning God created Heaven;"[1] but neither Tradition nor Scripture explains when the Angels were created. And the names of three only, admitted to Heaven after their probation, are given;—namely: St. Michael, St. Gabriel, and St. Raphael. Creation of Heaven.

The word "Angel" is derived from the Greek, and signifies "messenger." "Are they not all ministering spirits, sent to minister for them who shall receive the inheritance of salvation ? "[2] Angels of Heaven.

[1] Gen. i. 1.   [2] Heb. i. 14.

Angels, and their probation. It follows, from the general order of God's providence, that the Angels should pass through a certain probation, with full liberty of action during that time, to choose between good and evil. Some rebelled, and "God spared not the Angels that sinned, but delivered them, drawn down by infernal ropes to the lower Hell, into torments, to be reserved unto judgment."[1] Others gained eternal happiness, and have charge over us, for our Saviour said: "See that ye despise not one of these little ones: for I say to you, that their Angels in Heaven always see the face of My Father who is in Heaven."[2]

Influence of evil spirits. Satan and his Angels, under different guises, tempt to evil by influencing men in thought and desire; through fear and presumption; through false prodigies and diabolical seductions of all kinds. "And no wonder: for Satan himself transformeth himself into an Angel of light."[3]

Influence of Heaven's Angels. There are, among the Angels, messengers from Heaven entrusted with different commissions, and in whom each human being in particular finds an Angel guardian, frequently safe-guarding the well-doer from unlooked-for danger, as we may infer by our experiencing at times a sudden dread of what is actually before us, or in receiving some warning of evil that may be impending.

This is according to God's promise of protection to the just, thus expressed: "He hath given His Angels charge over thee; to keep thee in all thy ways. In their hands they shall bear thee up: lest thou dash thy foot against a stone."[4] Our guardian Angel helps us to rise when we fall, prompts us to good thoughts and desires, to acts of faith, and against the adverse promptings of evil: for

[1] 2 Pet. ii. 4.   [2] Matt. xviii. 10.   [3] 2 Cor. xi. 14.   [4] Ps. xc. 11, 12.

the Lord said : " Take notice of him, and hear his voice, and do not think him one to be contemned : for he will not forgive when thou has sinned, and My name is in him." [1]

" God created man to His own image : " [2] that is to say, the Divine Nature was shadowed forth in man when God " breathed into his face the breath of life, and man became a living soul." [3] This spiritual substance is the likeness of God in us, enduing us with understanding and free will, united to the body during life on earth, at death to be separated, but re-united hereafter.

Creation and nature of man.

Amongst the principal powers of the soul are reason and will, by which we think and act with freedom. If we were not free there would be neither vice nor virtue, because our sensibilities, thoughts, and actions would not be under our control; we should then have no liberty of choice, and it would not be in our power to adhere to virtue or to resist vice. Although circumstances may at times deprive us of freedom of action, our freedom of will is always under our own control; for " before man is life and death, good and evil, that which he shall choose shall be given him." [4] If any one cannot apprehend the accordance of our freedom of action with the fact that God foresees all events throughout eternity, it is none the less a certainty, although not wholly within his comprehension.

Man's soul and its powers.

The principal qualities of the soul are spirituality and immortality, which are absolutely unchangeable. The soul is a spirit, being without form, incorporeal and indivisible : and it is immortal, continuing to be after the death of the body. We find these facts mentioned in Scripture, and

Man's soul and its qualities.

[1] Exod. xxiii. 21. [2] Gen. i. 27. [3] Gen. ii. 7. [4] Ecclus. xv. 18.

our reason dictates such to be the case; for as, according to science, no particle of any matter can perish, notwithstanding the variety of changes it may undergo, so is it but consistent to infer that the soul, which is a spirit and immaterial, must be immortal. Furthermore, were the souls of sinners and the souls of the just to cease to exist when the body dies, sinners would remain unpunished and the just unrewarded.

The object of man's existence.

"The Lord hath made all things for Himself;"[1] therefore God created man to know Him, to love Him, to serve Him, and, by corresponding to His grace, to merit everlasting happiness. "Then shall the King say to them that shall be on His right hand: Come, ye blessed of My Father, possess you the kingdom prepared for you from the foundation of the world."[2] We are therefore placed in this world with the object of gaining our eternal salvation, and, in so doing, to learn to know and love God, to love others for His sake, and to do our duty in that state of life unto which it has pleased Him to call us.

God's omnipotence over man.

All that God has created gives evidence of His supremacy; "for God will not accept any man's person, neither will He stand in awe of any man's greatness: for He made the little and the great, and He hath equally care of all."[3] If we suffer from one cause or another, it is either through our own fault, —frequently from provocation of some more or less sinful character,—or because God, who is all-seeing and infinitely just, has reason for permitting now some suffering beyond our apprehension. Those who merely live to enjoy all the good things of this world, misusing their wealth or otherwise conducting themselves contrary to God's will; as well

---

[1] Prov. xvi. 4.   [2] Matt. xxv. 34.   [3] Wis. vi. 8.

as those who lead on earth a life of charitable endeavour, always striving to do good to every one, are undoubtedly all equally destined to be dealt with in Eternity according to their merits or demerits. God "giveth to all life, and breath, and all things: and hath made of one, all mankind, to dwell upon the whole face of the earth, determining appointed times, and the limits of their habitation. That they should seek God, if haply they may feel after Him or find Him, although He be not far from every one of us : for in Him we live, and move, and are."[1]

In our ignorance of God's reasons and motives, we have opportunity for manifesting our entire confidence in His wisdom and justice, by sacrificing to Him our will and the curiosity natural to our mind. By submitting in all humility and faith to those things which God ordains but does not explain we gain greater merit ; for it is evident that if we understood His reasons for everything, virtue would become less deserving of reward. In the words of the Preacher, " Seek not the things that are too high for thee, and search not into things above thy ability : but the things that God hath commanded thee, think on them always, and in many of His works be not curious. . . . For many things are shewn to thee above the understanding of men. And the suspicion of them hath deceived many, and hath detained their minds in vanity."[2] *Man's dependence on God.*

For the trials or sufferings many of us are obliged, without apparent cause, to endure we may easily bring to bear certain reasons of a consolatory nature. Affliction tends to lead our thoughts towards God, and away from the transitory comforts and luxuries of this world. By *God's justice towards man.*

---

[1] Acts xvii. 25-28.   [2] Ecclus. iii. 22, 25, 26.

suffering we may also expiate our sins here on earth instead of in Purgatory, gaining greater happiness in the future if we accept with resignation, patience, humility, and love of God, the trials Providence assigns to us; and resist with fortitude the temptations which assail us. "We know that to them that love God, all things work together unto good, to such as, according to His purpose, are called to be Saints."[1] St. James also says: "Count it all joy, when you shall fall into divers temptations; knowing that the trying of your faith worketh patience. And patience hath a perfect work."[2]

Adam and Eve and their fall. "The Lord God had planted a paradise of pleasure from the beginning: wherein He placed man whom He had formed;"[3] and having given him dominion over all the beasts of the earth, He commanded him saying: Of every tree of paradise thou shalt eat: but of the tree of knowledge of good and evil, thou shalt not eat. For in what day soever thou shalt eat of it, thou shalt die the death."[4] Then God created woman, and gave her, who was named Eve, to be the wife of Adam, requiring them to know, love, and serve Him, and to merit, by their fidelity, the continued possession of this terrestrial paradise called Eden, wherein He had placed them.

Adam and Eve, before incurring for themselves and their posterity the consequences of God's malediction, possessed gifts greatly superior to our own. God had given them entire liberty of action, with one exception, made for the sake of proving their fidelity:—by the body being deprived of the forbidden fruit, and by the soul having to make acts of faith and obedience.

[1] Rom. viii. 28.   [2] Jas. i. 2–4.   [3] Gen. ii. 8.   [4] Gen. ii. 16, 17.

But the woman, being tempted by the serpent, took of the forbidden fruit, "and did eat, and the eyes of them were opened."[1]

Thus they realized the loss they had sustained of good and of happiness, and understood sin, of which they had, till then, been ignorant. Their crime was the evidence of inordinate vanity, curiosity, greediness, unbelief, disobedience and ingratitude towards God. Their souls suffered loss in intelligence, will, peace, and power, and were immediately deprived of sanctifying grace: their bodies became subject to suffering, infirmity, and ultimate decomposition in the tomb. For God said: "Dust thou art, and unto dust thou shalt return."[2] *Consequences of Adam and Eve's sin.*

It is sometimes thought that the Cross of Calvary was placed over the tomb of Adam, and some have considered it probable that Christ would have so chosen that the great work of Redemption should be accomplished over the remains of the original sinner.[3]

By the transgression of Adam and Eve we inherit the consequence of their guilt, and therefore are all born with original sin, or privation of original justice. This means that the whole of the human race, as a result of the sin of our first parents, is deprived of the supernatural gifts freely bestowed upon them by God. Not that we took part in the actual disobedience before we existed, but we suffer from its effects, being subject to the losses and punishments they contracted, handed down to us by the transmission of life. Original sin is therefore not the mere absence of supernatural grace, but its privation, by reason *Original sin and its inheritance.*

---

[1] Gen. iii. 6, 7. [2] Gen. iii. 19.
[3] Cornelius à Lapide treats this matter at considerable length.

of a transgression. Consequently when we are born, our souls are without supernatural grace until we are baptized, or until, coming to the use of reason, we turn ourselves to God by the help of His grace. "Wherefore as by one man sin entered into this world, and by sin death; and so death passed upon all men, in whom all have sinned." [1] The inheritance of original sin is a mystery, but it is certain that, although God has permitted its transmission, God is infinitely just, and we have no right to any supernatural condition of life.

Apart from the holy humanity of our Lord, the sole exception to the inheritance of original sin, is the Blessed Virgin. But our faith dictates that the souls of children who die unbaptized, and the souls of adults who die exempt from mortal sin, but remain unbaptized without coming to the use of reason, and who consequently are still in a state of original sin, go to a place called Limbo. This is where the souls of the just went before the coming of our Saviour, and where they do not suffer, but even enjoy as complete a state of happiness as is possible out of Heaven.

God's promise of a Redeemer. After the fall of Adam and Eve, God gave them the promise of a Redeemer, in the coming of whom they were to place their faith. He said to the serpent, "I will put enmities between thee and the woman, and thy seed and her seed: she shall crush thy head, and thou shalt lie in wait for her heel." [2] God also ordained a primitive religion,

Institution of a primitive religion. revealing to Adam and Eve the manner in which they were to honour and serve Him. "He made an everlasting covenant with them, and He shewed them His justice and

[1] Rom. v. 12.   [2] Gen. iii. 15.

judgments. And their eye saw the majesty of His glory, and their ears heard His glorious voice, and He said to them: Beware of all iniquity."[1]

Subsequently this religion was called Patriarchal, from God's promises of a Redeemer having been by Him renewed to the Patriarchs, they handing down, by Tradition, their knowledge of this religion, which was to continue until the coming of the Redeemer who should efface the sin of the world. *Patriarchal religion.*

"When God had seen that the earth was corrupted,"[2] and that the world was becoming debased with crime, after warning man and giving him time for repentance, which was left unheeded, God punished all sinners in the deluge, saving only Noah and his children, with certain animals of different kinds in the ark. "And the flood was forty days upon the earth, and the waters increased, and lifted up the ark on high from the earth."[3] After the deluge, God made a promise to Noah and his children that man should never again perish in the same manner, saying : "I will establish My covenant with you, and all flesh shall be no more destroyed. . . . I will set My bow in the clouds and it shall be the sign of a covenant between Me, and between the earth."[4] *The Deluge.*

After the death of Noah, the world became again corrupt, and God then chose out Abraham for the preservation of the Patriarchal religion. He renewed to him the promise of a Redeemer who should be born from his posterity ; likewise repeating his promise to Isaac and to Jacob. Later, God gave to Moses the Decalogue and a code of civil laws for *Development of the Patriarchal religion.*

---

[1] Ecclus. xvii. 10, 11.   [2] Gen. vi. 12.
[3] Gen. vii. 17.   [4] Gen. ix. 11, 13.

His chosen people. This Patriarchal religion, in its more developed state, was afterwards called Jewish or Mosaic, either on account of the name of Moses, whom God had elected to establish it; or from the name of the people He had chosen.

CHAPTER III.

"And in Jesus Christ His only Son, our Lord."

BY saying, "and in Jesus Christ His only Son," we signify our belief, that our Blessed Saviour is God the Son, second Person of the Trinity, who took a body and soul like ours, who became Man without ceasing to be God, in whom we should place our entire hope and trust, and whose teachings we should accept with implicit confidence. *Belief in our Lord Jesus Christ.*

It is principally proved by the prophecies and miracles, that our Lord is the Messias promised by God, "shewing from the beginning the things that shall be at last, and from ancient times the things that as yet are not done, saying: My counsel shall stand, and My will shall be done." [1] *Christ, the promised Messias.*

There were several symbols or figures, typical of our Saviour, in ages preceding His coming; for example, the Paschal Lamb, sacrificed to God in the primitive religion, represented our Redeemer, the Lamb of God, "a lamb unspotted and undefiled, foreknown indeed before the foundation of the world." [2] The Paschal Lamb immolated at Easter was offered as a bloody but unbroken sacrifice, emblematic of Christ whose Blood flowed at His Crucifixion, but whose bones were unbroken. The blood of the *Our Lord Jesus Christ proved, by ancient symbols, to be the Messias.*

[1] Isa. xlvi. 10.   [2] 1 Pet. i. 19, 20.

C

18   *CATHOLIC DOCTRINE AND DISCIPLINE.*

Paschal Lamb, marked on the house-doors in Egypt, was
a sign of exemption from the slaying of the first-born;
and the merits of our Lord are a medium of salvation
against the powers of Hell. The Paschal Lamb was not
only sacrificed but eaten by the Jews; and our Saviour
was not only immolated on the Cross, but constituted
Himself the food of our souls in the Holy Eucharist.
The Paschal Lamb was eaten with unleavened bread, and
no alien was allowed to participate; and at the altar,
only those who have cleansed their souls by penitence and
are numbered amongst the faithful, are permitted to receive
Communion.

Prophecies relative to the Messias.

Predictions relative to the Messias were renewed successively by the prophets. "To Him all the prophets give
testimony, that by His name all receive remission of sins,
who believe in Him." [1] The principal predictions in the
Old Testament concerning our Lord, were: the people or
tribe from which He should come; [2] the miraculous
maternity of the Virgin who should be His mother; [3] the
place of His birth; [4] His Person at the same time human
and Divine; [5] the different appellations by which He
should be known; [6] the one who should be His precursor
in the desert; [7] His wonderful virtues and character; [8]
His miracles; [9] the opposition and incredulity He should
meet with from the Jews; [10] His Passion and violent death; [11]
the rich man's tomb in which He should be laid; [12] His
glorious Resurrection [13] and Ascension; [14] the rejection of

---

[1] Acts x. 43. [2] Jer. xxiii. 5, 6. [3] Isa. vii. 14.
[4] Micheas v. 2. [5] Isa. ix. 6. [6] Isa. xliii. 3.
[7] Malachi iii. 1; Isa. xl. 3. [8] Isa. xlii. 1, 3. [9] Isa. xxxv. 5, 6.
[10] Isa. liii. 2, 3; Dan. ix. 26. [11] Isa. liii. 4, 5, 7, 12.
[12] Isa. liii. 9, xi. 10. [13] Ps. iii. 6, lvi. 9. [14] Amos ix. 6.

the Jews, the establishment of the Church, and the word of salvation preached far and wide to the extremities of the earth.[1] These and many other prophecies were given thus clearly that all might recognize the Messias whose great mission was the redemption of the world and the establishment of a universal religion for the consolation and sanctification of all people, in all countries, and for all time. This development or completion of the Patriarchal and Jewish religions, was in after times called the Christian or Catholic religion.

Our Saviour declared Himself the Messias referred to in the prophecies, saying: "Search the Scriptures, for you think in them to have life everlasting; and the same are they that give testimony of Me. . . . Think not that I will accuse you to the Father. There is one that accuseth you, Moses, in whom you trust. For if you did believe Moses, you would perhaps believe Me also; for he wrote of Me."[2] And to the woman of Samaria, who spoke of the promised Messias, in whom she believed, our Lord said: "I am He, who am speaking with thee."[3] Also when apprehended and questioned by the high priest whether He was "Christ the Son of the Blessed God," our Redeemer answered: "I am."[4] And again, after our Lord's Resurrection, when discoursing to His disciples, "He said to them: These are the words which I spoke to you, while I was yet with you, that all things must be fulfilled, which are written in the Law of Moses, and in the Prophets, and in the Psalms, concerning Me. Then He opened their understanding that they might understand the Scriptures. And He said to

Our Saviour declared Himself the Messias.

---

[1] Isa. lv. 4, 5, xlix. 6.   [2] John v. 39, 45, 46.
[3] John iv. 26.   [4] Mark xiv. 61, 62.

them: Thus it is written . . . and you are witnesses of these things." [1]

Our Lord proved Himself the Messias, by prophecies.   To prove the Divinity of His mission, our Lord made many prophecies concerning it; among them His Passion, His violent death, and His Resurrection on the third day; [2] the descent of the Holy Ghost upon His Apostles; [3] the persecutions they should suffer for His sake; [4] and the establishment by them of His Church, founded on the supremacy of St. Peter, whose decisions and teachings should be infallible, because of our Lord's promises to be with His Church to the end of the world. [5]

Prophecy, and its value.   A prophecy is a certain prediction of future events, made without the possibility of human conjecture, and absolutely accomplished without any aid from coincidence. This supposes, therefore, an infinite intelligence, inevitably emanating from God. Consequently, the fulfilment of prophecies is a mark of Divine authority, giving an indubitable character of truth to the thing foretold and executed; thus affording veritable proof of the Divinity of revealed religion. Were a prediction in itself, in its motive, or its circumstances, bad or opposed to God, such would be sufficient to proclaim its imposture. "Understanding this first, that no prophecy of Scripture is made by private interpretation. For prophecy came not by the will of man at any time: but the holy men of God spoke, inspired by the Holy Ghost." [6]

Our Lord proved Himself the Messias, by miracles.   It is a historical fact that our Lord's life on earth, and His establishment of the Church, were accompanied by innumerable miracles. The first mentioned in Scripture

[1] Luke xxiv. 44–46, 48.   [2] Luke xviii. 32, 33.
[3] John xvi. 7; Luke xxiv. 49.   [4] Matt. xxiv. 9.
[5] Acts i. 8; Matt. xxiv. 14,' xvi. 18, 19, xxviii. 20.   [6] 2 Pet. i. 20, 21.

was His changing water into wine at a marriage feast. " This beginning of miracles did Jesus in Cana of Galilee ; and manifested His glory, and His disciples believed in Him."[1] He raised the dead to life, as in the case of Lazarus, who, at our Lord's command, " came forth, bound feet and hands with winding-bands; and his face was bound about with a napkin. . . . Many therefore of the Jews, who were come to Mary and Martha, and had seen the things that Jesus did, believed in Him."[2] On another occasion, our Saviour fed the multitude, who had followed Him, with a few loaves and fishes. " Now those men, when they had seen what a miracle Jesus had done, said : This is of a truth the Prophet, that is to come into the world."[3] Our Saviour healed the deaf, the dumb, and the blind. " And whithersoever He entered, into towns or into villages or cities, they laid the sick in the streets, and besought Him that they might touch but the hem of His garment : and as many as touched Him were made whole."[4]

" Many other signs also did Jesus in the sight of His disciples, which are not written in this book,"[5] is the testimony of St. John at the conclusion of his Gospel.

God thus evinced His approval and recognition of the veracity of Christ's doctrine, as being that of the Messias He had promised to the world. There were so many unprejudiced witnesses, and so great a multiplicity and variety of miracles, as to render imposture out of the question. The best authenticated events recorded in pagan writings cannot afford such numerous and incontestable proofs of truth.

---

[1] John ii. 11.   [2] John xi. 44, 45.   [3] John vi. 14.
[4] Mark vi. 56.   [5] John xx. 30.

Besides which, the Evangelists wrote in perfect harmony and simplicity, differing in their mode of expression, but never contradicting each other; which is in itself a testimony to the truth of their statements. People who still refuse belief in the miracles connected with the Christian religion, admit, by their denial, a most prodigious miracle in the existence of the religion of our Lord Jesus Christ, made universal and preserved intact through so many ages, without the aid of miracles! A doctrine, sanctioned thus by miracles, must infallibly be divine and true, otherwise God would be countenancing imposture and establishing error; which is impossible, for God cannot deceive us nor be deceived: whereas man is liable to deception of all kinds. God's power is infinite or illimitable, whereas man's is finite or limited. Therefore should we with all reason prefer to the sheer fallibility of our own minds, the infallibility of our Saviour's teachings, given us by His authority through the medium of His true Church.

Miracles, and their value.

A miracle is a supernatural fact exceeding all human power, which God alone can perform, or give power of performing; because God alone can derogate from the laws of nature which He Himself has established. Man must therefore discriminate between what is above his reason and what is contrary to it. For while God may achieve miracles that remain unfathomable mysteries to human beings, He never can call upon us to believe what is erroneous.

Our Saviour affirmed His equality with God.

Our Saviour affirmed the identity and equality of His Divine nature with that of God the Father, by saying: " I and the Father are one." [1]   " He that seeth Me, seeth the

[1] John x. 30.

Father also." [1] "I am the way, and the truth, and the life. No man cometh to the Father, but by Me." [2] By these and many like assertions our Saviour declared His identity with God.

In our Redeemer there is but one Personality; but in that one Person there is both a human and a Divine nature, and both a human and a Divine will. As man, our Lord came into the world in time,—as God, He exists from all Eternity; as man, He is inferior to the Father and to the Holy Ghost,—as God, He is their co-equal; which explains how our Saviour said, on one occasion: "My Father is greater than I;" [3] and on another: "I and My Father are one." [4] This hypostatic union is called the mystery of the Incarnation: "By this hath the charity of God appeared towards us, because God hath sent His only begotten Son into the world, that we may live by Him." [5]

Our Redeemer's nature, both human and Divine.

Scripture gives many proofs of the unity of the two natures in Christ: for example, our Lord answered the Jews who accused Him of blasphemy, saying: "Do you say of Him whom the Father hath sanctified and sent into the world: Thou blasphemest, because I said, I am the Son of God?" [6] "But that you may know that the Son of God hath power on earth to forgive sins, then said He to the man sick of the palsy, Arise, take up thy bed, and go into thy house." [7] And our Lord said to His disciples: "The Son of man shall come in the glory of His Father with His angels; and then will render to every man according to his works." [8]

The words, "Jesus advanced in wisdom, and age, and

---

[1] John xiv. 9.   [2] John xiv. 6.   [3] John xiv. 28.   [4] John x. 30.
[5] John iv. 9.   [6] John x. 36.   [7] Matt. ix. 6.   [8] Matt. xvi. 27.

grace with God and men,"[1] signify that our Saviour showed, in His human nature, fitting signs of that wisdom which, by His Divine nature, was ever inherent in Him.

Our Lord's will, both human and Divine.

The human will in our Lord was free like our own, but had not, as in our case, to contend against sin, nor was it exposed, as ours, to prefer evil to good. The perfection of His soul, especially through its union with the Godhead, made evil repugnant to Him. Our Saviour Himself spoke of His human will when saying: "Father, if Thou wilt, remove this chalice from Me: but yet not My will, but Thine be done."[2] It may be presumed, by this apparent weakness, or seeming incapacity of His Divine nature, that our Lord wished to teach us; first, never to pray to God for anything, the object of which would not be perfectly in harmony with His most holy will; secondly, to make us understand His natural repugnance to the cup of bitterness placed before Him, thereby to increase our appreciation of His sacrifice; and, thirdly, to teach us that it is not forbidden to feel strong aversion to the accomplishment of a duty; but that in all trials and sufferings, for which we are to gain so high a recompense, we should resign ourselves to the Divine will.

Divinity of Person in our Lord Jesus Christ.

There is in our Lord Jesus Christ only one Person, which is that of His Godhead: "For in Him dwelleth all the fulness of the Godhead corporally."[3] There could not be two persons in our Lord, any more than in our human nature the soul and body could constitute two persons. In man's soul, which is a spiritual substance, there is the power to feel, judge, and will; in man's body, which is a material substance, there is the power to eat, speak, and

---

[1] Luke ii. 52.   [2] Luke xxii. 42; Matt. xxvi. 39.   [3] Col. ii. 9.

move ; two entirely different substances, yet belonging to one and the same individual.

The Incarnation, of course, is a mystery we cannot fathom, still we know that it was the Son, the second Person of the Trinity, who became Man for the Redemption of the world —not the Father nor the Holy Ghost ; notwithstanding that the three Persons of the Trinity are but one God. " For God indeed was in Christ, reconciling the world to Himself, not imputing to them their sins ; and He hath placed in us the word of reconciliation." [1]   It is evident that God became incarnate for several principal reasons, namely : to make Himself visible to us; to manifest His love and goodness towards us; to atone for our sins; to enable us to yield perfect adoration, praise, and obedience ; and to obtain the salvation of man by meriting for us sanctifying grace on earth, and eternal glory in Heaven. *Mystery of the Incarnation.*

When saying, "our Lord," we signify that our Saviour is our Master. As God, He is our Creator; as Man, He is our Redeemer ; and therefore over us has absolute right as God and as Man. *Our Saviour is " our Lord " as God and as Man.*

[1] 2 Cor. v. 19.

CHAPTER IV.

THIRD ARTICLE OF THE CREED.

"Who was conceived by the Holy Ghost; born of the Virgin Mary."

Belief in the Incarnation as Divine.

I~ saying, "who was conceived by the Holy Ghost," we signify our belief in the miraculous accomplishment of the second of the three greatest mysteries in the Catholic religion. The miracle constitutes, as already explained, the union of the Godhead with the human nature, which came about, when the Archangel Gabriel said to Mary : "The Holy Ghost shall come upon thee, and the power of the most High shall overshadow thee : And therefore also the Holy which shall be born of thee shall be called the Son of God."[1]   This is assigned to the Holy Ghost, because, through the Incarnation is manifested God's love for mankind, and therefore is it suitable specially to ascribe this Divine act to the third Person of the Trinity, who proceeds from the mutual love of the Father and the Son ; although it must necessarily be the work of the three Persons of the Trinity, they having one and the same will, and one and the same power.

Belief in the virginal purity of our Lord's mother.

The words, "was born of the Virgin Mary," signify our belief that our Lord was born of the Virgin Mary, whose

[1] Luke i. 35.

purity miraculously remained intact to the end of her life; more clearly expressed by the literal translation of the Latin, "was born of Mary Virgin."

The Catholic faith regarding the Mother of the Son of God made man, teaches us, moreover, that the Blessed Virgin, by a privilege accorded to her alone, and in consequence of the future merits of her Divine Son, was preserved, as already stated, from original sin; that her chastity remained for ever inviolable; and that she is truly the Mother of God, by which appellation the Church, in its liturgical prayers, addresses her. The Blessed Virgin is then not only Mother of our Saviour as man, but Mother of God; there being in our Lord but one Person, which is that of the Son of God. For example: a mother is the source of the body or material portion of her son, but in no way of his soul, which is spiritual and created by God, and yet she is called the mother of the man, because the body and the soul of her son form but one person. *Belief that the Blessed Virgin is the Mother of God.*

Although our Lord could, undoubtedly, have taken the human form by other means, He chose to have a mother, in order that, for the reparation of the first man's sin and of the stigma attached to his descendants, the like agency should be employed which had served for the downfall of mankind. Our Saviour also wished to procure for us the consolation of being able to call His sacred Mother our mother, and of addressing ourselves to her as being brothers of her Divine Son, who, by the Incarnation, became a member of the human family. *Our Lord's motive for the means by which He took the human form.*

Our Saviour chose for His mother a virgin, because the Son of God could not unite Himself personally with a human being who had not always been pure and holy. He *Our Saviour's motive in choosing for His mother a virgin.*

ordained that the chastity of His Mother should remain
miraculously inviolable, because it was fitting that the
mystery of His conception should bear the character of a
miracle, as well as His birth, His life, and even His death,
at which time the miraculous cry, "My God, my God, why
hast thou forsaken Me?"[1] uttered with His last breath,
was beyond the exhausted forces of His human nature. Our
Lord willed that the chastity of His Mother should be perpetual, because it was fitting that the Mother of God made
Man should remain the virginal sanctuary of the Holiest
of the holy, and because this sacred Mother, whose virtues
and dignity were unequalled, was destined to become the
model and protectress of all souls who dedicate themselves to
God by the vow of chastity, and who break from all human
ties to consecrate themselves more freely and generously
to Him. Also, because the Son of God wished to raise in
our eyes the merit of virginity, teaching us to practise,
with the help of grace, the triumph of the spirit over the
flesh, this being the foundation of Christianity.

Our Lord's foster-father and "brethren." When the Scriptures speak of the "brethren" or
"sisters" of our Lord, a form of speech is used by which
cousins or even more distant relatives were denoted
amongst the Jews. He also passed for being "the son of
Joseph,"[2] who was in reality His foster-father, being the
spouse of the Blessed Virgin, as safeguard only of her
honour in the eyes of the Jews, and as serving to shelter the
mystery of the Incarnation till such time as it should be
disclosed by God. St. Joseph was the guardian and protector of the Child Jesus. By his devotion to the Blessed
Virgin and her Divine Son, he is entitled to our utmost

---

[1] Matt. xxvii. 46.   [2] Luke ii. 7.

reverence and respect, next after the Mother of our Saviour; and was solemnly declared by Pope Pius the Ninth the patron of the entire Church and spiritual protector of the faithful.

It is generally admitted that our Lord Jesus Christ was born on the twenty-fifth day of December, and He was born in a small town in Palestine called Bethlehem. *Our Lord's nativity.*

By order of Augustus Cæsar, the Roman Emperor, who possessed the suzerainty over Judea and Galilee, all the chiefs of different families were required, according to the custom of the Jews, to sign the public register in the city of their birth when the census was made.

St. Joseph and the Blessed Virgin, being of the race of David, left Nazareth, where they dwelt, and went to Bethlehem with the object of conforming to this decree thus fulfilling the prophecy of Micheas. Here our Saviour was born, and the Blessed Virgin "wrapped Him in swaddling clothes, and laid Him in a manger; because there was no room for them in the inn;[1] "and the Word was made flesh, and dwelt among us, (and we saw His glory, the glory as it were of the only-begotten of the Father) full of grace and truth."[1]

The life of our Saviour on earth is divisible into three epochs: the years of His infancy and early childhood; those of His hidden life; and those of His public life. The principal events of our Lord's childhood were: the adoration of the shepherds, the circumcision, the adoration of the Magi or philosophers of the East, the presentation in the Temple, the flight into Egypt, and the journey to Jerusalem at the age of twelve years. *The three epochs of our Saviour's life on earth. Our Lord's childhood.*

[1] John i. 14.

The warning given to the shepherds of Bethlehem of our Lord's birth.

An Angel of the Lord announced to some shepherds, "keeping the night watches over their flock,"[1] that the Saviour was born and they would find Him "in the city of David :"[2] and when the Angel had spoken, a multitude of heavenly spirits sang, "Glory to God in the highest, and on earth peace to men of good-will."[3] The first words of this hymn of praise signify that the new-born Christ rendered to God most perfect homage, and that, by Him, the highest in Heaven adored the Divine Majesty of God. The remaining words mean that our Saviour came to reconcile heaven and earth, bringing the peace of pardon for all men who have good will to profit by the grace of the Redemption. This reconciliation of man with God produces the supernatural peace of man with himself—that sweet peace the soul feels when united to God by sanctifying grace : "the peace of God which surpasseth all understanding."[4]

The shepherds' visit at our Saviour's birth.

The shepherds of Bethlehem were the first called to adore the Saviour, showing that our Lord had come to save all men ; the ignorant and poor as well as the opulent. Also that the establishment of His Church should be begun by men of the humbler class, who were unlettered and without influence of any kind. Further, as a commencement of the moral revolution which our Redeemer was to bring about in the world by substituting esteem, respect, and brotherly love, for the feelings of pride, selfishness, and arrogance, so prevalent with those in high position. He thus obliged the exalted and the rich to recognize the dignity of the poor and the humble, for they all equally became brothers of the Son of God made Man.

---

[1] Luke ii. 8.   [2] Luke ii. 11.   [3] Luke ii. 14.   [4] Phil. iv. 7.

The eighth day after our Lord's birth was dedicated to Circumcision of our Lord. the ceremony of circumcision, when "His name was called Jesus."[1] This was a rite of the Mosaic Law (metaphorically meaning purification of the heart) to which our Saviour submitted. He thus evinced His descent from Abraham, affirmed the Divinity of the Mosaic religion, and showed that its commandments were to be observed until replaced by the religion of which it was only the figure. He also wished to bear, from the first days of His mortal existence, the penalties of our iniquities, by taking the semblance of sin He was unstained with; and to teach us that all the life of a Christian should be a spiritual purification.

As our Saviour came on earth for the sake of all men, The Magi's visit at our the Gentiles were also called to adore Him, in the person of Saviour's the Magi, as the Jews had been called in the persons of birth. the shepherds of Bethlehem. A brilliant meteor appeared in the heavens to the Magi, who were philosophers and astronomers, called also kings of the East, perhaps because they had princely rank or were considered as princes of science. The Magi recognized this wonderful "star in the east"[2] as being that which had been foretold; and, enlightened by Divine inspiration, they followed its guidance to Jerusalem, where it was lost to sight. Here they heard from Herod—who was under the Emperor Augustus, king of Judea and Galilee—that it was in Bethlehem, the city of David, where the Messias should be born. Then Herod, "sending them into Bethlehem, said: Go and diligently inquire after the Child, and when you have found Him, bring me word again, that I also may come

---

[1] Luke ii. 21.   [2] Matt. ii. 2.

and adore Him."¹ This was but a pretext for murdering Him who as he feared might become his rival. The star reappeared, and the Magi continued their journey, "until it came and stood over where the child was."² Then, seeing Jesus, they fell down and worshipped Him, and made Him offerings of "gold, frankincense, and myrrh."³ After adoring Him, and having received a warning from God "that they should not return to Herod, they went back another way into their country."⁴

Among the presents offered by the Magi, gold was emblematic of the universal royalty of Him whose kingdom should extend to "the utmost parts of the earth:"⁵ incense symbolized the divine priesthood of Him who should be "a priest for ever:"⁶ and myrrh was an emblem of the burial of Him whose "sepulchre" should be "glorious."⁷

Our Lord's Presentation in the Temple. Forty days after His birth, our Lord was presented in the Temple, "according to the Law of Moses;"⁸ an obligation exacted from the mother of every first-born son, together with the offering of "a lamb of a year old for a holocaust, and a young pigeon or a turtle for sin,"⁹ to be delivered to the priest, "who shall offer them before the Lord."¹⁰

This may have been on account of the punishment of Eve's sin, which had become hereditary, or in consequence of the birth given to a child born with original sin. In the case of the poor, this double sacrifice was replaced by the offering of "two turtles, or two young pigeons, one for a holocaust, and another for sin."¹¹ Our Saviour submitted to the law of Presentation, and the Blessed Virgin to the

¹ Matt. ii. 8.   ² Matt. ii. 9.   ³ Matt. ii. 11.   ⁴ Matt. ii. 12.
⁵ Ps. ii. 8.   ⁶ Ps. cix. 4.   ⁷ Isa. xi. 10.   ⁸ Luke ii. 22.
⁹ Lev. xii. 6.   ¹⁰ Lev. xii. 7.   ¹¹ Lev. xii. 8.

law of Purification, either to evade the notice of the Jews, which would have been attracted by its omission, or to give us an admirable example of humility and obedience.

Supernaturally enlightened by the Holy Ghost, a just man named Simeon, who had been promised by God "that he should not see death before he had seen the Christ of the Lord,"[1] came to the temple when Mary and Joseph presented the Infant Jesus, and he took the Child in his arms, and blessed God, saying: "Now Thou dost dismiss Thy servant, O Lord, according to Thy word in peace; because my eyes have seen Thy salvation."[2] Also an aged widow named Anne, who served God with prayers and fastings, when she saw our Saviour, gave praise and thanks to the Lord, "and spoke of Him to all that looked for the redemption of Israel."[3]

Seeing that the Magi did not return, Herod's wrath knew no bounds, and he ordered the massacre of every male child of two years or less in and around Bethlehem. For, having learnt from the Magi when the miraculous star appeared to them, he judged that the new-born Child, whom he feared, would be among the slain. But "an Angel of the Lord appeared in sleep to Joseph, saying: Arise and take the Child and His Mother, and fly into Egypt: and be there until I shall tell thee. For it will come to pass that Herod will seek the Child to destroy Him. Who arose, and took the Child and His Mother by night and retired into Egypt: and he was there until the death of Herod."[4] Then the Angel again appeared to Joseph, and he took Mary and the Child Jesus and went as the Angel directed him, "into the land of Israel. But hearing that Archelaus

The massacre of children in Bethlehem.

[1] Luke ii. 26. [2] Luke ii. 29, 30. [3] Luke ii. 38. [4] Matt. ii. 13, 14.

D

reigned in Judea in the room of Herod his father, he was afraid to go thither: and being warned in sleep, retired into the quarters of Galilee. And coming he dwelt in a city called Nazareth." [1]

The finding of our Lord in the Temple.

At the age of twelve years, our Lord went with His Mother and foster-father to Jerusalem, for "the solemn day of the Pasch." [2]   When the feast was over and they were returning to Nazareth, they missed Jesus from among them, but thought He was with some of their company, always gladdened by the society of this Child showing so much of charm and intelligence through the veil which hid His real identity from the world.   But Mary and Joseph, becoming anxious at His absence, "sought Him among their kinsfolk and acquaintance, and not finding Him, they returned into Jerusalem seeking Him.   And it came to pass that after three days they found Him in the Temple, sitting in the midst of the doctors, hearing them, and asking them questions." [3]   The Blessed Virgin addressed our Lord with words that should not be taken as a reproach, but a tender expression of profound grief, saying : "Son, why hast Thou done so to us ? behold, Thy father and I have sought Thee sorrowing." [4]   Our Saviour answered, doubtless not less feelingly, "How is it that you sought Me ? did you not know, that I must be about My Father's business ? " [5]   By this Christ affirmed that He was the Son of the Father Eternal, and knew that Mary and Joseph could understand His reply and His presence in the Temple.   St. Luke's comment, "They understood not the word that He spoke unto them," [6] would imply that they

---

[1] Matt. ii. 21-23.   [2] Luke ii. 41.   [3] Luke ii. 44-46.
[4] Luke ii. 48.   [5] Luke ii. 49.   [6] Luke ii. 50.

did not comprehend how He should already be occupied, at the age of twelve years, about the accomplishment of His great mission in the world.

The Blessed Virgin's and St. Joseph's forbearance from all further questioning, affords us an admirable example of contenting ourselves with the light that God has given us without trying to penetrate more deeply into what it has pleased Him to keep secret. The practical lessons we may gain from our Lord's answer to His Sacred Mother are, that the authority of parents towards their children, is entirely subordinate to the supremacy of God. Also that, though.there is every obligation for children to consult their parents, they are not bound to obey them in case of opposition to what is decidedly a real vocation in life; and that parents should in no way hinder children in the practice of their religious duties, but, on the contrary, encourage and give them good example. *Lessons of obedience to higher authority.*

The hidden life of our Saviour, extending over the space of eighteen years, was passed at Nazareth, during which time He did not manifest Himself to the world, but lived with His Mother and St. Joseph, "and was subject unto them."[1] This submission on the part of our Lord should teach us duty and respect towards our parents; compliance with the laws of civil authority, of which domestic society is the model; and the merit of obedience in religious societies, which is an obligation voluntarily contracted by the vow of submission to superiors. The words, "and Jesus advanced in wisdom, and age, and grace with God and man,"[2] indicate, that as our Saviour increased in years, so did He progressively evince the wisdom and learning and *Hidden life of our Saviour, and what it teaches.*

---

[1] Luke ii. 51.   [2] Luke ii. 52.

holiness, that were in Him in all plenitude, and by which He glorified God, and edified man, more and more.

By the virtues our Lord practised in His hidden life, He teaches the rich to cultivate simplicity consistent with the position they occupy, and to avoid indolence and uselessness in their life, often engendered by wealth. He teaches the poor to accept with resignation and humility that state of life to which God has called them, and to learn that laborious hardships accepted with a Christian spirit are a help towards eternal happiness. His example teaches children to be respectful, submissive, docile, and fond of occupation and home, where they should find protection from injurious influences of the world—a safeguard productive of a salutary effect upon their whole lives : also members of religious communities to love poverty, obscurity, and obedience ; and all young people to imitate our Saviour in prayer, work, and submission to authority. Indeed, all Christians should take example on all occasions and in all circumstances from our Blessed Lord, whether in His hidden or His public life—so full of abnegation, charity, and suffering—"because in Him it hath well pleased the Father, that all fulness should dwell."[1]

Public life of our Saviour, prepared for by St. John the Baptist.

Our Saviour's public life occupied the three following years, when He preached the Gospel in Judea, openly proclaiming Himself the Messias, and prophesying and performing many miracles.

The way was prepared before Him by St. John the Baptist, who, after living in solitude and prayer in the desert, preached on the banks of the Jordan, calling all sinners to repentance, and saying: "Do penance; for the

[1] Col. i. 19.

Kingdom of Heaven is at hand;"[1] and baptizing them "in water unto penance,"[2] which was figurative of the real Baptism our Lord was to institute. St. John announced the near approach of the Messias, saying: "He that shall come after me, is preferred before me: because He was before me;"[3] and he finally designated our Lord as He that should come, saying: "Behold the Lamb of God, behold Him who taketh away the sin of the world."[4]

Our Saviour was called the Lamb of God, to show that He was the Redeemer promised to Adam and sacrificed figuratively "from the beginning of the world."[5] He was called, and also called Himself, the "Bridegroom;"[6] and the Church is alluded to as the "bride;"[7] significant of the indissoluble union between the Messias and His Church.

The principal events, and distinctive marks of the public life of our Lord, were His baptism by St. John; His fasting and temptation in the desert; His preaching of the Gospel; the selection of His Apostles; His miracles and prophecies; the Divine character of His doctrine; the Divine perfection of His virtues; His triumphal entry into Jerusalem; and the institution of the Holy Eucharist. *Principal events of our Lord's public life.*

The baptism St. John the Baptist gave, was a simple ceremony; the figure only, or representation of the real Sacrament of Baptism, which our Lord Himself was to institute; though it necessitated a certain penitence, otherwise the reception of it would have been hypocrisy. St. John recognized Christ as the Messias only at the moment that he baptized Him, and "gave testimony, saying: I saw *Baptism of our Lord by St. John.*

---

[1] Matt. iii. 2.   [2] Matt. iii. 11.   [3] John i. 15.   [4] John i. 29.
[5] Apoc. xiii. 8.   [6] Matt. ix. 15.   [7] Apoc. xxii. 17.

the Spirit coming down, as a dove from Heaven, and He remained upon Him . . . and I gave testimony, that this is the Son of God."[1]   Our Lord's baptism by St. John indicated His wish to confirm publicly the mission of His Precursor; and give example to others of what was to be the foundation of His gospel; to show that He had come as the Victim of the world to expiate the sins of all mankind: and to afford occasion for the miraculous manifestation which took place at His baptism: "the Spirit of God descending as a dove, and coming upon Him.   And behold a voice from Heaven, saying: This is My beloved Son, in whom I am well pleased "[2]—which was merely the outward revelation of all those gifts and virtues Christ already possessed, for He was "full of grace and truth."[3]   The Holy Ghost descended on our Saviour in the form of a dove, to make the presence of the Spirit known to all; probably, also, because a dove is the emblem of simplicity, innocence, and purity.   Perhaps, again, because as God sent a dove with an olive branch in its mouth, announcing to Noah the end of the deluge, so did He choose to send a dove proclaiming the speedy Redemption of man by "the Saviour of the world."[4]

Our Lord's fast in the desert.

After having been baptized, our Redeemer went into the desert, where He passed forty days and forty nights in prayer and fasting; in remembrance of which the Church established Lent.   Christ imposed on Himself this mortification before instituting the real Sacrament of Baptism, principally to prepare Himself for His public life, and also in order to show that, in adults, penitence must precede

---

[1] John i. 32–34.   [2] Matt. iii. 16, 17.
[3] John i. 14.   [4] John iv. 42.

this Sacrament, for it to be received with efficacy. Our Lord was "tempted by the devil"[1] in various ways, whose quotations from the Scripture Christ replied to from the same source, eluding his questions, and leaving him in ignorance of His identity. This is calculated to teach us that if we resist temptation it is glorious to God, meritorious to ourselves, and enables us to deserve grace. Also that the best way to vanquish temptation is by mortification, prayer, and diffidence of our own powers of doing any right without the help of God.

When He left the desert, after these forty days and nights, "Jesus began to preach"[2] in Judea and Galilee. Of all His instructions the Sermon on the Mount was the longest and most remarkable, giving the eight beatitudes, His chief precepts, and His counsels.

Our Saviour's preaching of the Gospel.

It is from our Redeemer Himself that the world learnt most of the mysteries of our faith. He threw a penetrating light on the revelations of anterior date, and developed that knowledge which was merely elementary until His coming. He made clear as much as human intelligence had the power of grasping and as much as was necessary for our guidance, at the same time placing before us the intricate and beauteous details of our religion. Our Saviour's teachings were spoken in simple words full of meaning, and generally parabolical, so as to render them easier of comprehension to the multitude. He explained our origin and our destiny, and showed us the two ways open to us: the one a wide and easy path leading to an eternity of misery; and the other a narrow road, thorny, hilly, and difficult of ascent, with the goal of sanctification and

[1] Luke iv. 2.   [2] Matt. iv. 17.

glory before our eyes as the reward of our efforts. Our Lord pointed out the virtues we should bring to bear in combating the miseries, temptations, and needs which are felt, with more or less acuteness, by all humanity, through the battle of life; for it was needful that a God should instruct us in those virtues which appeal instinctively to our admiration, but which are in many instances so adverse to our natural proclivities—virtues which infidel philosophers do not practise, but cannot refrain from extolling.

Apostles chosen by our Lord. Our Lord chose from among His disciples, twelve, " whom also He named Apostles ; "[1] Simon being the first among them, " whom He surnamed Peter,"[2] which signifies, Rock. Some time after, " the Lord appointed also other seventy-two, and He sent them two and two before His face, into every city and place whither He Himself was to come."[3] The twelve Apostles and the seventy-two disciples were representative of the hierarchy of ecclesiastical authority of bishops and priests, which Christ intended to institute. After the establishment of the Church and the Ascension of our Lord, He chose as an Apostle, St. Paul, whose name is associated with St. Peter because he exhibited immense industry in his work, great brilliancy in his writings, and also because he was imprisoned and suffered martyrdom in company with St. Peter.

Our Saviour's miracles and prophecies. Our Saviour performed endless miracles, already spoken of, of which Scripture only records fifty-five. The principal prophecies of our Lord have previously been narrated.

Our Lord's virtues and perfections. Our Lord's virtues and Divinity were apparent in every act of His life, as an everlasting example to mankind. He

---

[1] Luke vi. 13.   [2] Luke vi. 14.   [3] Luke x. 1.

"did no sin, neither was guile found in His mouth. Who, when He was reviled, did not revile; when he suffered, He threatened not; but delivered Himself to him that judged Him unjustly. Who His own self bore our sins, in His body upon the tree; that we, being dead to sins, should live to justice."[1] As His discourses showed a wisdom which was superhuman and Divine, so did His conduct evince a calm, a self-possession, and moral force beyond the power of man. In all, He was great, and grand, and holy, and could well say: "Which of you shall convince Me of sin?"[2] He preached humility, charity, and indifference to the wealth and pleasures of this world, practising what He preached. Even anti-christian philosophers speak with honourable justice of the Divine character of our Redeemer. For example, Jean-Jacques Rousseau, says: "If the life and death of Socrates were of a sage, the life and death of Jesus Christ were of a God."

When coming near to Jerusalem, "Jesus sent two disciples, saying to them: Go ye into the village that is over against you, and immediately you shall find an ass tied and a colt with her; loose them and bring them to Me."[3] He rode into the town, the people coming in numbers along the road to meet Him, strewing His way with branches of palms and olives, and crying out: "Hosanna to the Son of David: Blessed is He that cometh in the name of the Lord; Hosanna in the highest!"[4]

In our Saviour's triumphal entry into Jerusalem, it is to be remarked how He chose not to come as a conquering hero, but fulfilling the prophecy: "Behold the King cometh

Our Saviour's entry into Jerusalem.

---

[1] 1 Pet. ii. 22-24.   [2] John viii. 46.
[3] Matt. xxi. 1, 2.   [4] Matt. xxi. 9.

to thee, meek, and sitting upon an ass."[1] He was attended
by a train of followers from among the indigent and lowly
born; His coming being marked by poverty, humility, and
charity to all, more especially towards the unfortunate, the
suffering, and the destitute.

Preparation of the Last Supper.

The two Apostles our Lord elected, to make ready the
Last Supper, were Peter, who was to be the head of the
Church, and John, His favourite Apostle, to whom He said:
" Go, and prepare for us the pasch."[2] The place selected
was a large and garnished hall; thus to represent that
Christ's Church should be ample, so that all may have
access to the feast of the Eucharist; and that we should
come with our souls adorned by sanctifying grace.

Principal incidents of the Last Supper.

The principal incidents attending the Last Supper were:
The eating of the paschal lamb, which preceded the
institution of the Holy Eucharist, because it was the figure
of the Lamb of God who was to be sacrificed on the altars
of the Church. Secondly, Christ washing the feet of His
disciples, which is interpreted that we should be ever
ready to render each other services of charity, even the
most humble, and that we should never come to receive
the Sacrament of the Holy Eucharist without, not only
being cleansed from our graver sins by Baptism or Penance,
but also after purifying ourselves of smaller faults by acts
of humility and charity, done in a spirit of sincere repentance. Thirdly, our Saviour predicting that Judas would
betray Him, saying, "Amen, amen, I say to you, one of
you shall betray Me;"[3] in consequence of which betrayal
this Apostle became guilty of two crimes: by causing, or
helping to cause, the death of another; and by effecting his

---

[1] Matt. xxi. 3.   [2] Luke xxii. 8.   [3] John xiii. 21.

own death. Fourthly, the institution of the Holy Eucharist, which was the great miracle constituting a Sacrament, so well calculated to relax the hold of our worldly interests, and elevate our thoughts and desires towards Heaven; also to be our consolation in life and at the hour of death: a Sacrament eminently worthy of our utmost admiration and gratitude. Fifthly, our Lord's promise of doctrinal infallibility made to Peter, chief of the Apostles, to whom He said, "Simon Simon, behold, Satan hath desired to have you, that he may sift you as wheat. But I have prayed for thee, that thy faith fail not: and thou being once converted, confirm thy brethren."[1] Our Lord then predicted that Peter would deny Him three times, saying, "The cock shall not crow this day, till thou thrice deniest that thou knowest Me."[2] Having first promised him infallibility of doctrine, and then speaking of how he would fail in his allegiance, seems to imply that the privilege did not mean he would be impeccable.

Our Saviour's discourse after His Last Supper contained prophecies of the descent of the Holy Ghost, the persecutions of His disciples, their victory over the world, and the eternal happiness that awaited them.

Our Lord prayed not only for His Apostles, but for all who should believe in Him; teaching us to be charitable to one another in our prayers as well as in our deeds. In accordance with the Jewish custom of reciting a hymn after the Passover, we also should ever give thanks after assisting at the Sacrifice of the Mass, and more especially when we have participated in the Holy Communion.

Our Saviour's discourse after the Last Supper.

---

[1] Luke xxii. 31, 32.   [2] Luke xxii. 34.

CHAPTER V.

"Suffered under Pontius Pilate; was crucified, died, and was buried."

Belief in the Redemption.

THE words, "suffered under Pontius Pilate; was crucified, died, and was buried," signify our belief that our Lord Jesus Christ, the second Person of the Trinity, Son of God made Man, endured the agonies of His Passion and died on the Cross as representative of guilty and fallen humanity, for the salvation of the whole world. These events constitute the third great mystery of the Catholic religion, which is called the mystery of the Redemption.

Mystery of the Redemption.

Our Saviour's sufferings.

In saying that our Saviour "suffered," we include all the agonies of His Passion until the moment of His death;—a suffering which was felt by His human nature only, subject, like our own, to sorrow and pain. His Divine nature being immortal and impassible, was therefore unaffected by all pains of the flesh. Nevertheless, His sufferings were those of a God, because His humanity was that of a Divine Person.

Date of our Lord's Passion.

The words, "under Pontius Pilate," fix precisely the time of our Lord's Passion and death, written of in the prophecies: Pontius Pilate being governor of Judea under the Roman Emperor Augustus.

The five principal incidents in our Lord's suffering were : Principal events of our Lord's Passion. His Agony in the garden of Gethsemani, His Scourging by Pilate, the Crowning with thorns, the Carrying of the Cross, and His Crucifixion,—in addition to which our Saviour's moral sufferings were many and acute, because, being the Mediator between us and God, for our reconciliation with Him, He bore mental distress as well as physical pain. The most prominent afflictions to His Soul were the innumerable sins of mankind; the betrayal of Judas; the flight of His disciples; the triple denial of Peter; the unjust accusations brought against Him; the ingratitude of all those who had ever received benefits at His hands—not one of whom tried to defend Him or proclaim His innocence; the clamorous and wrathful appeals for His death; the infamous derision of which He was the object; and the ineffable grief of His Sacred Mother, whom He loved intensely.

Our Saviour went to the garden of Gethsemani, on the Our Saviour's prayer in the Garden of Olives. Mount of Olives, followed by His disciples; and leaving them at a certain distance, He said, "Pray, lest ye enter into temptation."[1] Then, going a little further, "and kneeling down, He prayed, saying : Father, if Thou wilt, remove this chalice from Me : but yet not My will, but Thine, be done :"[2]—and His agony was such that His sweat was as of blood which fell on the ground.

When our Lord came back to His disciples He found them asleep, and said, "Why sleep you? arise and pray, lest you enter into temptation."[3] While He spoke, a multitude of people came with swords and staves, accompanying the chief priests and soldiers, who were to take

[1] Luke xxii. 40. [2] Luke xxii. 41, 42. [3] Luke xxii. 46.

Him captive. From among them came Judas and betrayed our Saviour with a kiss, who said, "Judas, dost thou betray the Son of man with a kiss?"[1] but He spoke no word of rebuke, or reproach, or threat.

They then took our Lord Jesus Christ and led Him away to the house of the high priest Caiphas, and sought false testimony against Him, in order to put Him to death. All the disciples had forsaken our Blessed Lord except Peter, who followed at a distance, and was among the servants of the high priest when he denied Him three times. Immediately the cock crew, "and Peter remembered the words of the Lord, as He had said, Before the cock crow, thou shalt deny Me thrice."[2]

Our Lord taken before Pilate and Herod.

On the morrow our Lord was taken before Pontius Pilate, the Governor, the people making accusations against Him; but Pilate said, "Why, what evil hath He done?"[3] The multitude becoming fierce and importunate for His death, our Saviour was sent to Herod,—the tetrarch or governor of Galilee, under the Roman Emperor,—who questioned Him, had Him arrayed in a white garment, and sent Him again to Pilate. "And Pilate, calling together the chief priests, and the magistrates, and the people, said to them, You have presented unto me this Man, as one that perverteth the people; and behold I, having examined Him before you, find no cause in this Man, in those things wherein you accuse Him."[4] But they cried out the more, to crucify Him; and when Pilate saw he could not prevail against them, he took water, and "washed his hands before the people, saying, I am innocent of the Blood of this just Man: look you to it."[5]

---

[1] Luke xxii. 48.   [2] Luke xxii. 61.   [3] Matt. xxvii. 23.
[4] Luke xxiii. 13, 14.   [5] Matt. xxvii. 24.

Then the soldiers of the Governor took our Saviour and The crowning with thorns. scourged Him, and put on Him a purple robe, and smote Him, and mocked Him, and placed on His head a crown of thorns, and saluted Him derisively, saying : " Hail, King of the Jews." [1] Afterwards, they took off the robe, and Pilate, to satisfy the people, " delivered up Jesus, when he had scourged Him, to be crucified." [2]

Our Lord was then compelled to carry His cross, under The carrying of the Cross. the weight of which, Tradition tells us, He fell several times, the strength of His human nature being exhausted by the great moral and bodily sufferings He had undergone. Therefore, the soldiers made Simon a Cyrenean, who was passing by, carry the Cross.

This incident teaches us not to expect miraculous assistance when human aid can suffice ; and that we should bear our crosses in life with resignation and patience, uniting our hearts to the heart of our Redeemer in all our griefs.

Tradition recounts that, on the road to Calvary, a good Veronica's handkerchief. woman, moved by commiseration, came forward, and, with respectful tenderness, wiped the face of our Lord, which was covered with dust and blood ; and that miraculously, the impression of the holy face of the Saviour remained on the linen handkerchief she used for this act of compassionate devotion. This circumstance gave to the woman, whose real name is not known, the appellation of Veronica, signifying, it is believed, " true image."

Our Saviour " was crucified " about midday, on a hill The Crucifixion. to the north of Jerusalem, called Calvary, or in Hebrew, Golgotha, from the skull-shaped rock on which criminals were crucified. It is supposed that our Lord chose this

[1] Mark xv. 18.   [2] Mark xv. 15.

place for His crucifixion, because He wished to drink, "even to the dregs,"[1] His cup of humiliation and bitterness, by being crucified on the spot destined for the execution of criminals.

Our Saviour's last words before dying. In the midst of insults and blasphemies from the populace, our Redeemer prayed for His accusers and torturers, saying: "Father, forgive them, for they know not what they do;"[2] which teaches us to show mercy and charity even to our enemies, and those who treat us unjustly.

There were two malefactors crucified, one on either side of our Blessed Lord. To the one who was penitent and said: "Lord, remember me when Thou shalt come into Thy kingdom;"[3] Jesus answered: "Amen I say to thee, this day thou shalt be with Me in Paradise."[4] By this our Lord meant the place where He would, after His death, visit the souls of the just who had died before His coming. From His words we may learn that faith and sincere repentance from a sinner is availing, even at the last hour.

Then our Saviour, seeing His Mother standing by the Cross with the disciple "whom Jesus loved," said to her, "Woman, behold thy Son;"[5] and turning to John, He said, "Behold thy Mother."[6] In His refraining from calling either by name, Catholics believe that these words of our Lord indicate His wish, that the Blessed Virgin should be considered as the Mother of all the Faithful, to be honoured by us in the highest degree, as the Second Eve; St. John personifying the children of the Second Adam and the New Eve.

---

[1] Isa. li. 17.   [2] Luke xxiii. 34.   [3] Luke xxiii. 42.
[4] Luke xxiii. 43.   [5] John xix. 26.   [6] John xix. 27.

By the cry of anguish, "My God, my God, why hast thou forsaken Me ?"[1]—an anguish which the sight of His Mother's suffering could but increase,—our Saviour, on the Cross, showed us that we may make heard a cry of grief which calls for consolation and comfort; just as in the garden of Gethsemane, He taught us that we may ask God to take from us a cup of bitterness, provided that our will is resigned to His.

His saying, "I thirst,"[2] may be interpreted symbolically of our Saviour's thirst for the salvation of our souls, for which He became "obedient unto death, even the death of the Cross."[3]

Our Lord's words, "It is consummated,"[4] expressed the completion of His atonement for the sins of the world, and the accomplishment of the prophecies from beginning to end.

Then, with His last breath, our Redeemer said in a loud voice, "Father, into Thy hands I commend my Spirit."[5] As all the forces of His human nature must necessarily have been previously consumed, He thereby proved His divinity by a great miracle. We are reminded by His very last words, that the destiny of the body depends on that of soul ; that we should never neglect all in our power that will enable us, at the hour of death, with confidence to commit our souls into the hands of God ; and that, not knowing when that hour may come upon us, we should practise penitence and continually live in that state of grace, through which we, too, may say with our Saviour, " Father, into Thy hands I commend my spirit."

---

[1] Matt. xxvii. 46. [2] John xix. 28. [3] Phil. ii. 8.
[4] John xix. 30. [5] Luke xxiii. 46.

E

Our
Redeemer's
death.

And now, our Redeemer had died ; that is to say in His human nature only, which, as in all human deaths, consisted in the separation of the soul from the body. Our Saviour expired about three o'clock on a Friday in the full moon of the month of March. From the elevation of the Cross until our Blessed Lord died, darkness overspread the land; an eclipse, recounted in other writings besides the Scriptures, and impossible, except by supernatural agency. The veil of the Temple was rent from top to bottom, the earth trembled, and the rocks were rent asunder. The rock on Mount Calvary, as may be seen to this day, is split in a contrary direction to its veining, which could only have been caused by a supernatural earthquake producing this change in the course of nature. " The graves were opened ; and many bodies of the saints that had slept arose, and coming out of the tombs after His Resurrection, came into the holy city, and appeared to many." [1]

The piercing
of our Lord's
Body with a
lance.

Then the soldiers, by order of Pilate, came to break the legs of the two malefactors, but seeing that Jesus was already dead, they refrained from doing the same by Him, but pierced His side with a spear, and forthwith issued " blood and water. . . . These things were done, that the Scripture might be fulfilled: You shall not break a bone of Him." [2]

The Redemption of
mankind.

And thus our Saviour died for the Redemption of mankind, past, present and future: for the salvation of all who have the will to profit by the means that is offered them of sanctification and eternal happiness; for " He is the propitiation for our sins : and not for ours only, but also for those of the whole world." [3]

[1] Matt. xxvii. 52, 53.   [2] John xix. 34, 36.   [3] 1 John ii. 2.

We may remember Christ's sufferings, endured with the most sublime generosity, silence, calm, and unshrinking intrepidity, as an encouragement to bear our own afflictions, both moral and physical, with patience and fortitude; for how can we forget that " the disciple is not above his master, nor the servant above his lord " ? [1]

Towards the evening of the same day, Joseph of Arimathea, a rich man and a distinguished citizen, who was secretly a disciple of our Saviour, went to Pilate and begged that he might take the Body of our Lord. Then he, with another called Nicodemus, followed by the women from Galilee, took the Body down from the Cross, and wrapped it in linen, " and laid it in his own new monument which he hewed out in a rock ; and he rolled a great stone to the door," [2] closing all entrance. Our Redeemer was buried, to render more incontestable His death, upon the reality of which depended the truth of the great miracle of His Resurrection. *Our Saviour's burial.*

The next day, the chief priests and Pharisees, remembering the words of our Lord, that on the third day He would rise again, came to Pilate, asking that a guard might be placed near the sepulchre, so that the disciples might not come and take away the Body of their Master, " and say to the people, He is risen from the dead." [3] So Pilate commanded that it should be done as they wished ; " and they departing, made the sepulchre sure, sealing the stone, and setting guards." [4] It is therefore certain that no precaution was neglected, by those acting against our Saviour, to ensure the impossibility of His Body being removed by any human agency. *The sealing and guarding of the tomb.*

[1] Matt. x. 24.   [2] Matt. xxviii. 60.   [3] Matt. xxvii. 64.   [4] Matt. xxvii. 66.

CHAPTER VI.

FIFTH ARTICLE OF THE CREED.

"He descended into Hell; the third day He rose again from the dead."

Hell and what it signifies.

HELL, in its wide, as distinguished from its narrower meaning, signifies three completely different and separate abodes for the souls of the dead: Purgatory, Hell, and Limbo.

Purgatory is for the souls of those whose sins have been forgiven, but have still to expiate the punishment due for sin before they are sufficiently pure to enter Heaven; for our Saviour said, "Thou shalt not go out from thence, till thou repay the last farthing."[1] Hell, in the commonly used sense, is for the eternal punishment of the damned; and Limbo, for the souls of the just who died before the coming of our Lord, where they enjoyed an almost complete degree of happiness, but were deprived of the sight of God and the joy of Heaven. That there is an insuperable separation existing between these three places, is shown by the words of Abraham to the rich man tormented in Hell: "Between us and you there is fixed a great chaos : so that they who would pass from hence to you, cannot, nor from thence come hither."[2]

[1] Matt. v. 26. [2] Luke xvi. 26.

When saying that our Lord Jesus Christ "descended into Hell," we signify our belief that His Soul went down into Limbo to announce to the just—who died before His coming—the great mystery of the Redemption, and their approaching deliverance by their glorious ascension with Him into Heaven. "He preached to those spirits that were in prison,"[1] and, "ascending on high, He led captivity captive."[2] *Belief in our Saviour's descent into Hell.*

In saying, "the third day He rose again from the dead," we signify our belief that on the third day after His death on the Cross, the Soul of our Redeemer was re-united to His Body by the miracle of His Resurrection. *Belief in our Lord's Resurrection.*

The absolute certainty of the reality of our Saviour's death is proved in several ways. For example, the agony in the Garden, the ill-treatment, and scourging He underwent could but exhaust His bodily strength and quicken the extinction of life, immolated as He was on the Cross, while the piercing of His side with a spear made death the more undeniable. The fact of blood and water issuing from the wound rendered it evident that death had taken place. Renan's view that Jesus was in a trance and not dead, is too absurd to need refutation. *Proofs of our Saviour's death.*

In evidence of the certainty of our Saviour's Resurrection, there are also many proofs. For instance, the Jews, who were so interested in not admitting this great miracle, were never able to establish anything against the truth of it. Their only attempt to produce evidence of our Lord's body having been stolen by His disciples, was the testimony of the guards who watched the sepulchre; by which they offered witnesses who slept! the chief priests and elders *Proofs of our Saviour's Resurrection.*

---

[1] 1 Pet. iii. 19.   [2] Eph. iv. 8.

of the city having given "a great sum of money to the
soldiers, saying : Say you, His disciples came by night, and
stole Him away when we were asleep." [1]   Thus our Lord's
very enemies gave testimony to the truth by their inability
to prove imposture, notwithstanding that they were in the
best position to do so, and most concerned about effecting
it if they could.

Evidence,
through the
Apostles, of
our Lord's
Resurrection.
The Apostles bring incontestable attestation to bear in
their accounts of the numberless miracles which followed
during the forty days our Redeemer spent on earth before
His Ascension.   Their words were in every way worthy of
credence, for the conscientiousness and piety of these men
exclude any idea of deception on their part, which would
have necessitated removing the Body of our Lord, and
persuading the Jews that He had come to life again—
both things impossible of accomplishment under the circumstances.   There could not possibly be fraud in the
testimony of so many people of different characters, tem-
peraments, and imaginations, who saw, heard, and touched
the Saviour after His Resurrection.   If there had been
any imposture, what benefit could the disciples reap ?
Whereas, they remained steadfast to their assertions and
the cause of Christ through imprisonment, torture, and
death.

Evidence,
through
miscellaneous
witnesses, of
our Lord's
Resurrection.
Over five hundred ocular witnesses of unprejudiced
minds, spoken of by St. Paul, rendered deception or hallu-
cination impossible, concerning the number and variety
of our Lord's apparitions ; and unbelievers, in the persons
of Jews and pagans, were vanquished by the consequent
evidence of things.   Again, they who have tried to

[1] Matt. xxviii. 13.

explain our Saviour's Resurrection, otherwise than as a miracle of God, have seldom denied the fact itself; and countless are the miracles which have been performed in favour of the Catholic teaching, from the time of the Apostles even to the present day.

The Divinity of our Lord Jesus Christ is the basis of the Catholic religion, and the miracle of His Resurrection is the fundamental proof of that Divinity, predicted as such, to the Jews, long in advance, by our Lord Himself, when He said, "I lay down My life, that I may take it again. No man taketh it away from Me: but I lay it down of Myself, and I have power to lay it down: and I have power to take it up again." [1] *Proofs of our Lord's Divinity.*

Judging by the passages of Scripture, which speak of how the elect of Heaven shall appear at the last day, it is evident that the Body of our Saviour was, after His Resurrection, gloriously transformed, being endued with spirituality, subtility, agility, impassibility, and immortality; for our Lord must have been the model of what those called to everlasting life will be. We may derive practical lessons from this miraculous transfiguration of our Saviour after His Resurrection; that being dead to sin by Baptism, we should rise above temptation, as He rose from death, and "walk in newness of life," [2] thinking of heavenly things, and seeking "the things that are above; ... not the things that are upon the earth." [3] For that which is at present momentary and light of tribulation, worketh for us above measure exceedingly an eternal weight of glory." [4] *Transfiguration of our Saviour.*

[1] John x. 17, 18.   [2] Rom. vi. 4.
[3] Col. iii. 1, 2.   [4] 2 Cor. iv. 17.

The forty days following our Lord's Resurrection.

Our Lord "showed Himself alive after His Passion, by many proofs, for forty days," [1] and instructed His Apostles respecting the government, ordinances, and ceremonial of His Church, saying : " Teach ye all nations ; baptizing them in the name of the Father, and of the Son, and of the Holy Ghost : teaching them to observe all things whatsoever I have commanded you : and behold, I am with you all days, even to the consummation of the world." [2]

[1] Acts i. 3.   [2] Matt. xxviii. 19, 20.

CHAPTER VII.

SIXTH ARTICLE OF THE CREED.

"He ascended into Heaven, and sitteth on the right hand of God the Father Almighty."

IN saying, "He ascended into Heaven," we signify our belief that on the fortieth day after the Resurrection of our Redeemer, He ascended bodily into Heaven by the power of His Divinity. Belief in our Saviour's Ascension.

Our Lord, followed by His Apostles, went to the Mount of Olives, near Bethany. At this place, "He commanded them that they should not depart from Jerusalem, but should wait for the promise of the Father,"[1] in the coming of the Holy Ghost, who, as He had already given them to understand, was to fill them with a supernatural power and wisdom for the accomplishment of their mission, "even to the uttermost part of the earth."[2] Then, lifting up His hands, He blessed them; and it came to pass, that while He blessed them, He departed from them, and was carried up to Heaven."[3] Our Blessed Lord did not disappear suddenly, but was gradually lost to sight. It is interesting to read in the accounts given by ancient travellers that the vestige of a footprint exists on the rock of the Mount of Olives, which was believed to be that of our Saviour. Events connected with our Lord's Ascension.

---

[1] Acts i. 4.   [2] Acts i. 8.   [3] Luke xxiv. 50, 51.

Belief
regarding the
place our
Redeemer
occupies in
Heaven.

By the words, "and sitteth at the right hand of God the Father Almighty," we signify our belief that our Redeemer, as Man, occupies the first place, after the Father; but that, by His Divinity, He has, as He Himself declared, "all power . . . in Heaven and in earth."[1]

Equality of
the Son with
the Father.

In saying that He "sitteth," is to express in figurative language, the tranquillity and immutability of His eternal reign; and "at the right hand of God the Father Almighty" means the communication of the Divine almighty power to the humanity of our Blessed Lord which the Son of God possesses, being consubstantial with the Father.

Humanity
personated
in Heaven by
our Lord.

"God—who is rich in mercy—for His exceeding charity wherewith He loved us, even when we were dead in sins, hath quickened us together in Christ . . . and hath raised us up together, and hath made us sit together in heavenly places, through Christ Jesus."[2]   We should therefore exert ourselves to gain in grace as we walk through life, that we may be worthy to take our place in this realm of heavenly bliss, where our humanity has been elevated and impersonated by our Saviour.

[1] Matt. xxviii. 18.   [2] Eph. ii. 4–6.

CHAPTER VIII.

"From thence He will come to judge the living and the dead."

By the words, "from thence He will come to judge the living and the dead," we signify our belief that our Lord Jesus Christ will descend from Heaven, in all His Majesty and glory, at the last day, to judge mankind before the whole world, and reward each one according to his merits. "All nations shall be gathered together before Him, and He shall separate them one from another, as the shepherd separateth the sheep from the goats."[1] *Belief in the last judgment.*

In addition to the literal meaning of these words, "the living and the dead," the expression is taken in a figurative sense to indicate the just and the sinful. The just are called "living," because they possess the supernatural life of sanctifying grace; and sinners are called "dead," because they have lost that vital spark, and, by sin, are dead to the life and to the impulses of grace. *Signification of the "living and the dead."*

There are two judgments after death: "as it is appointed unto men once to die, and after this, the judgment."[2] There is the separate or particular judgment of each individual, which takes place immediately after the soul *Judgments of the dead.*

[1] Matt. xxv. 32.   [2] Heb. ix. 27.

departs from the body; and the general judgment at the end of the world, to which the seventh article of the Creed refers : " but of that day or hour no man knoweth." [1]   The latter will be the solemn and public confirmation of the former, when soul and body will be re-united for ever to receive eternal recompense or condemnation.

Anti-Christs.   Scripture mentions the coming of many anti-Christs, against whom we must combat and maintain our faith victoriously to the end, keeping our souls in a state of grace, so that we may be ever ready to meet death without fear of what shall await us.   Happy then, are they, whose names shall not be blotted out of " the book of life." [2]

[1] Mark xiii. 32.   [2] Apoc. xx. 12, 15.

CHAPTER IX.

"I believe in the Holy Ghost."

IN saying, "I believe in the Holy Ghost," we signify our belief in God the Holy Ghost, third Person of the Trinity, who proceeds from the Father and the Son, and is their equal, having one and the same nature, power, and Divinity.

Belief in the Holy Ghost.

By several passages in Scripture, we know that there is this third Person in God, whom our Lord called "the Spirit of truth, who proceedeth from the Father."[1] The third Person of the Trinity is designated by the name of Holy Ghost or Holy Spirit, meaning in Latin and Greek, "breath," because the third Divine Person emanates, as it were, from the mutual love of the Father and the Son, as a bond of perfect union, producing one single and substantial love, in the person of the Holy Ghost. He is also called the Divine Spirit of consolation, and Giver of life, because, in the Sacraments especially, the Holy Ghost gives to our souls that supernatural life of sanctifying grace, which is inseparable from the love of God; and He descended upon our Lord Jesus Christ, "as a dove from Heaven,"[2] symbolical of innocence, gentleness, and fecundity.

Evidence in Scripture of the Holy Ghost.

[1] John xv. 26.　　　　[2] John i. 32.

Descent of the
Holy Ghost
on the
Apostles.

After our Lord's Ascension, the Apostles "were persevering with one mind in prayer with the women, and
Mary the Mother of Jesus, and with His brethren," [1]
awaiting the day of Pentecost. Being all assembled, the
Holy Ghost descended upon them in the form of "parted
tongues as it were of fire," [2] emblematic of light and love.
The Apostles, who were simple, uneducated men, received
knowledge of the truths of religion, power of speaking
different languages, and courage to suffer the persecutions
that awaited them; "rejoicing that they were accounted
worthy to suffer reproach for the name of Jesus." [3] They
were likewise given power of communicating to others the
gifts of the Holy Ghost. This was the Sacrament of Confirmation as administered by the Apostle St. Paul after the
Sacrament of Baptism, when he imposed his hands on
certain disciples, and "the Holy Ghost came upon them,
and they spoke with tongues, and prophesied." [4] The
manifestation of the Holy Spirit was thus miraculously
great at the foundation of the Church, to strengthen and
encourage the faithful, and to favour the propagation of the
Gospel.

Influence of
the Holy
Spirit.

The presence of the Holy Ghost is clearly revealed
among us in most striking examples: by inspiring with
ardour the heart of the missionary who leaves his home,
his country, and his friends, to cross the seas and face
dangers and suffer hardships for the sole purpose of
bringing souls to the true belief; by stimulating with zeal
the priest in his guardianship and protection of the souls
committed to his care, the execution of painful and laborious
tasks, and even the braving contagion and death; by

---

[1] Acts i. 14.   [2] Acts ii. 3.   [3] Acts v. 41.   [4] Acts xix. 6.

inculcating love of charity and indifference for the comforts and luxuries of this world, among those who are thus spurred on to give their lives for the teaching of the young, consolation of the afflicted, and devotedness to the suffering and infirm.

Although God is everywhere, He makes His presence felt by the Holy Ghost who gives His love in sanctifying grace to the souls of the just. Therefore ought we to glorify God in our bodies as well as in our souls, and ask of the Holy Ghost, who is Giver of life and wisdom, light and understanding, to know our duties and real interests in this world, namely, our sanctification and salvation. We should also pray for divine love to make us devotedly and faithfully fulfil those duties; and for supernatural strength to surmount our weaknesses, and vanquish temptations and difficulties.

[margin note:] The Holy Ghost, Giver of grace.

CHAPTER X.

NINTH ARTICLE OF THE CREED.

"The Holy Catholic Church ; the communion of Saints."

Belief in the Church.

IN saying, "the Holy Catholic Church," we signify our belief in the Church founded by our Lord Jesus Christ; its holiness, and Catholicity; and consider ourselves bound to submit to its authority as Divine and infallible.

The Church founded by our Saviour.

The word "Church" is derived from the Greek, denoting assembly, and in the Creed means Religious Society. The Roman Catholic Church is, therefore, the religious society of all those who profess the true doctrine of our Lord Jesus Christ; who, having entered it by the Sacrament of Baptism, recognize, as means of salvation, all the other Sacraments instituted by our Saviour, and who submit and adhere to the teaching of those placed by Him in authority for the instruction of the faithful and the government of His Church.

The Church mentioned under three headings.

There is but one true Church, as our Saviour declared at its foundation, saying, "There shall be one fold and one shepherd."[1]   But it is spoken of under three headings : the Church militant, the Church suffering, and the Church triumphant.   The Church militant, means those members

[1] John x. 16.

of the true Church who are still on earth, fighting until death, against the devil, the world, and themselves. The Church suffering means those who are in purgatory, painfully expiating the punishment due for their sins, with a view to ultimate purification. The Church triumphant means those who are already in possession of the everlasting glory of Heaven.

Our Redeemer gave power and authority to His Apostles, saying: "Teach ye all nations; baptizing them in the name of the Father, and of the Son, and of the Holy Ghost. Teaching them to observe all things whatsoever I have commanded you: and, behold, I am with you all days, even to the consummation of the world."[1] "He that heareth you, heareth Me; and he that despiseth you, despiseth Me."[2] Therefore, refusing to be a member of the true Church is refusing to hear the successors of the Apostles, entrusted by our Blessed Lord to teach His doctrine; and is declining also to keep His commandments; consequently, is to despise Him; and despising God, is to will not to be saved. Our Lord said: "I am the door. By Me, if any man enter in, he shall be saved."[3] "He that is not with Me, is against Me."[4] Therefore, to willingly remain away from the true Church is to be against our Saviour; and those who are obstinately against Him, cannot obtain salvation. Again, our Saviour said that he who "will not hear the Church," shall be considered as a "heathen;"[5] and added, "Amen, I say to you, whatsoever you shall bind upon earth, shall be bound also in Heaven; and whatsoever you shall loose upon earth, shall be loosed

The power and authority given by our Lord to His Church.

---

[1] Matt. xxviii. 18-20.   [2] Luke x. 16.   [3] John x. 9.
[4] Luke xi. 23.   [5] Matt. xviii. 17.

F

also in Heaven."[1]   Consequently those who refuse to receive the doctrine and authority of Christ's Church, reject the one true means of salvation : "for there is no other name under Heaven given man, whereby we must be saved."[2]

Aliens from the Church.

There is no salvation for any who willingly, of their own fault or free accord, die out of the bosom of the true and only Church of our Lord Jesus Christ; for those who obstinately refuse to accept the teaching of the Church, and to submit themselves to its authority as its members, are heretics, and make shipwreck of the faith. "They profess that they know God ; but in their works, they deny Him ; being abominable, and incredulous, and to every good work reprobate."[3]   It is, however, a Catholic doctrine that those who follow faithfully the dictates of their own conscience, without wilfully putting obstacles in the way of Divine grace ;—who would, in short, become members of the Church if they knew it to be the true Church, belong by inward faith to the Church without being externally members of it,—sin not against the truth.   It is those who know, but knowing will not believe, and those who culpably continue in ignorance, that remain sinners; for as our Lord expressed it, " If you were blind, you should not have sin : but now you say, We see ; your sin remaineth."[4]

Very many Protestants have a most incorrect idea of Catholicism, and frequently content themselves with considering that, if they do their duty to the best of their ability in that state of life in which they find themselves placed, it is not for them, as laity, but for the clergy in general to dispute about, and decide upon the various

---

[1] Matt. xviii. 18.   [2] Acts iv. 12.   [3] Titus i. 16.   [4] John ix. 41.

abstruse points of doctrine. They therefore conclude, that it is beyond them to find any reason sufficient for inducing them to desert the religion of their fathers, in which they themselves have been brought up; or they do not care to think about embarrassing questions and to encounter difficulties, but prefer to agree to differ; —a mark of sloth almost amounting to indifference, which is scarcely excusable on any most important subject in life. They, meanwhile, seem to forget that if their ancestors had remained of the same faith as their forefathers of old, the chances are, that the greater number of those, who are now heretics or schismatics, would belong to the Catholic Church.

We ought to help each other towards the light of truth, but it is for the servant of the Lord to be "mild towards all men, apt to teach, patient, with modesty admonishing them that resist the truth." [1]

In constituting His Church, our Saviour committed the faithful to the care of pastors, who should teach and govern them under the authority of the bishops, themselves under the supremacy of the Roman Pontiff, His vicar on earth. *Supreme authority instituted by our Saviour for His Church.* Our Lord, in His love for him, wished St. Peter to be first, and, choosing him as head among the Apostles, He changed his name to one that should have reference to his future position, saying, "Thou art Simon, the son of Jona : Thou shalt be called Cephas, which is interpreted Peter." [2] And when St. Peter proclaimed Jesus to be "Christ, the Son of the living God;" [3] our Lord said, "Thou art Peter, and upon this rock I will build my Church; and the gates of Hell shall not prevail against it." [4] Our Redeemer thereby declared, not only that St. Peter should be the head of the

[1] 2 Tim. ii. 24, 25.   [2] John i. 42.   [3] Matt. xvi. 16.   [4] Matt. xvi. 18.

Church, but also that the Church should stand during all generations. Then our Saviour said, "I will give to thee the keys of the kingdom of Heaven. And whatsoever thou shalt bind upon earth, it shall be bound also in Heaven, and whatsoever thou shalt loose on earth, it shall be loosed also in Heaven." [1]   By this declaration our Lord gave St. Peter supreme ecclesiastical authority and power of teaching, ministry, and government; power to define doctrine, and instruct all nations; to regulate all religious functions for the due fulfilment of Divine worship; to validate or invalidate impediments of marriage, and grant indulgences. This gave equal privileges to St. Peter's successors, the Pope for the government of the whole Church, the bishops for diocesan jurisdiction, and the priests for parochial management. Again, our Lord gave spiritual supremacy of teaching to St. Peter personally, when He said, " Confirm thy brethren;" [2] and also when He said, " Feed My lambs, . . . Feed My sheep; " [3] meaning that St. Peter, as principal controller of the Church, and shepherd of the flock, should nourish the souls of those under him in · authority, designated by the name of "sheep," with the doctrine of truth; and that they, in their turn, should instruct the faithful or "lambs " of the fold.

St. Peter exercised his function as first head of the Church.

St. Peter was thenceforth recognized by the Apostles as their chief in all most solemn circumstances; his name always being at the head; "first, Simon, who is called Peter." [4]

After having preached the Gospel about Jerusalem and Antioch, he established his Episcopal See in Rome, then capital of the heathen world, in the reign of the Emperor

[1] Matt. xvi. 19.   [2] Luke xxii. 32.   [3] John xxi. 15, 17.   [4] Matt. x. 2.

Claudius, A.D. 42; where he was eventually martyred, and where is still his tomb, in what is now the capital of the Christian world.

In order that the Church might ever be under a supreme head, it was necessary there should be successors to St. Peter. This our Lord intended when He said, "Going, therefore, teach ye all nations, . . . and, behold, I am with you all days, even to the consummation of the world;"[1] giving to St. Peter personally, "the keys of the kingdom of Heaven,"[2] as power of authority to him and those who should follow in his place. From that time St. Peter has been succeeded in direct line by two hundred and fifty-nine Popes, about sixty of whom are honoured as saints, and about half of that number have merited the appellation of martyr. *Perpetuity of pastors.*

A small kingdom belonged to the Holy See for nearly twelve hundred years, until Italy became united under a King, who appropriated the Papal States. The principality forming the Papal States originally belonged to the rulers of the Byzantine or Eastern Empire, who proved incapable of defending it against the Lombards; and the Kings of France, conquerors at different times of the Lombards, who had invaded that country, presented it as a donation to the Holy See. *Papal States.*

Providence so willed that the Pope should have temporal power in the possession of a small Kingdom, because it is necessary that he, who is head of the Church, father and supreme guide of all Christians, should be independent of all other temporal government, and subject to no political ruler, in order that he may freely communicate and be communicated with, by any Catholic in the world, *Temporal power of the Pope.*

[1] Matt. xxviii. 19, 20.　　　　[2] Matt. xvi. 19.

as to all that concerns religious matters. Being sovereign guide of the souls of those who govern, as much as of their subjects, it is requisite for the Pope to be as unconstrained in his direction of the one as the other. An independent kingdom was considered indispensable to place any act of the Pope above all suspicion of having been dictated or inspired by any temporal power upon which he might be dependent; to exempt him from being mistrusted in respect of partiality on account of different nationality ; and that he might be always neutral in their disputes, whether political or otherwise, without obligation to submit to the temporal power of one country or another. It was also deemed desirable that the Episcopal See should have independent resources, contributing at least towards the many demands upon the Pope's aid. And in all ways the temporal power of the Pope is calculated to render his spiritual power more efficacious, and more fruitful, for the well-being and free government of the Church.

Temporal possessions of the Church.

There is nothing in the words of our Saviour that would give reason for disapprobation on this head, for although our Lord said, " My Kingdom is not of this world;"[1] He was clearly understood to mean that He had no thought of seeking to destroy the Roman empire in Palestine. His words do not, in any manner, insinuate that the Church should never have any temporal possessions.

Usurpation of the Church's temporal possessions.

The Pontifical Patrimony is sacred and inviolable, belonging, not to the Pope personally, but to the whole of the Catholic Church. It is inviolable as all legitimate possessions are, the partial or total usurpation of which the seventh commandment forbids. It is sacred, because that

[1] John xviii. 36.

which is given to the Church is consecrated to God; the spoliation of the Church being punished by excommunication.

Our Saviour established in His Church an infallibility of teaching, choosing twelve from among His disciples, whom also He named Apostles,"[1] which word signifies "messengers;" and said, "To you it is given to know the mysteries of the Kingdom of Heaven;"[2] "You are the light of the world;"[3] "That which I tell you in the dark, speak ye in the light: and that which you hear in the ear, preach ye upon the housetops."[4] "Whatsoever I have heard of My Father, I have made known to you. . . . I have chosen you; and have appointed you, that you should go, and should bring forth fruit; and your fruit should remain: that whatsoever you shall ask of the Father in My name, He may give it you."[5] "And I will ask the Father, and He shall give you another Paraclete, that He may abide with you for ever; the Spirit of truth, whom the world cannot receive, because it seeth Him not, nor knoweth Him: but you shall know Him; because He shall abide with you, and shall be in you."[6] In saying "for ever," it is evident that the Spirit of truth was promised by Christ, not only to His Apostles, but to their successors, to preserve them from error, for our Lord said: "The things that are to come, He shall show you;"[7] "He will teach you all things, and bring all things to your mind, whatsoever I shall have said to you."[8] Then, again, when our Saviour prayed for His Apostles, He said:

Infallibility of the Church.

[1] Luke vi. 13.   [2] Matt. xiii. 11.   [3] Matt. v. 14.
[4] Matt. x. 27.   [5] John xv. 15, 16.   [6] John xiv. 16, 17.
[7] John xvi. 13.   [8] John xiv. 26.

"Sanctify them in truth : Thy word is truth. As Thou
hast sent Me into the world, I also have sent them into
the world . . . and not for them only do I pray, but for
them also who, through their word, believe in Me."[1]   And
giving them command to act as His ministers throughout
the universe, He said : "Teach ye all nations; baptizing
them in the name of the Father, and of the Son, and of the
Holy Ghost; teaching them to observe all things whatsoever I have commanded you : and, behold, I am with you
all days, even to the consummation of the world."[2]

Infallibility of the Church, proved by reason.   When our Lord instituted His Church, He gave certain
commandments as to belief and practice. It is evident
that, in order that the government should be wisely
and efficiently carried out, there was needed a visible
head on earth, representative of our Lord Jesus Christ;
otherwise controversies would be interminable, not only
about appointments to ecclesiastical offices and respecting
matters of discipline, but also concerning doctrine; every
one interpreting the Scriptures according to his own ideas
or interests. Many texts of Scripture can admit of two
interpretations ; such, for example, as are concerned with the
two great subjects questioned by Protestants—the Sacraments of Penance and of the Holy Eucharist. How, then,
should a definite decision be arrived at, if not by the
authority of the Church ? As it is impossible that our
Lord would have condemned us to error, it is equally
impossible that He should subject our intelligence and will
to a power capable of leading us astray. Consequently it
is out of the question that He should not have made this
authority infallible.

[1] John xvii. 17, 18, 20.   [2] Matt. xxviii. 19, 20.

As the Scriptures were written by men whom God inspired for that purpose, their guidance must have been by Him rendered infallible. Why, then, should it be harder to believe that God still provides an authority in His Church whose teaching is infallible ?

Whatever may have been the character of some few Roman Pontiffs, among the great number who have reigned since the Apostle St. Peter, their conduct is no reason for condemnatory judgment of the existence of the institution itself, which was established by our Saviour. No more than the perfidious behaviour of Judas, whose traitorous actions by no means lessened the dignity or authority of the remaining portion of the Apostolic body. It is therefore indisputably, according to reason, that our Lord should have established a superior authority to give definite decisions, and thereby to close controversies.

Christian faith is contained in Holy Scripture, and in Tradition, conveyed direct from the Apostles; and the Catholic Church is the infallible interpreter thereof. Those who refuse submission to her teachings are declared heretics, and cut off, as such, from the body of the Church. This question of the authority of the Church is the root of all differences and discussions between Catholics and heretics. Were that settled, the rest would follow. A true disciple of Christ should have no dealings with heterodoxy, except with a view to bringing to the true faith those who are misled. " A man that is a heretic, after the first and second admonition, avoid : knowing that he, that is such an one, is subverted, and sinneth, being condemned by his own judgment." [1]

Infallibility of the Church, proved by the false principle of private interpretation.

[1] Titus iii. 10, 11.

Protestants refuse to admit that our Saviour instituted
this means of making known with certitude His doctrine,
and they reject the impossibility of His having established
the principle of free examination which they adopt, each
one studying the Scriptures and interpreting them according to his own ideas, forming his beliefs, devotions, and
mode of worship for himself. Thus Protestants set up
free examination, and individual reasoning and judgment,
in place of the Divine and infallible authority given by our
Redeemer to His Church. In the accusations brought
against the Catholic Church, it is necessary to make a clear
distinction between doctrine and discipline. Many practices which the Church has adopted are condemned, or at
least called in question, by Protestants, as being contrary
to doctrines of faith, because they cannot be found in
Scripture. But as our Lord gave His Church infallible
authority to govern and teach, He meant her members
to live in subservience to her laws; and there is certainly
nothing in Scripture which excludes the authority of the
Church, nor which presents the written word of God to us,
as offering the only rule of faith.

It being manifest, therefore, that the Church of Christ
was, by Him, given authority to teach and govern, it seems
incongruous that the various Protestant sects should dispute
the matter at all. The more so as they vary greatly in their
notions as to when they suppose error to have crept into
the Church. Some affirm that the Church first erred from
the true faith at the Council of Nicæa, when the Divinity of
our Saviour was defined. Others accept the authority of
the Church until the Council of Trent, thus admitting the
Church of Rome to have been the true Church of Christ up

to that period, whatever, till then, may have been her errors. However, all the rights we possessed before Protestants threw off their allegiance to us, still remain ours. A change took place in them, but we forfeited nothing.

The Apostles received their teaching verbally, and afterwards recorded part, at least, in writing; but there is no intimation in the New Testament that the Christian code was to be given in writing, although the written, as well as the verbal teaching of the doctrines, were mentioned as requiring an equal degree of respect, as is shown in St. Paul's Epistle to the Thessalonians : " Therefore, brethren, stand fast; and hold the traditions which you have learned, whether by word, or by our epistle." [1] We do not find that our Lord, or His Apostles after Him, gave any intimation whatever that the Christian rule of faith should be grounded on individual examination of written matter and on private interpretation of Scripture. On the contrary, our Saviour, in commanding His Apostles to "go forth and teach all nations," unquestionably intended their hearers to learn from their teaching, and be governed by them. It is, then, quite evident that we are not to make our own rule of faith, each one according to his own reading and judgment; but that we are to follow that which is taught us verbally by our priests, who are the descendants of Christ's Apostles. St. Paul, in writing to his disciple Timothy, does not tell him to give copies of his writings to those under him, in order that the doctrines, handed down by him, might be more surely delivered without danger of alteration; but he says, "The things which thou hast

[1] Thess. ii. 14.

heard of me by many witnesses, the same commend to faithful men, who shall be fit to teach others also." [1]

The fact of there existing none but manuscript Bibles for several centuries, would have been a decided impediment to individual deciphering and understanding of the Scriptures. Also, the art of reading could be by no means universal, especially before the invention of printing; and indeed, until books became common, this means of study would have been physically impracticable for the populace, even were the people in a position to be certain of the Bible they read being the true translation of the original manuscripts. This, however, is a cause of dispute, as is manifest by the diversity of translations that have been made. It is, then, logically impossible that our Lord should have established a means of knowing the truth, that must inevitably result in controversy, contradiction, and division of opinion, thereby producing an effect the reverse of that which He designed; all of which is incontestably the case among Protestant sects.

It is evident that the soul, in its greatest needs, requires and experiences comfort in leaning with certainty on an infallible authority which speaks definitely and decisively; and also in being able to feel that this authority teaches the truth. And, therefore, Catholics are consoled by the words of one who speaks in Christ's name, and whenever he says " Go in peace, thy sins are forgiven thee."

What the infallibility of the Church consists in.

The infallibility established by our Lord in His Church, regards matters of faith and morals, as well as discipline connected with those matters, when applying to the universal Church. Our Saviour established this infallibility

[1] 2 Tim. ii. 2.

concerning matters of faith and morals, when He gave His Apostles command to go and teach all nations; and this infallible sureness concerning matters of general discipline, when He bestowed on them divine authority of government, in consequence of which authority the Church's action can never be contrary to faith and morals. This infallibility of authority and of teaching being given to St. Peter personally, and to the other Apostles under his guidance, passed on to their successors, the Pope and the bishops. It is, therefore, clear that the Church must be preserved from error, for it is impossible that anything deviating from right and truth could "be bound also in Heaven."

There are two kinds of Councils for the determination of Two kinds of Councils. religious questions. First, those which consist of a sufficient assembly of bishops to represent the entire Church— that is to say, the Church in all parts of the world. These are called General Councils. They are presided over by the Pope or his Legate—a Cardinal, Bishop, or other ecclesiastic authorized by the Pope to act in his name at a General Council. The decrees formed by them, if approved of by the Pope, are infallible. Secondly, there are National, Provincial, or Diocesan, Councils or Synods. These are assemblies of the bishops of one nation or province, whose decrees are not meant for the universal Church, but concern only part of it—one country or one province. They are not infallible. But they may be approved of by the Pope as obligatory for the whole Catholic world. They then receive an infallible sanction. They can likewise be, by him, completely annulled, or sanctioned only for the nation or district where the Council was held. Our Lord said, "If two of you shall consent upon earth, concerning

anything whatsoever they shall ask, it shall be done to
them by My Father who is in Heaven. For where two
or three are gathered together in My name, there am I in
the midst of them."[1] This, of course, meant such assemblies as are gathered together in the name and authority
of the Church: in which manner it was practised by the
Apostles, when "Paul, choosing Silas, departed . . . and
he went through Syria and Cilicia, confirming the Churches,
commanding them to keep the precepts of the Apostles and
the ancients."[2] "And as they passed through the cities
they delivered unto them the decrees for to keep, that
were delivered by the Apostles and ancients who were at
Jerusalem."[3]

The institution of the Church's infallibility by our Lord.   In founding His Church, our Saviour addressed Himself
to the Apostle He intended should assume pre-eminence,
saying, "Thou art Peter; and upon this rock I will build
my Church; and the gates of Hell shall not prevail against
it."[4] The foundation stone must be firm, otherwise the
whole edifice would inevitably fall to the ground. The
foundation of the Church must be imperishable and infallible. It was, then, to St. Peter, as chief of the Apostles
and of the whole Church in futurity of time, that our
Saviour spoke the solemn words which assured to him the
privilege of infallibility, and of its becoming permanent in
the person of his successors. When, therefore, the Pope
speaks *ex-Cathedra*, that is to say, when he makes use of
his office as pastor of all Christians, and exercises his
supreme Apostolic authority, to define a doctrine on matters
of faith or morals, he does so by the divine assistance promised to St. Peter, and consequently such definitions are

[1] Matt. xviii. 19, 20.   [2] Acts xv. 40, 41.   [3] Acts xvi. 4.   [4] Matt. xvi. 18.

free from error. But, for the Pope's determination to be Indispensable conditions for the Pope's decisions to become infallible. infallible, and for that reason obligatory on every Catholic, under penalty of heresy, the decision must be concerning faith or morals,—which includes all general discipline bound up with faith or morals,—and must be given by the Pope, not as a private person, or merely as a counsellor, or as head, in a special sense, of local Churches at Rome, or in Italy, but as supreme head of the whole Church and pastor of all Christians.

All tenets or articles of faith are contained or involved Articles of faith. in what was revealed to the Apostles, and transmitted by them, through Scripture or Tradition; but all beliefs so transmitted by the Apostles are not necessarily articles of faith—the Catholic Church not having attached to every one of them the seal of authority. The Church makes no changes, creations, or innovations regarding the Catholic doctrine as taught by our Saviour, but simply interprets and explains faithfully the revelation handed down by the Apostles. It makes progress, but no other alteration. By progress everything expands or enlarges, but remains itself; by alteration it is transformed into something else. However worthy and wise a Pope may be, nothing he may say, either in private conversation or public allocution, in writing or in speaking, to his bishops or to other individuals, has the privilege of infallibility, unless, in his position as chief guide to all Christians, he gives, to the entire Church, a decision on the subject of faith or morals in the manner described; the prerogative of doctrinal infallibility appertaining to the Pope's supreme authority, and by no means depending on his personal merits. It therefore, in no way, renders him incapable of sinning.

Characteristic marks of the Church.

The true Church is One, Holy, Catholic, and Apostolic, and by these characteristic marks may be recognized. In the Creed, the word "Church," in the singular—not "Churches," in the plural—indicates its Unity. Its Holiness and Catholicity are expressly mentioned. Its Apostolicity is implicitly and tacitly understood; for the Church could not be Catholic or universal as to time, unless it could be traced back without interruption to the Apostles, and consequently were Apostolic.

Unity of the Church.

The Unity of the true Church of our Lord Jesus Christ consists in concord of pastoral ministry and of faith; that is to say, that its members are in submission to its legitimate pastors, and profess the same doctrine for the attainment of the same end. Obedience to the same authority, from which proceeds the profession of the same faith, produces unity of religion, giving to all the same rights, and imposing on all the same duties for the acquirement of the same supernatural end—one head, one faith, one worship. Our Saviour said, "There shall be one fold and one shepherd."[1] And when praying for His Apostles, He said, "That they may be one, as Thou, Father, in Me, and I in Thee; that they may also be one in Us."[2] Caiaphas, the high priest, prophesied that our Lord should die, "not only for the nation, but to gather together in one the children of God that were dispersed.[3] St. Paul, in his Epistle to the Ephesians, speaks of the Unity of the Church, exhorting them "carefully to keep the unity of the Spirit in the bond of peace. One body and one Spirit; as you are called in one hope of your calling. One Lord, one faith, one baptism."[4] And again, St. Paul mentions the Unity

[1] John x. 16.   [2] John ii. 21.   [3] John xi. 52.   [4] Eph. iv. 3–5.

of the Church, saying, "If any one preach to you a gospel besides that which you have received, let him be anathema." [1]

The true Church is Holy, inasmuch as it teaches a holy doctrine, and offers to all means of holiness. It surpasses and eclipses every sect by the efficacy of its doctrine and worship, and by its laws for the sanctification of souls. The reality of such holiness is manifest in many of its members by matchless external effects, such as are evinced through holy teaching, holy acts and miracles. For instance, there have been Martyrs of all ages, both sexes, all conditions, all nationalities, who have suffered willingly for the love of God, giving proof of the sanctity of the Church. The apostle or missionary who voluntarily quits his country and sacrifices all his earthly well-being, even his very life, for the conquest of souls to Christ, is a living proof of the Holiness of the Church to which he belongs. Virtues of charity, patience, chastity, or alienation from the world, carried to a degree of heroism, prove that Holiness exists in that Church, whereof those who practise these virtues are members. Real miracles can only be performed by divine power, and consequently it is to the Saints, and to no others, that God accords the privilege of working them unceasingly in the true Church; and this is an undeniable demonstration of its Holiness. We have but to contemplate the acts of the Martyrs, the lives of the Saints, and the histories of the religious orders, to recognize the Holiness of the Church, even as we recognize a tree by its fruit. Our Saviour founded His Church to bring souls, through sanctification, to the eternal life of Heaven.

Holiness of the Church.

---

[1] Gal. i. 9.

He "delivered Himself up for it . . . that it should be holy and without blemish,"[1] in a large degree, even in this world. And St. Paul speaks of the Church as made up of those "called to be Saints."[2] If, therefore, the Church did not produce Saints, it would not fulfil its purpose.

Catholicity of the Church.

The true Church is Catholic, inasmuch as it is universal, existing over the greater part of the world; exercising its jurisdiction, either successively or simultaneously, in all those countries, which, in communion with each other, form one spiritual kingdom or body. The Roman Catholic Church is the only one truly Catholic, because it alone is universal, and alone teaches the same doctrine that our Lord commanded should be "preached in the whole world, for a testimony to all nations."[3] The word "Roman" is in no way a geographical limitation, but a term signifying which amongst Christian bodies are in communion with the Bishop of Rome. It is manifestly unfair to argue from the expression that the Roman Catholic Church is not universal. It is universal, subsisting in all ages, existing in all nations, teaching all revealed truth. "But I say: Have they not heard? Yea, verily, their sound hath gone forth into all the earth, and their words unto the ends of the whole world."[4]

Apostolicity of the Church.

The true Church is Apostolic, inasmuch as it has never separated itself from the Church, whose doctrine has descended, through a direct line of pastors, from the Apostles, under the supreme chief, St. Peter. The Apostles established the Church according to the direction of our Lord Jesus Christ Himself, who founded it on St. Peter,

---

[1] Eph. v. 25, 27.   [2] Rom. i. 7; 1 Cor. i. 2.
[3] Matt. xxiv. 14.   [4] Rom. x. 17, 18.

and his successors, perpetuated in a line unbroken. The Church has certainly never held any doctrine, previously declared by it to be heretical, and never has declared heretical any doctrine, formally defined as an article of faith. It teaches, and always has taught, the true doctrine of our Saviour. Being Apostolic is a distinctive mark appertaining to the Roman Church, and to no other; for with all sects the point of interruption or commencement can be so defined as to be beyond dispute. For our Lord established in His Church one single Apostolic body under a supreme head, deputed for its instruction and government. Consequently, as the Catholic Church is the only one having certain and uninterrupted and direct successors to these Apostolic teachers and rulers, it must necessarily be the true Church.

The principal contemporary sects, separated from the Church, are the Protestant heretics and the Greek and Russian schismatics, who, wishing to modify the true doctrine somewhat, have chosen to depart from the Catholic Church to which they originally belonged. For the very absence of any one of the four characters, or distinctive "notes," of the true Church founded by our Lord Jesus Christ, is sufficient to condemn theirs as being false. *Sects separated from the Church.*

Protestantism is a shapeless, antagonistic medley of a multitude of sects, protesting against the true Church, and rejecting, as a fundamental cause for dissent, the divine and infallible authority of teaching, belonging to it. Protestantism is divided into three principal branches: Lutheranism, Calvinism, and Anglicanism; which are again subdivided into a heterogeneous collection or crowd of other sects. *Protestant heretics.*

Schismatics.   The Greek and Russian schismatics have alienated themselves from the true Church by their refusal to recognize the divinely instituted supremacy of the Pope over the Church Catholic, thereby rejecting the sovereign authority of Governance established by our Saviour.

Unity of the Church, not applicable to sects.   In comparing Protestantism with Catholicism, relatively to the four characteristic marks of Unity, Holiness, Catholicity, and Apostolicity, it is easy to see how absolute is the super-eminence of the latter over the former. The Roman Catholic Church is the only one which possesses unity of ministry and exacts complete unity in faith, sentiment, and action; oneness is the dominant idea which gives it exclusive individuality. Its members are one in belief, worship, and submission, conformably with the teaching and ordinance of our Blessed Lord ; so that when questioned on this or that point, in any part of the globe, they will always give answers identical. Protestant heretics have neither unity of faith nor of ministry, and when interrogated, will tender a diversity of contradictory replies, after the manner in which each one understands his Scriptures. For their principle of individual examination and private judgment creates dissension only, and harbours every kind of variation of opinion.

Holiness of the Church, not applicable to sects.   The Roman Catholic Church possesses sanctity or Holiness; its dogmatic and moral doctrine embracing every virtue, perfection, and good work, and condemning every vice, evil thought, word, or action; hence affording every means and incentive for the sanctification of the soul. Among backsliders and apostates, is there one who has ever, in consequence of desertion from the true faith, become more virtuous, more pure in mind or body ? Is there one who has, on abandoning the Catholic Church, made any great worldly sacrifice for the sake of heresy or schism ? Is there any Catholic who, at the hour of death, regrets the doctrine he professes, and turns for consolation, salvation, and sanctification towards some sect ? The Catholic Church gives proofs, even to the most prejudiced, of the sublime virtues of its saints. Protestants, on the other hand, since their alienation from it, would be at a loss to present authentically proved instances of heroism carried to its highest pitch, and cannot point to a single miracle. Although Protestantism may form certain charitable communities, they can never produce anything worthy of comparison with the Catholic religious orders, whether of men or of women, except by imitating them, and more or less disobeying their Bishops placed in a position of rule. Without entering into the comparative merits and moral character of the public representatives of the Catholic and Protestant Churches, our contention is, that the Church of Christ is, through His promise, preserved from error and corruption; whereas Protestants can only strive to justify their separation from us by supposing that our Lord's Church did not always possess the character of Holiness. In short, they can solely ground their formation of a new system of belief on the assumption that the Church was at some time unholy.

The Roman Catholic Church possesses universality of doctrine and communion in space and in time. On the other hand, although Protestants may be found in divers parts of the world, they hold opinions heretical, and beliefs never universally identical; nor have they Catholicity of time, since they only date as far back as the sixteenth century. *Catholicity of the Church, not applicable to sects.*

Our right to the title of Catholic is amply shown by the designation given in all ages to the Church of Christ, through its spread in universality of communion throughout the Christian world. Further, the Protestant Church not only varies in its teaching, but is not unfrequently so limited in range as to be narrowed to the particular nationality where, for the time being, it happens to find acceptance. The very name "Protestant," in its antagonism to the Catholic Church, is expressive of absence of universality.

Apostolicity of the Church, not applicable to sects.   The Roman Catholic Church is Apostolic by its certain and legitimate succession of supreme Pastors in direct and uninterrupted line from St. Peter and the Apostles to our own time ; whereas, amongst the sects "protesting," inasmuch as they have only existed since the sixteenth century, in that number of centuries there stands a gap between their origin and the time of the Apostles. No tangible proof is forthcoming of any Protestant religion having been heard of before that date ; they have hence clearly no legitimate right to call themselves Apostolic. The origin of the word "Apostolic," as one of the characteristic marks of the Church, is not that its doctrines are Apostolical—although certainly the doctrine now taught is the same as that believed by the Apostles,—but that the Apostolic succession has come direct from the first holder of the Roman See, who was nominated by our Redeemer Himself as chief of His Church, down to the present Pope. By a special dispensation of Divine Providence the Roman See is the only one in which the succession of pastors has been preserved without interruption. Therefore, as seen from the foregoing pages, there are four "notes" pointing

out which is the true Church of Christ, and the Catholic
Church alone combines these four notes, for it alone is
One, Holy, Catholic, and Apostolic.

In saying, "the communion of Saints," we signify our Belief in the
communion of
belief in the communication of spiritual benefits between Saints.
the members of the Church Militant, the Church Suffering,
and the Church Triumphant, all of whom form one body;
" for the body also is not one member, but many. If the
foot should say, because I am not the head I am not of the
body ; is it therefore not of the body ? "[1] "For as in one
body we have many members, but all the members have
not the same office : so we being many, are one body in
Christ, and every one members one of another."[2]

The Faithful in Heaven are called " Saints," because they Explanation
of the
are already in possession of eternal happiness. The Faithful communion of
Saints.
in Purgatory are called " Saints," because they are in a
state of grace which they can never lose, and are destined
to enter Paradise when their term of expiation is ended.
The Faithful on earth are called " Saints," because all are
consecrated to God by Baptism, and are offered the opportunity of sanctification by the other Sacraments of the
Church. Members of the Church Militant are in communion with each other, by professing the same faith,
obeying the same authority, and helping each other by
their prayers and good acts. They are in communion
with those in Heaven, by honouring them and supplicating
the charity of their prayers ; they are in communion with
those in Purgatory, by praying in their behalf; and the
faithful in Purgatory are in communion with the holy
ones on earth, by craving help and protection. Thus the

---

[1] 1 Cor. xii. 14, 15.   [2] Rom. xii. 4, 5.

Church Militant and Suffering is united with the Church Triumphant. This is the Communion of Saints.

We may be certain that this communication of spiritual benefits is distributed by God in just proportion to the good disposition of each individual, according to his deserts and his personal participation in the common treasury of merits and indulgences. For how can one who gives little expect to receive much ? or share largely in the merits of others, if he deserve but little or no reward on his own account; except perhaps by obtaining the grace of conversion to a purer and more saintly state of living, which is, after all, a priceless treasure to be sought for with all diligence ? " I say to you, that even so there shall be joy in Heaven upon one sinner that does penance, more than upon ninety and nine just who need not penance." [1]

[1] Luke xv. 7.

CHAPTER XI.

"The remission of sins."

BY "the remission of sins," we signify our belief that the pastors of the Church have divine authority from our Saviour for the forgiveness of sins. He bestowed that power on St. Peter and His other Apostles, and through them to their successors, saying : "Whose sins you shall forgive, they are forgiven them ; and whose sins you shall retain, they are retained." [1]

Belief in the remission of sins.

Absolution is administered in an external manner through the Sacrament of Penance. The remission of sins in the Sacrament of Penance is the pardon of the guilt itself, not including the remission of the temporal punishment due for the expiation of the sin forgiven. Theologians suppose that there was from the very beginning a ceremonial rite for the remission of original sin, given in prevision of the future merits of the Divine Redeemer ; and that the remission of actual sin could be obtained only by means of perfect contrition. How immensely grateful, then, should we be for the precious benefits that we receive in the Sacraments, established by our Lord

Sin remitted through Baptism and Penance.

[1] John xx. 23.

Jesus Christ, for the present sanctification and ultimate salvation of our souls; particularly for the strength given us by the Sacrament of Penance in our ever recurring weaknesses! Those who reject the light of the Holy Spirit, and thus die incredulous and unfaithful, are necessarily unrepentant, and consequently their sins remain unforgiven in this life and cannot be pardoned after death. This may explain the words of our Lord, when He said : "Every sin and blasphemy shall be forgiven men, but the blasphemy of the Holy Spirit shall not be forgiven . . . neither in this world, nor in the world to come." [1] It is, therefore, our own fault if we do not give ourselves up to repentance, do not profit by so easy a means of recovering the supernatural gift of sanctifying grace, and do not gain everlasting salvation.

[1] Matt. xii. 32; Luke xii. 10.

CHAPTER XII.

"The resurrection of the body."

IN saying, "the resurrection of the body," we signify our belief that at the end of this world the body of each one will be restored to life and be re-united to the soul to which it belonged on earth. "For the hour cometh, wherein all that are in the graves shall hear the voice of the Son of God. And they that have done good things, shall come forth unto the resurrection of life; but they that have done evil unto the resurrection of judgment."[1] *Belief in the resurrection of the body.*

The resurrection of the dead will immediately precede the last judgment, when the sentence pronounced by our Supreme Judge, will forthwith be put into execution, and the soul adjudged for ever, according to its merits. The sea will give up her dead, and so will the earth and the under-world, and they shall be "judged every one according to their works."[2] The righteous man will have life everlasting when Christ "will raise him up in the last day."[3] For although all things change, nothing is lost, and "death is swallowed up in victory."[4] But those who are not "found written in the book of life," will be "cast into *The resurrection of the dead before the last judgment.*

[1] John v. 28, 29.   [2] Apoc. xx. 13.   [3] John vi. 40.   [4] Cor. xv. 54.

the pool of fire. . . . This is the second death,"[1] which to avoid, we should ever lead a life that is pure, keeping our souls free from sin and prepared for judgment, " for we know not the day nor the hour "[2] when the Son of Man shall come.

As our body contributes to the evil and to the good we do, so will it share in whatsoever is awarded, whether of condemnation or glorification, to the soul. " For we must all be manifested before the judgment seat of Christ, that every one may receive the proper things of the body, according as he hath done, whether it be good or evil."[3]

The resurrection of the bodies of the just.   On the day of resurrection, the bodies of the just will be glorified in a manner similar to that of our Blessed Lord at His Resurrection, " who will reform the body of our lowness, made like to the body of His glory, according to the operation whereby also He is able to subdue all things unto Himself."[4] We shall not be in the state of our childhood, nor in that of old age, nor in that of deformity in which we may happen to die ; but shall be endowed with the qualities of agility, subtility, spirituality, and impassibility, in due proportion to our supernatural virtues on earth. Thus St. Paul says, " One is the glory of the sun, and another the glory of the moon, and another the glory of the stars : for star differeth from star in glory, so also is the resurrection of the dead."[5] By agility is meant a supernatural quality, imparting perfect submission of the body to the spirit, in the power of transporting itself from one place to another, with light and ethereal speed ; " the just shall shine, and shall run to and fro like sparks among

---

[1] Apoc. xx. 15, 14.   [2] Matt. xxv. 13.   [3] 2 Cor. v. 10.
[4] Phil. iii. 21.   [5] 1 Cor. xv. 41, 42.

the reeds."[1] By subtility is meant a supernatural quality, giving the body the power of penetrating other bodies that pure spirits have; "sown a natural body, it shall rise a spiritual body."[2] By spirituality is meant a supernatural quality, giving the brilliancy and glorious effulgence of the soul to the body; "then shall the just shine as the sun."[3] By impassibility is meant a supernatural quality, rendering our bodies exempt from all material troubles and infirmities, from suffering and pain. "Sown in corruption, it shall rise in incorruption . . . sown in dishonour, it shall rise in glory,"[4] to enjoy complete repose and satiety of all desires. "No more hunger nor thirst,"[5] no grief nor sadness; for "God shall wipe away all tears from their eyes; and death shall be no more, nor mourning, nor crying, nor sorrow . . . for the former things are passed away;"[6] and we shall possess eternal life. The soul will be re-united to the body for ever, to live in the blessedness with which God has invested His rewards, for "this mortality must put on immortality."[7]

"We shall all indeed rise : but we shall not all be changed."[8] On the day of resurrection the bodies of sinners will remain materially the same. That is to say, they will not be endowed with the four first-named privileges of the just, but will pass their eternity in " everlasting punishment."[9] "What things a man shall sow, those also shall he reap. For he that soweth in his flesh, of the flesh also shall reap corruption : But he that soweth in the spirit, of the spirit shall reap life everlasting."[10] The bodies of

The resurrection of the bodies of the unjust.

---

[1] Wisdom iii. 7.   [2] 1 Cor. xv. 44.   [3] Matt. xiii. 43.
[4] 1 Cor. xv. 42, 43.   [5] Apoc. vii. 16.   [6] Apoc. xxi. 4.   [7] 1 Cor. xv. 53.
[8] 1 Cor. xv. 51.   [9] Matt. xxv. 46.   [10] Gal. vi. 8.

sinners in Hell will be re-united to their souls, only that they may, with them, and partly by them, eternally suffer penalty for the abuse they have made of them ; retaining remembrance of the cause of their punishment, and the miserable pleasures of this life, for which they bartered their souls.

Judgment leading to everlasting happiness or punishment. From horror of what awaits the unjust, the consolation afforded us in anticipation of the eternal happiness we may so easily gain, should sustain us with confidence and courage to lead a moral and even highly virtuous existence, in the practice of mortification of the body for the salvation of the soul. By penitence, we may redeem the time we have wasted in the pursuit of the vanities of this vain world, and seek after whatever may beautify the soul, moulding ourselves to honour rather than dishonour, bearing in mind St. Peter's words : " Labour the more that by good works you may make sure your calling and election." [1]

[1] 2 Pet. i. 10.

CHAPTER XIII.

"And life everlasting."

By the words, "and life everlasting," we signify our belief in the eternal life of happiness which is reserved for the just. It is alluded to in this absolute manner, as being the only true and immortal life, in contradistinction to the everlasting death of those "who obey not the Gospel of our Lord Jesus Christ: who shall suffer eternal punishment in destruction from the face of the Lord, and from the glory of His power."[1] "Life everlasting," also implies death and judgment, because every one must pass through both before entering Heaven. It implies Purgatory, because the greater number have sins to expiate, before they can possess the happiness of Paradise; and it also implies Hell, because as Heaven is life eternal to the souls of the just, so is Hell ever-abiding continuance in torment, and absence from God. *Belief in life everlasting.*

Death that "passed upon all men,"[2] as the inheritance of original sin, is the temporary separation of the soul from the body, snatching us away from those who are dear to us on earth. The body may decompose, but its *The death of man.*

---

[1] 2 Thess. i. 8, 9.　　　　[2] Rom. v. 12.

minutest particles are never lost; and the soul passes immediately to judgment and from thence to Heaven, Purgatory, or Hell. As there is nothing in Scripture or Tradition, that contradicts the belief, we may suppose that those who are living at the last day, will die in the conflagration of the universe, when "the heavens shall pass away with great violence, and the elements shall be melted with heat, and the earth and the works which are in it, shall be burnt up."[1]

Eternity.   Our Eternity depends upon the state of our soul at the time of our death. We do well, therefore, to curtail pleasures and luxuries on earth during our span of existence; for if we risk dying in sin by neglecting to live in a state of grace, we are in constant danger of giving ourselves up to eternal desolation and suffering. Not knowing what shall be on the morrow, we should not make light of the thought of death, nor content ourselves with some distant preparation, but be ever "ready"[2] for that which is so inevitable and decisive. For what is life? "It is a vapour, which appeareth for a little while, and afterwards shall vanish away."[3] Sad though the thought of death may be to many, it would be sadder indeed not to have bestowed upon it sufficient consideration. And why should that be sad which ends so much of misery, poverty, suffering, and temptation, taking us to a life of joy without end! The thought of death, too, helps to preserve us from sin, and to console us in the afflictions of life. Because "that which is at present momentary and light of our tribulation, worketh for us above measure exceedingly an eternal weight of glory; while we look not at the things which

1 2 Pet. iii. 10.   2 Matt. xxiv. 44.   3 Jas. iv. 15.

are seen, but at the things which are not seen: for the things which are seen are temporal ; but the things which are not seen are eternal."¹ The thought of death makes us realize the worthlessness of worldly riches and pleasures, "for what doth it profit a man, if he gain the whole world, and suffer the loss of his own soul ? "² Should we not then seek, with all the fervour of our souls, to die in sanctifying grace by righteous living, re-membering this, that "where our treasure is, there will our heart be also." ³

At the moment the soul is separated from the body by death, it receives the judgment of irrevocable salvation or damnation. For God, "without respect of persons, judgeth according to every one's works." ⁴ Those who have been favoured with fuller instruction and enlighten-ment as to their duties, will be more severely judged than the heathen. Likewise those who have been called to higher religious training, and have received spiritual graces in more abundance than ordinary members of the Church : for "unto whomsoever much is given, of him much shall be required." ⁵ And each one will be obliged to give account of his smallest faults as well as of his greatest sins ; " every idle word that men shall speak, they shall render an account for it ; "⁶ if we cannot give this, then shall we be judged without indulgence. We should, then, practise penitence and mortification, for "if we would judge our-selves, we should not be judged ; "⁷ remembering that our sins do not pass into oblivion, but are counted one by one in record against us.

Judgment immediately after death.

---

¹ 2 Cor. iv. 17, 18.   ² Matt. xvi. 26.   ³ Luke xii. 34.   ⁴ 1 Pet. i. 17.
⁵ Luke xii. 48.   ⁶ Matt. xii. 36.   ⁷ 1 Cor. xi. 31.

H

Purgatory. Purgatory is an exile and a prison where the acute
realization of being denied the possession of Heaven and
the presence of God is ever present to the mind as punishment for sin; where there is neither power to gain nor to
lose in merit; where the one desire of the heart is for
Heaven, and the great chastisement is banishment from the
Divine Presence. Those in Heaven are already redeemed
from sin, and those in Hell are beyond redemption; but
souls in Purgatory can benefit by our prayers and supplications in the life of purification, through which they must
pass to be cleansed and made worthy of God. For "the
fire shall try every man's work, of what sort it is." [1]

Purgatory proved by reason. Reason alone proves the existence of Purgatory. If two
souls are taken from this earth, one having led a virtuous
and pious life from first to last, the other having lived in
vice and crime, but finally repenting, is converted, and
receives absolution, both leave this world in a state of grace.
But if both straightway entered Heaven, there would merely
be a difference of greater glory for the one than for the
other. Therefore it is consistent with the infinite justice of
God, to assume with certitude the existence of Purgatory.

Prayers for the dead. It is "a holy and wholesome thought to pray for the
dead, that they may be loosed from sins." [2] In praying for
souls suffering the punishment due for sin, we perform a
duty to God by aiding in the speed of their entry into
Heaven, where they increase, by their presence, the praise
and adoration offered by the Saints and Angels, who
glorify God during all eternity. We perform a duty to
our neighbour by acting towards him as we would he
should act towards us, besides offering to those we have

[1] 1 Cor. iii. 13.   [2] 2 Mac. xii. 46.

known and cared for on earth, just recognition of the love, friendship, or gratitude we may owe them. We perform a duty to ourselves by profiting personally through that which we do in their favour; for Christ said, "As long as you did it to one of these My least brethren, you did it to Me."[1] If, then, acts of charity in this world are esteemed by God as though done to Himself, how much greater merit is there in what we do towards benefiting souls in Purgatory! We gain their gratitude, and consequently reap advantage from their prayers and powerful intercession when their term of expiation being ended they enter Heaven, where forgetfulness and want of charity are impossible. Although we may feel convinced as to those who enter Heaven, we can make no assertion about who shall be lost in Hell; for who knows what may pass between God and the soul of any one of us at the last moment! So our prayers can, with God's mercy, be efficacious for a sinner whom He alone can judge. Venial sin should not, as is too frequently the case, be lightly regarded, or dismissed from our minds as unimportant, when we consider the grievous penalty that it engenders. But all precautions possible should be observed, to escape, or at least lessen, the period of our retention in Purgatory, by the avoidance of sin, even venial; aided by penitence, piety, charity, and good works.

Heaven is that kingdom far "above all heavens,"[2] where Heaven. our happiness is complete and eternal, in the contemplation of God by the beatific vision, the ever-enduring union with our Saviour, and the joy which results therefrom; thus completing our heavenly happiness in this triple

---

[1] Matt. xxv. 40.   [2] Eph. iv. 10.

recompense of the three theological virtues, of which the one that is everlasting in Heaven is Charity. Faith, which we possess on earth, in the steadfast belief of beholding God, cannot have place in Paradise, when there we see what we have here believed without seeing. Likewise the Hope we experience in this world, that causes us to await with patience and confidence the realization of our Redeemer's promises, disappears when we possess that for which we have hoped. Charity alone remains, to become more and more perfect, and more like the charity of Him who is ever merciful, and ever great in His love for all mankind.

Beatific vision.

The elect of Heaven are sure of the vision of God, "for we see now through a glass in a dark manner; but then face to face."[1] And our Lord Himself declared this by saying, "Blessed are the clean of heart: for they shall see

Union with God.

God."[2] They are sure of unchanging union with God, because "we are the sons of God: and if sons, heirs also; heirs indeed of God, and joint heirs with Christ;"[3] and

Everlasting happiness.

partakers of the Divine nature."[4] They are sure of the joy which results from this vision of, and union with God, rejoicing, as St. Peter describes it, "with joy unspeakable and glorified."[5] For it is written, "Eye hath not seen, nor ear heard, neither hath it entered into the heart of man, what things God hath prepared for them that love Him."[6] We are certain that these three rewards are changeless and everlasting. Our Saviour described them as the "joy no man shall take from you:"[7] and St. Peter "as an inheritance incorruptible, and undefiled, and that cannot fade."[8]

[1] 1 Cor. xiii. 12.   [2] Matt. v. 8.   [3] Rom. viii. 16, 17.
[4] 2 Pet. i. 4.   [5] 1 Pet. i. 8.   [6] 1 Cor. ii. 9.
[7] John xvi. 22.   [8] 1 Pet. i. 4.

We are sure of eternal rest and peace of mind and body, for " God shall wipe away all tears ;"[1] and we shall have liberty for good alone, and shall be sinless as are the Angels of Heaven.

As we have a natural aversion for suffering and a natural desire for happiness, Heaven is the crown of our life, and ending of every misery and pain, a realization of joy for ever, beyond all that our imagination can conceive. What, then, can seem too hard a task to fulfil in order to win the glories that await us ?—We work so vigorously for position, affluence, and pleasure in this transitory life, and surely we had better devote our time, mind, and will, in more exact proportion to the eternal wealth of riches we are free to merit in Heaven.

Contemplation of our ultimate happiness.

Hell is a place of anguish and torment, where those who have voluntarily and finally defied God suffer the everlasting punishment of their sins, proportioned in its violence to their deserts. It consists of absolute and eternal separation from God, enchained in darkness, as " the Angels who kept not their principality;"[2] where the fire of remorse for having voluntarily merited damnation, and of despair for this incomparable and unending anguish, is unextinguishable: " where the worm dieth not, and the fire is not quenched."[3] If sinners die with determined will for evil, they freely place themselves beyond recall of good, and in ceaseless degradation and torture.

Eternal punishment of Hell.

Death, Judgment, Heaven, and Hell are collectively the end of life, because we are obliged to pass through each of the two first stages in turn, and these definitely determine our eternal future of salvation or damnation. Purgatory is

The end of life.

---

[1] Apoc. xxi. 4.   [2] Jude i. 6.   [3] Mark ix. 47.

not thus named, being but a temporary condition between earth and Paradise; therefore the Creed closes expressing the object of all our desires, the haven of rest and happiness on which our hopes are centred, the life of tranquillity and joy that shall have no end, and to which it should be our one greatest aim in this transitory existence to attain.

Conclusion of the Creed.

The word " Amen " is derived from the Hebrew, meaning " So be it," and signifies acquiescence or confirmation of all that has preceded it. Thus, in the Creed, it is a final protestation of firm belief in the twelve articles. It is the expression of a desire to obtain the unending life of happiness promised to those who believe and follow all that the Church teaches; and it is a prayer for the highest of our desires, to reach, in truth and in godliness, "the life everlasting."

CHAPTER XIV.

" If thou wilt enter into life, keep the Commandments." [1]

THE Commandments of the Christian religion were taken from the Mosaic religion, with modifications made by the Divine authority of our Lord Jesus Christ and of His Church. They are laws expressing the will of our Creator, and are imposed by Him on all men throughout the universe. They are the twofold fundamental precept of God; the development of the great law of Charity. They are obligatory, general, just, useful, permanent, legitimate, and promulgated for the well-being of our transitory existence in this world, with a view to our ultimate salvation. Therefore the violation of one commandment may involve forfeiture of attainment of eternal happiness, for it is written, " Whosoever shall keep the whole law, but offend in one point, is become guilty of all." [2] *The Commandments in general.*

The Commandments of God are called the Decalogue, which is a word derived from the Greek, meaning Ten Words ; they are also called the Tables of the Law, because God gave them to Moses on Mount Sinai, engraved on two tablets of stone. The first three concern our duty towards *The Commandments of God.*

[1] Matt. xix. 17.   [2] Jas. ii. 10.

God, and the seven others our duty towards our neighbour; and they were ratified by our Lord when He said, " On these two commandments dependeth the whole law and the prophets." [1] Whether preceptive or prohibitive, the Commandments impose an equal obligation of obedience, one as much as the other. Those in the affirmative need not necessarily be binding under all circumstances, whereas those in the negative are obligatory on every occasion. All Christians, having reached the age of reason, are required to know the words of the Decalogue, and the meaning of the Commandments, at least as to substance.

The Command-
ments of the
Church.

Among other ecclesiastical laws of various descriptions regarding hierarchical superiors, parish priests, religious orders, etc., certain Commandments have been constituted by the legislative power of the Church, through the Divine authority of government and teaching established by our Lord Jesus Christ, when He said, " Whatsoever thou shalt bind upon earth, it shall be bound also in Heaven: and whatsoever thou shalt loose on earth, it shall be loosed also in Heaven." [2] These Commandments are for the direction of all members of the Church, and to help us in the better accomplishment of the Commandments of God and the maxims of the Gospel.

Necessity of
keeping the
Command-
ments.

If we keep the Commandments, we are treading the path that leads to eternal happiness; and the non-observance, whether of those ordained by God, or by the Church, is punishable, not only in this world, but in the next. For the open and scandalous violation of the Commandments, the Church can inflict temporal punishment by the prohibition of certain Sacraments; by the deprivation of

---

[1] Matt. xxii. 40.   [2] Matt. xvi. 19; xviii. 18.

religious burial; by excommunication; and by the suspension of the rights of office in the case of an ecclesiastic. Disregard for civil laws is also an offence against God, "for there is no power but from God. . . . Render therefore to all men their dues. Tribute, to whom tribute is due: custom, to whom custom: fear, to whom fear: honour to whom honour:"[1] though, when it is a question of choosing between obedience to the Church or obedience to civil authority, "we ought to obey God, rather than men."[2]

[1] Rom. xiii. 1. 7.   [2] Acts v. 29.

CHAPTER XV.

VIRTUES NECESSARY FOR KEEPING THE COMMANDMENTS.

Virtues
necessary for
keeping the
Command
ments.

FOR the strict observance of the Commandments, we must habitually practise good and abjure evil, in order to cultivate the inestimable and indispensable quality of real virtue. Virtue has two elements : virtuous disposition and virtuous action. The disposition may remain after the action is performed, or sometimes the effect of the action continues when the disposition has vanished. A person may accidentally commit an error against the virtue he usually practises, just as a person may, on occasions, do right, without habitually possessing virtue. For instance, a moment of transitory patience may be found in those of an impatient character, and a passing impatience in those who are generally inclined to be most patient. There are two kinds of virtue : that which is natural, and is originated by the light of reason and natural principles, from a natural motive, and for a natural end ; and that which is supernatural, and is the fruit of Divine grace, with a motive taught by Faith, and for an end leading towards Heaven, without which supernatural aid by Divine grace we cannot practise true Christian virtue.

The
theological
virtues.

The theological virtues are " Faith, Hope, Charity, these

three; but the greater of these is Charity."[1] The name
"theological" is taken from two Greek words, signifying
that which relates directly to God. The three theological
virtues are supernatural gifts of God, diffused in our souls
by the grace of God, and having God for their direct object
and motive. By Faith, we believe in and know God in a
supernatural manner; by Hope, we trust in God's promise
that we shall be with Him in the life to come; by Charity,
we love God above all things. We may lose Charity through
sin; Hope through despair; and Faith through incredulity.
It is therefore our duty to profit by these supernatural gifts
received in Baptism: if lost through mortal sin, to regain
them by contrition in the Sacrament of Penance; and to
increase our spiritual strength in possession of them by
their continual and fervent practice, by prayer, and by
the Sacraments. Faith, Hope, and Charity are necessary
for salvation, and are the source of all other virtues.
"Without Faith, it is impossible to please God."[1] We are
of the house of God "if we hold fast the confidence and
glory of Hope unto the end:"[2] and St. Paul said, "If I
should distribute all my goods to feed the poor, and if I
should deliver my body to be burned, and have not Charity,
it profiteth me nothing."[3]

Faith is a supernatural virtue by which we firmly believe, The virtue of
on account of God's perfect truth, all that He has revealed Faith.
and requires us to believe undoubtingly.   The word "supernatural" expresses the principle of Faith, because it signifies
that this virtue comes direct from God; that it is an interior
light and gratuitous gift of God, which, without illuminating all the darkness of mystery, expels error from the

---

[1] Heb. xi. 6.   [2] Heb. iii. 6.   [3] 1 Cor. xiii. 3.

intelligence. The words, "on account of His perfect truth," give the motive, signifying that God can neither deceive us nor be deceived; and the words, " all that God has revealed," denote the object, being expressive of the truths God demands of us to believe. "For by grace you are saved through Faith, and that not of yourselves, for it is a gift of God." [1]   Faith is interior, when existing in the heart and mind; exterior, when professed by words and signs; implicit, when our belief is of truth in general; explicit, when the article which we believe is distinctly known to us; and dead, when not animated by sanctifying grace.

The virtue of Hope.

Hope is a supernatural virtue, by which we trust with entire confidence, that God will give us possession of the eternal life of happiness with Him, and the means of obtaining it, promised to us through the merits of our Saviour, by God who is truth itself. The principle is represented by the word "supernatural," significant of Hope being a direct gift from God, a filial confidence in Divine Providence amidst all the events of life. " Possession of the eternal life of happiness with Him, and the means of obtaining it," denotes the double object of our Hope; and "promised to us, through the merits of our Saviour, by God who is truth itself," gives the motive; expressing the infallibility of God's pledges, without which we cannot attain salvation. We must therefore live " unto the hope of life everlasting, which God, who lieth not, hath promised before the times of the world." [2]

The virtue of Charity.

Charity is a supernatural virtue, by which we love God above all things, on account of His infinite perfection, and love our neighbour as ourselves, for God's sake. The word

[1] Eph. ii. 8.　　　　　[2] Titus i. 2.

"supernatural" expresses its principle, because Charity is a gift direct from God. To say, "We love God above all things, and our neighbour as ourselves," indicates the double object of our love; Charity being the essence of the two greatest Commandments. The motive is given by the words, "on account of His infinite perfection," and "for God's sake;" signifying the reason why we love God and our neighbour. Perfect Charity is the sovereign love of God above all things; and imperfect Charity is a love of God in a lower degree. Perfect Charity excludes the commission of venial sin. Imperfect does not. Charity is the greatest of the three theological virtues, because, without it, and by Faith and Hope alone, we cannot gain salvation; also because it is the one virtue, out of these three, that remains through all eternity: for "God is charity;"[1] and Christ said, "Love one another, as I have loved you."[2] Charity, too, "never falleth away."[3]

The four principal moral virtues are "temperance, pru- *Moral virtues.* dence, justice, and fortitude."[4] They are called "Cardinal," from a Latin word signifying "hinge," and are so named because all other virtues depend on or are controlled by them. They are called "moral," because they concern what is right and good for the just regulation of our lives, and refer to God indirectly to distinguish them from the theological virtues, which have God for their direct object. They are supernatural, because they are promoted by a supernatural motive. They are infused by the gift of God, and can be increased in strength by the help of divine grace.

Temperance is a virtue, which regulates and moderates *Temperance.* our taste for those things that appeal to our senses, thereby

---

[1] 1 John iv. 8, 16. [2] John xv. 12. [3] 1 Cor. xiii. 8. [4] Wisdom viii. 7.

preventing any excessive indulgence. It teaches restraint in all things, abstinence in food, sobriety in drink. Also chastity in maintaining the purity of that state of life to which we are called, whether virginity, celibacy, matrimony, or widowhood. Temperance embraces mortification in words and actions, " as becometh saints ;" [1] for no " obscenity, or foolish talking, or scurrility . . . no fornicator, or unclean or covetous person, hath inheritance in the kingdom of Christ." [2]

Prudence. Prudence is a virtue, by which we may discern between the good to be done and the evil to be avoided. It regulates other virtues in preventing us from going to extremes; it teaches us to use precaution, and to act only after mature judgment; and it gives us power of weighing the consequences of our actions, so as to realize in advance what will be helpful, and what detrimental to our undertakings.

Justice. Justice is a virtue, teaching us to render what is due to God, to our neighbour, and to ourselves. It dictates the duties of superiors to inferiors, of inferiors to superiors, and of equals one to another; it implies penitence, humility, obedience, integrity, gratitude, courtesy, and liberality.

Fortitude. Fortitude is a virtue, giving us courage to overcome all difficulties that may be in the way of doing good or of gaining salvation, and to bear bravely all our trials in life. It helps us in action or in suffering to cultivate patience, firmness, and perseverance; and to endure all without murmuring, for love of God. " Blessed are they that suffer persecution for justice' sake : for theirs is the Kingdom of Heaven;" [3] and "he that shall persevere unto the end, he shall be saved." [4]

---

[1] Eph. v. 3.   [2] Eph. v. 5.   [3] Matt. v. 10.   [4] Matt. x. 22.

CHAPTER XVI.

VIOLATIONS of the Commandments of God and of the Church, Actual sin. are sins consisting in acts of commission or omission, both kinds of sin being interior by thoughts and desires, or exterior by words and actions. Besides original sin, already explained, there is actual sin, so called because it is committed by an act of our own free will. It is sinful voluntarily to expose ourselves to temptation, for under such circumstances, how can we expect the help of Divine grace to preserve us from evil? "A hard heart shall fear evil at the last: and he that loveth danger shall perish in it."[1]

Actual sin is divided into mortal sin and venial sin. Mortal sin. The former is so called because it takes from the soul the supernatural life of sanctifying grace, and those "who, having known the justice of God,"[2] commit mortal sin, are worthy of "eternal punishment in destruction, from the face of the Lord, and from the glory of His power;"[3] and not only they who commit the sins, "but they also that consent to them that do them."[4] The gravity of mortal sin, and its punishment, may vary according to the

[1] Ecclus. iii. 27.   [2] Rom. i. 32.   [3] 2 Thess. i. 9.   [4] Rom. i. 32.

malice or motive inspiring it; for "by what things a man sinneth, by the same also he is tormented."[1] That which constitutes mortal sin is some matter of grievous offence against God, executed with entire consciousness of its serious importance, and with full consent of will. The absence of one of these three conditions, changes its nature to venial sin. All the evils we can have to put up with, all the sufferings we can endure in this world, are as nothing, when they end with death; but mortal sin brings punishment that shall last throughout eternity. We need not fear "them that kill the body, and are not able to kill the soul; but rather fear him that can destroy both soul and body into Hell."[2]

Venial sin.   The word "venial" is taken from the Latin, and signifies pardonable; it is, therefore, by this name we distinguish those sins which are offences against God, but are not grave enough to make us entirely forfeit God's love or sanctifying grace. Compared to mortal sin, it is as a wound to the soul that can be healed, where mortal sin itself would be fatal. It is as a stain on the soul, which, with those who are well disposed, can be removed, leaving us subject to the temporary punishment of Purgatory, in place of the eternal sufferings of Hell. Although no number of venial sins can equal one mortal sin, yet if we do not avoid the lesser offences, we may fall little by little into committing greater evil, amounting to mortal sin. As we are all subject to sin, it should be an object with us to render our term of Purgatory shorter and easier by making every effort not to displease God, even in small things.

Capital sins.   There are seven capital sins; so called because they

---

[1] Wisdom xi. 17.   [2] Matt. x. 28.

represent the sources from which many others spring. All mankind is more or less under the influence of these vices, one among them predominating in each individual, and generally causing the other sins that are committed. Therefore, to practise virtue, we should discover what is our master passion and destroy it, or at least bring it under proper control, that our lives may not be tainted throughout by its pernicious influence.

The capital sins are pride, covetousness, lust, envy, gluttony, anger, and sloth.

Pride is an irregular and inordinate self-esteem, leading Pride. us to magnify our own merits unjustly above those of others, and to attribute to ourselves the glory of the good that is in us, instead of considering it as coming from God, from whom all goodness proceeds. Pride is placed first among the capital sins, because it brought sin into the world; because it is found in all other sins, which are acts of proud rebellion against the will of God; because it glides even into virtuous actions to convert them into sin, or at any rate decrease their merit; and because, as humility was characteristic of our Saviour's life, so is pride the figure-head of all that is in opposition to that life. "Pride is the beginning of all sin: he that holdeth it, shall be filled with maledictions, and it shall ruin him in the end."[1] Pride produces presumption, boastfulness, hypocrisy, opinionativeness, contention, disobedience, contemptuousness, vanity, egoism, over-sensitiveness, and love of luxury in dress and surroundings.

The opposite virtue to Pride is Humility, which should Humility. make us realize that we are nothing without assistance

---

[1] Ecclus. x. 15.

I

from above. It should teach us to estimate at a proper value the merits and the good to be found in others; it should induce us to avoid vain reputation, and to bear honourable distinction without ostentation; to remember our own faults and the frailty of our own nature.

Covetousness. Covetousness is an excessive and unrestrained love of the good things of this world, rendering the accumulation of wealth, and the desire for riches of every description, a kind of idolatry. It causes injustice, deceit, perjury, ingratitude, unnecessary anxieties and preoccupations about one's self and one's surroundings; our worldly interests making us negligent concerning our future salvation.

Liberality. The opposite virtue to Covetousness is Liberality, which should dispose us towards a just medium between cupidity and prodigality. It should teach us charity towards the poor, and a certain indifference to heaping up riches, except when wealth can be well and rightfully employed—not for the indulgence of our passions and caprices, but for our just requirements and the needs of others. If misused, the saying applies literally, " How hardly shall they that have riches, enter into the kingdom of God."[1] Our Saviour lived among the poor and dealt with generosity to all, but especially to the indigent and afflicted; promising "reward "[2] to those who should help the needy; and saying, " thou shalt be blessed, because they have not wherewith to make thee recompense: for recompense shall be made thee at the resurrection of the just:"[3] " For with the same measure that you shall mete withal, it shall be measured to you again."[4] Thereby we shall

[1] Mark x. 23.　　[2] Matt. x. 42.　　[3] Luke xiv. 14.　　[4] Luke vi. 38.

reap the good of what we give according to our means;
remembering that "it is a more blessed thing to give,
than to receive." [1]

Lust denotes an irregular and depraved desire for impure Lust.
pleasures. To keep ourselves free from this vice, we
should avoid bad companionship, because "evil communications corrupt good manners;" [2] and we make enemies
to ourselves if we frequent society that may lead to our
own destruction, or allow others under our protection to
come in contact with such pernicious influences. We
should shun entertainments that are dangerous and blameworthy, such as immodest plays or dances. We should
be careful what we read, and be on our guard against
immoral principles, only too often found ingeniously clothed
in seductive language calculated to poison our minds, even
without our immediately realizing its fascination for us.
We should contemn that apparel which is not within the
strict limits of decorum, and turn away from what is
impure or dangerous for the eye to rest on, for "hereby
lust is enkindled as a fire." [3]

The opposite virtue of Lust is Chastity, which renders Chastity.
us moderate in all that might tend to impurity, and induces
us to abstain from what is illicit. Chastity is obligatory
on all in a general sense, but it is a special duty for
ecclesiastics and those in religious communities, who have,
by their vows, bound themselves to an increased obligation
of obedience to the sixth commandment. It is a virtue of
exceeding rarity when accorded as a peculiar privilege to
the few who may be said to possess Angelic Chastity; for
"incorruption bringeth near to God." [4] We should cultivate

---

[1] Acts xx. 35.   [2] 1 Cor. xv. 33.   [3] Ecclus. ix. 9.   [4] Wisdom vi. 20.

purity of thought and action by avoiding any occasion of defilement; fleeing from the world of dissipation, and devoting ourselves to serious occupations; seeking help by prayer, mortification of the senses, and penitence.

Envy.   Envy is a feeling of discontent at the prosperity, whether spiritual or temporal, of others, which we regard as diminishing our own merits or advantages. It is not to be connected with any effort to equal or surpass our neighbour in just competition; nor with the distress we may experience at the unworthy reception, by another person, of some benefit; provided that our feeling is accompanied with charity. Envy is closely allied to Pride and Covetousness, provoking a longing to attain the merits of others or bring them down to our own level, disliking to find in them the virtues we have not the courage or perseverance to gain for ourselves. It creates in us an intense jealousy, by which we torment ourselves at the success of our neighbour, and take delight in his misfortunes. "By the envy of the devil, death came into the world: and they follow him that are of his side."[1] Envy produces hatred and slander; pleasure in hearing those of whom we are jealous maligned; and satisfaction in misinterpreting their words and actions. "Where envying and contention is, there is inconstancy, and every evil work."[2]

Charity.   The opposite virtue of Envy is Charity, which moves us to love God above all things, and feel contented with what it has pleased Providence to bestow upon us. Also to love our neighbour as ourselves; thereby wishing him good as strongly as to ourselves; and it diverts our ambition from earthly successes towards the attainment of heavenly treasures.

---

[1] Wisdom ii. 24, 25.   [2] James iii. 16.

Gluttony is an inordinate love of eating and drinking, Gluttony. engendering an excess pernicious to health; causing useless expenditure; and sometimes sinful waste of valuable time, in what should be merely a proper and suitable satisfying of the appetite, as necessary for our physical well-being. St. Paul says, "Whether you eat or drink, or whatsoever else you do, do all to the glory of God."[1] Extravagant love of food and alcoholic liquids makes beasts of gluttons, "whose end is destruction, whose God is their belly."[2] It unfits a man for the right accomplishment of his duties; renders him a slave to his sensual inclinations, coarse in appearance, manner, and conversation; it tends to disorderly conduct, lasciviousness, drunkenness, and gambling; stupefying his intellect, or exciting his mind to wanton folly, and forgetfulness of the day of judgment, concerning which our Lord said, "Take heed to yourselves, lest perhaps your hearts be overcharged with surfeiting and drunkenness, and the cares of this life, and that day come upon you suddenly."[3] Children should be made to realize that we must eat to live, and not live to eat. They should be educated to have a wholesome horror of the consequences of gluttony, which, if not instilled into their youthful minds, may cause disaster or ruin to their whole future.

The virtue contrary to Gluttony is Temperance, teach- Temperance. ing moderation in all things that are agreeable to our taste; leaving our minds and bodies full scope in the energy they possess for the fulfilment of our occupations, and the preservation of our health. "The grace of God our Saviour hath appeared to all men; instructing us that, denying

---

[1] 1 Cor. x. 31.   [2] Phil. iii. 19.   [3] Luke xxi. 34.

ungodliness and worldly desires, we should live soberly, and justly, and godly in this world." [1]

Anger.   Anger is a passion which is excited by our feelings of resentment or indignation against people or things that displease us; and awakens or calls forth the evidence of all that is vicious in our natures. Giving way to anger must inevitably lower us in the eyes of others, as well as in our own estimation, if we have still sufficient consciousness of the effect of its degradation to perceive the result of our abandonment to this vice. It makes us lose peace of mind; it disturbs the powers of judgment and reason; it causes us to be rash in our acts and words; it produces injustice, violence, enmity, and revenge.

Meekness.   The opposite virtue to Anger is Meekness, which moves us to treat the words or actions of others, who may hurt or offend us, with gentleness and patience. This meekness does not originate from conventional politeness nor feebleness of character, but from Christian charity and self-respect. For calmness is the best line of conduct in moments of impatience, and silence is often a very powerful manifestation of wisdom. We should walk through life " with all humility and mildness, with patience, supporting one another in charity." [2]

Sloth.   Sloth is a strong rooted habit of inaction of mind and body, inducing us to neglect or completely omit those duties that are right for every Christian to perform, and conducing to spiritlessness and frequently to feelings of despair. If we are, by nature, of an idle temperament, we may find room for self-correction, and consequently means of merit, by overcoming our inclination to laziness,

---

[1] Titus ii. 11, 12.   [2] Eph. iv. 1, 2.

remembering that "idleness hath taught much evil."[1] As we cannot surmise what may happen on the morrow, we should never pass the day in vain, for in a few hours it will be gone beyond retrieving. We should not be satisfied to accomplish just sufficient for the reward which is our salvation, but strive to be fervent and exemplary in our conduct and in the service of God : "in carefulness not slothful; in spirit fervent; serving the Lord."[2] We should bear in mind that our eternal happiness is the end of all our efforts for good, and we should strain every nerve to gain our end, knowing that "they that run in the race, all run indeed, but one receiveth the prize."[3]

The virtue opposed to Sloth is Diligence, which should Diligence. render us zealous for the glory of God, the sanctification of our own souls, the spiritual and temporal well-being of our neighbour, and the love of an honest occupation at which we should work to the best of our endeavour.

[1] Ecclus. xxxiii. 29.   [2] Rom. xii. 11.   [3] 1 Cor. ix. 24.

CHAPTER XVII.

FIRST TABLE OF THE LAW, AND FIRST COMMANDMENT

OF GOD.

"I am the Lord thy God . . . thou shalt not have strange gods before Me." [1]

Command-
ments of the
first Table of
the Law.

IN the first of the three Commandments concerning our duty towards God, we offer to Him the worship of our intelligence by Faith, and of our hearts by Hope and Charity. In the second, the worship of our words; and in the third, of our works. In all three we offer the worship of our body and soul to God alone.

Worship due
to God alone.

The first Commandment, in the words of our Saviour, is, "The Lord thy God shalt thou adore, and Him only shalt thou serve;" [2] by which we are bound to acknowledge God with sentiments of Faith, Hope, Charity, and Religion, rendering to Him that devotion and worship He exacts from us.

Faith neces-
sary in
adoring God.

In reference to the virtue of Faith, the first Commandment ordains that we should believe in and adore God through the homage of our intelligence and will. For it is requisite that we should believe in the existence of God as our Creator and Remunerator; also in all the truths He has revealed and teaches us by the infallible authority of

---

[1] Exod. xx. 2, 3.   [2] Matt. iv. 10.

His Church. "Without faith it is impossible to please God. For he that cometh to God, must believe that He is, and is a rewarder to them that seek Him."[1] The precept of Faith, being an affirmative one, we should, from time to time, express our faith in God; but we are not called upon to display it continually, except when the occasion demands. Such as at the hour of death, and when it is necessary to manifest an exterior profession of faith in temptation, in the reception of a Sacrament, and under all circumstances where silence would be interpreted as denial: which Christ rebuked in these terms, "Every one therefore that shall confess Me before men, I will also confess him before My Father who is in Heaven. But he that shall deny Me before men, I will also deny him before My Father who is in Heaven."[2]

There are three principal kinds of sin opposed to Faith: infidelity, heresy, and apostasy. Infidelity is the rejection of any article of faith, of which we have sufficient knowledge and understanding; and having this knowledge, "he that believeth not shall be condemned."[3] Heresy is obstinately maintaining an error against Faith, which we are well aware is declared such by the Church: any person wilfully refusing admonition, "being condemned by his own judgment."[4] Apostasy is renouncing the Christian faith as received in Baptism, which may occur from giving unreasonable credence to the words, whether written or spoken, of unbelievers, with whom simple-minded members of the Church may not be competent to argue. St. Paul tells us to "shun profane and vain babblings: for they grow much towards ungodliness."[5] Affiliation with secret

Sins against Faith.

---

[1] Heb. xi. 6. [2] Matt. x. 32, 33. [3] Mark xvi. 16
[4] Titus iii. 11. [5] 2 Tim. ii. 16.

societies that are hostile to the Church or State; taking active part in any heretical religious ceremonies; or reading certain heretical literature, are connected with sins against Faith, and are strictly prohibited by the Church.

Hope necessary in adoring God. Regarding the virtue of Hope, the first Commandment ordains we should have firm confidence that, if we fulfil our duties towards God, He will be steadfast to His promises, according us the recompense of eternal happiness in Heaven, and the means and grace necessary in this world to merit the same. But we must "hold fast the confession of our hope without wavering (for He is faithful that hath promised)."[1] Hope, being an affirmative precept, the reasons for making frequent acts of this virtue are, as in the case of Faith, more particularly urgent on certain occasions. As, for example, at the moment of death, also in our religious devotions and practices, and again in temptation to despair. "Seek ye, therefore, first the kingdom of God, and His justice;"[2] were the words uttered by our Lord in His Sermon on the Mount, and they inculcate the virtue of Hope.

Sins against Hope. There are two sins against Hope: despair and presumption. By the first, we lose courage to live our life out, or to practise our religious duties and temporal calling, with confidence in God for help in this world, and for our reward in the next. By presumption, we assume, with undue assurance, the certainty of our ultimate salvation, without taking the proper trouble to correct our faults, or avail ourselves of the authorized means for the pardon of our sins.

Charity or love necessary in adoring God. Relating to the virtue of Charity, the first Commandment ordains that we should love God above all things, for He will have no rival in our hearts, and exacts from us a

[1] Heb. x. 23.   [2] Matt. vi. 33; Luke xii. 31.

devotion that shall be exclusive in its force and pre-eminence. Our Saviour thus quoted this Commandment, "Thou shalt love the Lord thy God, with thy whole heart, and with thy whole soul, and with thy whole mind, and with thy whole strength."[1] In respect to acts of Charity, it is the same with this virtue as with those of Faith and Hope, the reasons being analogous.

All mortal sins are in opposition to Charity, because they show a want of love towards God; but more especially sins of hatred of God, which induces us to lead others from Him; or complete forgetfulness, which permits us to live without thought of God, without prayer, or any religious act.

Sins against Charity.

Religion is a virtue impelling us to render to God that worship which we owe Him as our Creator and Re-munerator. The name "Religion" is taken from the Latin, signifying a "lien" or "tie," and thus expresses the bond attaching us to God.[2] We are all under paternal and civil authority, to which are due obedience and consideration. How much more, then, do we owe adoration and complete submission to God: "for there is no power but from God: and those that are, are ordained of God. Therefore he that resisteth the power, resisteth the ordinance of God. And they that resist, purchase to themselves damnation."[3] Because God obliges even the most incredulous to bow their intelligence and will before those very many things in the natural order that are as undeniable as they are incompre-hensible. "Let them know how much the Lord of them is more beautiful than they . . . let them understand by

Virtue of Religion

---

[1] Mark xii. 30.
[2] Or more probably from the Latin word signifying *attentive*, instead of *negligent* study and practice. See Skeat's Dictionary.
[3] Rom. xiii. 1, 2.

them, that He that made them, is mightier than they: for by the greatness of the beauty, and of the creature, the Creator of them may be seen, so as to be known thereby." [1]

The adoration we render to God is called " latria," from a Greek word, meaning the highest kind of worship. The homage we offer to the Blessed Virgin is called " hyperdulia," being above that given to the Angels and Saints, called " dulia," both names being Greek words. Although we may worship God and pray in silence, without exterior demonstration, yet outward marks of reverence and piety are necessary, helping us to raise our minds to God, and being of immeasurable value as example to each other. But we cannot do either, in a public manner, with right feeling and due honour, unless the heart speaks also; for we must adore God " in spirit and in truth." [2]

Sins against the virtue of Religion are of two kinds, in excess or deficiency: that is to say, by superstition or irreligion. The principal sins of the latter class, closely concerning the first Commandment, are temptation of God, sacrilege, and simony.

By tempting God, is meant, presuming too strongly on the goodness of Providence; expecting, with unreasonable rashness, some extraordinary proof of God's bounteous charity, when we, either explicitly and of set purpose, or implicitly and heedlessly, try to call forth upon ourselves some particular and providential favour, supposing that God should derogate from the laws of nature, exclusively for our edification or caprice. " It is written again : thou shalt not tempt the Lord thy God." [3] This in no way prevents the right of asking, with humility and confidence,

---

[1] Wisdom xiii. 3–5.   [2] John iv. 24.   [3] Matt. iv. 7; Luke iv. 12.

some special grace from God that may be for our good, and for the greater manifestation of His glory.

Sacrilege is the profanation of sacred things, alienating Sacrilege. to common uses that which is consecrated to God. Sacrilege may be the profanation of persons, places, or things, such as an ecclesiastic or member of a religious community bound to God's service; a Church, Chapel, or cemetery consecrated or blessed by a bishop; a relic, vestment, or Church ornament. The most audacious and criminal sacrilege is that touching the Holy Sacrament.

Simony is the buying or selling of anything consecrated Simony. to God and of spiritual benefit only. This name originates from Simon Magus, who begged the Apostles to sell him the power of conferring the gifts of the Holy Ghost. "He offered them money, saying : Give me also this power. . . . But Peter said to him : Keep thy money to thyself, to perish with thee, because thou hast thought that the gift of God may be purchased with money."[1] The sin of simony has nothing to do with the just fees of an ecclesiastic, for these are not a temporal price set upon a spiritual thing, which is ever freely given ; but the pay-ment of some outward function, or a contribution for the support of the ministers of the Church, and for their distribution among the poor, and various good works. According to St. Paul, our Lord ordained that "they who preach the gospel, should live by the gospel;"[2] and Christ also said, "The labourer is worthy of his hire."[3]

Those sins against the virtue of Religion, understood under the name of superstition, are idolatry, divination, magic, spiritualism, table-turning, and vain observances.

---

[1] Acts viii. 18-20. [2] 1 Cor. ix. 14. [3] Luke x. 7.

Idolatry.

By idolatry is meant the inward adoration and the outward worship bestowed on some created being, or some passion preferred to God, "which is the service of idols,"[1] and distinctly prohibited by God in the first Commandment.

Divination.

Divination is the employment of various demoniacal ways of trying to ascertain hidden events of the past, present, or future; like the heathens, who "sacrifice to devils."[2]

Magic and spiritualism

Magic, or the production of extraordinary effects by unnatural means; and spiritualism, or intercourse with spirits by the aid of mediums or table-rappings, must necessarily be communication with the evil one, who produces false appearances and impressions. "The soul that shall go aside after magicians and soothsayers"[3] is condemned by God.

Vain observances.

Vain observances are engendered by foolish fear, and consist in excessive credulity concerning outward circumstances, with unfounded belief in remarkable incidents taken for omens and portents; the placing of undue dependence on dreams, which generally are the effect of natural causes, or of demoniacal artifice, and, if not, would bear the impress of heavenly origin.

Relative honour.

The inferior worship, more properly called relative honour, that we pay to the Blessed Virgin, Angels and Saints, relics and images, is by no means contrary to the first Commandment, which only forbids idolatry.

Veneration towards the Blessed Virgin.

God first honoured the Blessed Virgin, and raised her above all women, as she acknowledged so humbly yet confidently in her hymn of praise called the Magnificat— saying, " Behold, from henceforth all generations shall

[1] 1 Cor. iii. 5.   [2] 1 Cor. x. 20.   [3] Lev. xx. 6.

call me blessed. Because He that is mighty, hath done great things to me; and holy is His name." [1] Our Lord gave us the example of honouring the Blessed Virgin in the highest degree, when He lived with her and St. Joseph at Nazareth, by the fact of being Himself "subject to them." [2]

We regard the Angels as companions and messengers of God, and therefore honour them accordingly, as sharing in His great glory. For it is written, "There shall be joy before the angels of God upon one sinner doing penance." [3] *Veneration towards God's Angels.*

We honour as Martyrs and Saints those whose right to the titles of beatification and canonization has been authentically proved by the judgment of a special assembly of Cardinals, appointed by the Pope for the examination of their lives, actions, virtues, and the miracles, heroic deeds or sufferings attributed to them. Upon the evidence thus gathered and considered with scrupulous care, the Pope declares that there is reason to suppose the soul of the person in question is blessed in Heaven, and has right to the title of Blessed. Or he pronounces a decree of canonization, which is infallible, because it comes from "the house of God, which is the Church of the living God, the pillar and ground of the truth." [4] The Pope could not declare a person enrolled as a Saint, if there were any possibility of his falling into error by bestowing upon a soul not in Heaven the right to that veneration and honour called "dulia." For our Saviour said, "If any man minister to Me, let him follow Me; and where I am, there also shall My minister be. If any man minister to Me, him will My Father honour." [5] The Church does not *Veneration towards the Saints and Martyrs.*

---

[1] Luke i. 48, 49. [2] Luke ii. 51. [3] Luke xv. 10.
[4] 1 Tim. iii. 15. [5] John xii. 26.

guarantee the revelations of Saints as coming from God, and, in approving of them, simply asserts that they contain nothing contrary to faith or morals.

Veneration for relics of Saints.

We honour the bodies or the relics of Saints in a similar manner that we respect the dead whom we have loved, or anything that has belonged to them. This honour paid to the servitors of God is manifestly agreeable to Him, as He has evinced by miracles. For example, when "God wrought by the hand of Paul more than common miracles. So that even there were brought from his body to the sick, handkerchiefs and aprons, and the diseases departed from them, and the wicked spirits went out of them."[1] The holiness of those, whose bodies or other relics have been given to a Church or religious community by the Pope, is not incontrovertible, unless proved by the decree of canonization.

Veneration for statues and images.

We honour, with respect and affection, the Crucifix, as the image of our Saviour crucified; and the statues or pictures of the Blessed Virgin and Saints, as we venerate the likeness of those of our fellow-creatures whom we have cared for. The words, "Thou shalt not make to thyself a graven thing," etc.,[2] are qualified and explained by those that follow : "Thou shalt not adore them, nor serve them."[3] This honouring of images is to the glory of God, in whose service those who are represented have been faithful. It is to the encouragement in us of an attempt to imitate their virtues; it is to the acknowledgment by us of the favours received by their intercession, and the examples given us by them; and it is to the attainment of their protection and interposition for our welfare and ultimate possession

[1] Acts xix. 11, 12.   [2] Exod. xx. 4.   [3] Exod. xx. 5.

of eternal happiness. In the ceremony called "the adoration of the Cross," we manifest the most respectful devotion possible to the representation of Christ crucified. It must be remembered that the highest external form of worship manifested towards the Cross on Good Friday, is exceptional, on account of the day, and is a relative worship given to the Cross, only as carrying our minds to Christ, to whom alone absolute worship is due.

CHAPTER XVIII.

SECOND COMMANDMENT OF GOD.

"Thou shalt not take the name of the Lord thy God in vain."[1]

Profanation of God's name. IN the second Commandment, God forbids us to take His name in vain; that is, to profane His holy name by blasphemy, imprecation, by irreverent and contemptuous use of it, etc.

Blasphemy. Blasphemy is the uttering of contumelious and disparaging words against God, or the dissemination of such in writing. It is direct, when pointedly referring to God; indirect, when it refers to the Blessed Virgin, the Angels, Saints, or others known to be special servants of God, the ministers of the Church, or even things connected closely with our holy religion, if there be intentional contempt of God. It is interior, by thought; exterior, by word; heretical, when against the Catholic faith; execratory, when expressing a curse against God, or any very special creation of God. It is derisive, if, in regard to a truth referring to God, the Blessed Virgin, Angels, or Saints, the words or manner employed are irreverent or contemptuous. Blasphemy is a mortal sin of its own nature, for it is written, " He that blasphemeth the name of the Lord, dying let him die."[2]   " And let not the naming

[1] Exod. xx. 7.   [2] Lev. xxiv. 16.

of God be usual in thy mouth, and meddle not with the
names of Saints, for thou shalt not escape free from them." [1]

Imprecation is the wishing some great evil to ourselves Imprecation.
or some other person or being; or the uttering of vindictive
words, generally spoken in a moment of violent anger, and
often accompanied by the name of God. An imprecation
or malediction is an offence to God, whether directly or
indirectly, because it is a calling down evil on some being
of His creation, and explicitly or implicitly expressing a
desire that God should execute, or at least permit, the
evil that is wished. " A man that sweareth much, shall
be filled with iniquity, and a scourge shall not depart from
his house." [2] In its most serious sense, an imprecation or
malediction is a mortal sin, though there are many occasions
when it may be considered as a venial sin. For instance,
when the evil desired is not of a very grave nature, or
when a passing display of temper calls forth words that
are not really meant.

An oath is a solemn affirmation in which we invoke the Oaths.
name of God, tacitly or explicitly, as witness to the truth
of a statement. It may not be used lightly, neither in God's
name, nor in the name of things that specially represent
Him, for "whosoever shall swear by the temple, sweareth
by it and by Him that dwelleth in it: and he that sweareth
by Heaven, sweareth by the throne of God and by Him that
sitteth thereon." [3] An oath is permissible in justice and in
truth, when circumstances are of sufficient importance. We
read : " To God thou shalt adhere, and shalt swear by His
name;" [4] as St. Paul did when saying, "The things which
I write to you, behold, before God, I lie not." [5] With an

---

[1] Ecclus. xxiii. 10.   [2] Ecclus. xxiii. 12.
[3] Matt. xxiii. 21, 22.   [4] Deut. x. 20.   [5] Gal. i. 20.

oath, we render homage to God's knowledge by attesting that nothing is hidden from Him: to His infallible veracity, by certifying that He cannot be accessory to untruth: to His perfect justice, by testifying that He will not allow the perjurer to go unpunished. An oath should be taken "in truth, and in judgment, and in justice:"[1] that is to say, affirming or promising with adequate motive a thing, of which we are morally certain or mean to perform. Without these three conditions of integrity, namely, a solemn affirmation or promise, importance of matter, and equity of motive, an oath would unquestionably be disrespectful to God, and must therefore be a mortal or venial sin, according to the gravity of the circumstance, or intention and opinion of the person taking the oath. For example, when swearing to a thing we either know or think to be false or doubtful, or when the words of the oath are ambiguous, or when there is no intention of carrying out the promises sworn to. An oath should be considered as most solemn and binding, hence swearing can never be allowed to become habitual. "You have heard that it was said of them of old, Thou shalt not forswear thyself: but thou shalt perform thy oaths to the Lord."[2] Whatever we promise or vow in God's name we should adhere to, though there are certain causes that may nullify the obligation to accomplish a promissory oath. For instance, when a person under age, or a married woman, makes a vow of which the father or the husband at once disapproves; when the circumstances have been misrepresented to the person who gives the promise, or the conditions afterwards become

<hr />

[1] Jer. iv. 2.   [2] Matt. v. 33.

totally altered in an unforeseen manner ; when the person to whom the promise is made does not accept it, or having accepted it, withdraws the obligation; when the thing promised is, or becomes impossible; when it is, or becomes illicit, for the execution of such a promise would be an additional sin; finally, when the fulfilment of a promise precludes the accomplishment of a greater good.

A vow is a solemn and deliberate promise, given with Vows. full understanding of the gravity of the obligation and duty entered upon, and with free consent, by which we make some formal engagement with God, and in His service, from which we cannot release ourselves without sin, either mortal or venial, according to the character of the vow made. "If a man make a vow to the Lord, or bind himself by an oath ; he shall not make his word void; but shall fulfil all that he has promised." [1] A vow may be positive, that is, unconditional; conditional, that is, to be executed under certain circumstances; personal, that is, binding no other person ; real, that is, concerning the gift of some object, an obligation which may descend to successors; temporary, that is, for a time only; perpetual, that is, for ever; private, that is, peculiar to one's self; of religion, that is, a vow made to enter a religious order. A vow ceases to be binding only when a change of circumstances renders its accomplishment impracticable, or so exceedingly difficult as to cause undue detriment to the person concerned. Also when the obligation is annulled or suspended by a superior, to whom the person taking the vow is really subject. Also when dispensation or commutation is obtained by ecclesiastical authority in the power

---

[1] Num. xxx. 3.

our Lord gave His Church to "bind" and to "loose."[1]
A vow should never be undertaken without mature reflection, ample time for consideration, and advice from a
spiritual director who knows all the circumstances and
conditions involved, and who has full power to judge and
counsel.

[1] Matt. xvi. 19, xviii. 18.

CHAPTER XIX.

THIRD COMMANDMENT OF GOD.

" Remember that thou keep holy the sabbath day." [1]

THE third Commandment ordains that we should con- Sanctification of Sunday. secrate Sunday specially to God, to whom, as already explained, we owe not only private but public worship; and it has pleased Him to designate one day of every week for particular observance of this duty.

Saturday, the "Sabbath" or seventh day of the week, was set apart in old times, and the Jews were commanded to sanctify the mystical "seventh day" as corresponding with that on which, figuratively speaking, God "rested" [2] from the work of creation. Sunday was afterwards substituted by the Apostles, and was called Dies Dominica, or "the Lord's day," [3] as being consecrated to the public worship of God. Hence St. Paul ordered the collection of alms to be made "on the first day of the week," [4] which is chosen for sanctification in perpetual remembrance of the great mystery of Christ's Resurrection, and of the descent of the Holy Ghost on the Apostles.

God Himself gave this law : "The first day shall be most Public worship ordained by solemn unto you, and holy : you shall do no servile work God. therein." [5] Nothing that is not of serious consequence

---

[1] Exod. xx. 8.   [2] Exod. xx. 11.   [3] Apoc. i. 10.
[4] 1 Cor. xvi. 2.   [5] Lev. xxiii. 7.

absolves us from the obligation of abstaining from servile works and assisting at Holy Mass on Sundays and the other days the Church orders should be thus observed. On these days the Church's command is that the faithful should be united in prayer, taking their part in the Sacrifice offered through the instrumentality of the priest in commemoration of the great mystery of the Redemption. It is our unquestionable duty to be present at the adorable Sacrifice, the mere figure of which, before the coming of Christ, was awaited by the Jewish people, who attended with regularity those sacrifices which were but the types of what we, in fulfilment of them, possess the reality.

Servile works prohibited on holy days.

By servile works, from which we must abstain on Sundays—and, when possible, on holy days of obligation—is meant arduous bodily labour, constituting a trade or profession of everyday occupation and payment. The employment of others is in like manner forbidden. It is not only a sin against God to desecrate the day He has commanded us to sanctify or keep apart, but the non-observance of this command is injurious to soul and body. It deprives us of religious instruction and meditation, that would elevate our minds above the hollow frivolities and passing trials of this world, and inspire us with sentiments and desires of future happiness prepared for us in the life to come. Also, it makes impossible that physical relaxation so essential for the good health of those who work during the week, whether at manual or intellectual labour. People of all classes and all ages should be in comparative repose on holy days, and should evince, by their presence at public worship, their equality and good-fellowship, one with another, in the house of God.

If, by disobedience to the law enjoining the sanctification of Sunday, we despise the authority of God, paternal and civil authority must inevitably lose our respect. Many occupations, however, are permissible, as necessity or utility demands—even if productive of remuneration—provided that they are not laboriously pursued during a considerable time, and do not result in causing scandal to others. There are instances, too, which warrant the performance of some laborious work on Sunday : such as the requisite decoration of the Church, and preparation of those things needed in religious ceremonies, which cannot be prepared in advance. Hence Christ said : "On the sabbath days the priests in the Temple break the sabbath, and are without blame."[1] There is also the daily care of the animals in our possession ; the alleviation of suffering, or the execution of any other good deed, which cannot be deferred or anticipated ; for our Lord said : "What man shall there be among you, that hath one sheep : and if the same fall into a pit on the sabbath-day, will he not take hold on it and lift it up ? How much better is a man than a sheep ? Therefore it is lawful to do a good deed on the sabbath-days."[2] In any doubtful cause for infringement of the precept, dispensation is accorded by an ecclesiastic duly appointed, but it is not needed in a plain case. Work of absolute necessity for public benefit, prevention of accident, or remedy of disaster, is all, at least tacitly, approved of by the Church, and her consent is not given, even by silence, to anything opposed to faith or morals. Because, honouring God by the sanctification of Sunday, is a positive precept, and the Church merely fixes the details, and grants dispensation when the obligation is too hard of accomplishment.

(margin note: Occupations permitted on holy days.)

[1] Matt. xii. 5.   [2] Matt. xii. 11, 12.

CHAPTER XX.

SECOND TABLE OF THE LAW.

Command-
ments of the
second Table
of the Law.

THE seven Commandments of the second Table of the Law, concern our duties towards our fellow-creatures, as laid down by our Saviour, who said, "Thou shalt love thy neighbour as thyself :"[1] "All things therefore, whatsoever you would that men should do to you, do you also to them. For this is the law and the prophets."[2] This second Commandment is like unto the first, inasmuch as it also embraces the love of God, for whose sake, and by whose will, we are bound to feel charity towards all mankind, and act accordingly. "Let us not love in word, nor in tongue, but in deed, and in truth ;"[3] remembering that in the accomplishment of what we owe to God and to our fellow-creatures we, at the same time, fulfil our duties towards ourselves, and shall reap the harvest of right doing; for, "Blessed are they who hear the word of God and keep it."[4]

Spiritual
duties of
charity.

Our spiritual duties of charity towards our neighbour are : we must instruct those who are ignorant of religion, helping them to understand the most essential points, and to realize and appreciate the preciousness of the holy gift of faith our Lord has given us. We must give

[1] Matt. xxii. 39.   [2] Matt. vii. 12.   [3] 1 John iii. 18.   [4] Luke x. 28.

fraternal correction in matters of importance, but with great prudence, if the person doing wrong is a dependent or constant companion ; as also correction in cases of scandal to all those to whom the admonition may be of avail. And fraternal correction should be accepted by ourselves with feelings of gratitude ; for, from a service thus rendered, we can glean much that may be most profitable to ourselves. We must counsel those who stand in need of advice, and whom we can hope to benefit by it. We must console the afflicted with words of sympathy, kindness, and encouragement, leading them to bear the trials and sufferings of this world with patience and resignation, as a means to attain the endless happiness for which we all strive : sorrowing not hopelessly for the dead, but rather comforted by the thought that, if they are in Heaven, their work is done, and their reward gained; and if in Purgatory, we may have the further comfort of helping them by our prayers, and of winning their aid through gratitude. We must bear with the faults of others without angry complaint or impatience ; repressing even inward feelings of rancour, recollecting that no one is without blemish, and that they have perhaps more to endure from our faults than we from theirs ; "for if any man think himself to be something, whereas he is nothing, he deceiveth himself." [1] We must pardon the sins of others ; not only by showing forgiveness, but by driving out revenge or hatred from our hearts. It is one thing to hate sin, but quite another to hate the sinner. Our Redeemer said, " If you love them that love you, what thanks are to you ? for sinners also love those that love them. And if you do good to them who do good

[1] Gal. vi. 3.

to you, what thanks are to you? for sinners also do this."[1] We must pray for the living and the dead, as Christ taught us by praying for all, even for His persecutors.

Corporal duties of charity. Our corporal duties of charity towards our neighbour, such as hospitality to those who hunger or thirst, clothing the poor, visiting the sick, etc., may all be included under the heading of almsgiving, and must necessarily be observed in the charity we owe towards our fellow-creatures, as our Lord commanded, saying, "Open thy hand to thy needy and poor brother;"[2] "Do good and lend, hoping for nothing thereby: and your reward shall be great."[3] The violation of this precept may be only a venial sin, though in cases of pressing exigency, or extreme misery, the refusal of the charity we know to be of immediate need, even necessitating some sacrifice to ourselves, may become a mortal sin. While distributing our charity with a generous hand, we should be just in giving that only which is strictly our own, and should offer this with joy and without regret; "every one as he hath determined in his heart, not with sadness, or of necessity; for God loveth a cheerful giver."[4] We should be prudent in alleviating the distress of those who are really poor, not giving alms to those who can work, but have not the will to exert themselves; for, as St. Paul says, "If any man will not work, neither let him eat."[5] We should be prompt in not delaying till to-morrow the help essential for to-day. "Afflict not the heart of the needy, and defer not to give to him that is in distress."[6] We should be humble in our gifts, not boasting to what extent we are charitable;

[1] Luke vi. 32, 33.   [2] Deut. xv. 11.   [3] Luke vi. 35.
[4] 2 Cor. ix. 7.   [5] 2 Thess. iii. 10.   [6] Ecclus. iv. 3.

for our Lord said, "When thou dost an alms-deed, sound not a trumpet before thee, as the hypocrites do in the synagogues and in the streets, that they may be honoured by men. Amen, I say to you, they have received their reward. But when thou dost alms, let not thy left hand know what thy right hand doth." [1]

[1] Matt. vi. 2, 3.

CHAPTER XXI.

FOURTH COMMANDMENT OF GOD.

"Honour thy father and thy mother."[1]

Honour due to parents.

THE fourth Commandment ordains that we should honour our father and mother; that is, love, respect, and obey them. This is "the first Commandment with a promise:"[2] the only one to which God has attached a temporal recompense, by assuring long life on earth to those who obey His injunctions concerning parental authority. Not only a long, but a happy life; for naturally a lengthy existence, that is not joyful, would scarcely be a reward. Of those who die young, notwithstanding their obedience, one may suppose that God foresees they will be in danger in later years of losing eternal salvation, or that their sorrow and suffering would inevitably be rendered very great, or that disobedience to other commandments would counterbalance their right to the prolongation of a life, marred by crimes of different kinds. Therefore, we may believe that by premature death, they are given an easy escape from sin, or misery, or suffering, and taken to a life of greater happiness even than was promised them. Those who are obedient, but suffering in this world, doubtless gain a tenfold recompense hereafter.

[1] Exod. xx. 12.   [2] Eph. vi. 2.

We must love, honour, and respect our parents, because they are the secondary authors of our existence, and the natural representatives of God's authority. To honour our parents we should respect them in our hearts, with a sentiment of veneration; and in our manner and words, by the consideration and attention it is our unquestionable duty to evince. We should love them with that instinct of affection, which shows itself spontaneously in all nature, however inferior to our own. How greatly, therefore, ought we to cultivate this tenderness of feeling, and assiduously practise its dictates for the comfort and benefit of our parents! It is our duty to administer to their spiritual and temporal requirements; to help them in distress, or poverty; to tend them in illness; to comfort them in affliction; to see that they receive the consolation and support of religion in their last moments; to pray for the repose of their souls after death; and to acquit ourselves with punctuality and exactitude of the obligations with which they have charged us, either by writing or word of mouth. We are taught obedience to our parents by the example of submission our Saviour showed towards His sacred Mother and St. Joseph, when He was "subject to them,"[1] during His hidden life; and by several passages in Scripture, among which is the clearly expressed injunction of St. Paul, "Children, obey your parents in the Lord, for this is just."[2]

The authority of parents extends over all that concerns morality, education, and home government, to which obedience should be yielded in everything that is not against the laws of God or of the Church. Should parents take undue advantage of their position, children are

[1] Luke ii. 51. [2] Eph. vi. i.

not only absolved from the obligation of submission, but
are strictly bound to adhere to the supreme decrees of
God and of His Church ; as our Lord taught us, saying,
" He that loveth father or mother more than Me, is not
worthy of Me : and he that loveth son or daughter more
than Me, is not worthy of Me." [1]

Care due from parents to their children.   The obedience imposed on children towards their parents,
supposes that the parents merit the right to that filial
devotion; a matter omitted in the Decalogue, because,
as we have a love for ourselves, which is innate in us,
so may it be presumed that parents love and care for
their offspring, who are part of themselves. " If a man
have not care of his own, and especially of those of his
house, he hath denied the faith, and is worse than an
infidel." [2]   Parents should love their children, not merely
from natural motives, and for their own pleasure, but from
a Christian point of view, and for the eternal salvation of
the souls God has entrusted to their keeping: children
created, not for them, but for Himself; and not for the purely
natural satisfaction of their parents, but for the supernatural
object and end of their own temporal existence. Parents
fail in this duty of love for their children, by the absence
of any of those duties we owe one to another in charity
towards our neighbour; or by unjust antipathy to or special
fondness for one among several, without reasonable motive.

Duties of parents to their children.   The particular duties of parents, for the spiritual and
corporal well-being of their children, are : that they should
watch over their health; preserving them from danger,
moral and physical; tending them in sickness; and educating them as fully as means permit, and position demands.

---

[1] Matt. x. 37.   [2] 1 Tim. v. 8.

They should give them religious instruction, teaching them, at an early age, the rules of morality, and the Commandments of God and of the Church, that, being responsible for them, they may not in after years have reason to reproach themselves for neglect of their duty towards their children. They should watch over them with vigilant care by studying their characters, and separating them from people and things that might prove of injurious or dangerous influence; for, "he that toucheth pitch, shall be defiled with it: and he that hath fellowship with the proud, shall put on pride."[1] They should correct them in all things detrimental to their souls or bodies, in their own interest as well as that of their children: "he that spareth the rod, hateth his son: but he that loveth him, correcteth him betimes;"[2] tempering, by gentleness and justice, the adequate chastisement. It is written by St. Paul, "Provoke not your children to anger; but bring them up in the discipline and correction of the Lord."[3] They should afford them good example in words and actions, for from whom would a child naturally take the impress of good or evil, if not from those in nearest relationship and closest contact? Example given in tender years remains almost indelible, more especially if evil example, because of the usually corrupt inclinations of our nature. Parents should procure for their children, as well as they are able, a situation or occupation in life suitable to their tastes, dispositions, and capabilities; directing, advising, and consulting with them on the selection, with every care and consideration; but not opposing them in the choice of a "vocation," when there is full reason for feeling convinced that they have found

[1] Ecclus. xiii. 1.   [2] Prov. xiii. 24.   [3] Eph. vi. 4.

L

their calling in life. Such opposition would be unjust towards God, towards their children, and towards themselves; because we ought all to follow that way, which God has marked out to lead us to Himself, more especially when there is question of a person called in a special manner to His service. There must always be one occupation, for which we have more taste, and aptitude, and in which are provided the particular graces necessary for the better fulfilment of our duties, and the leading of a worthy life. In resisting the will of God in such matters, parents compromise the happiness of their children in this world and in the next, and assume, by so doing, an immense responsibility, involving their own temporal and eternal peace.

Reciprocal obligations of superiors and inferiors.

The fourth Commandment includes also the reciprocal obligations and duties of superiors and inferiors, servitors and masters; because the name "father" is applicable to all those higher in rank or position than others. There are various passages in Scripture alluding to the love, honour, respect, and submission due to those whom we serve. St. Peter writes: "Be ye subject therefore to every human creature for God's sake : whether it be to the king, as excelling ; or to governors, as sent by him for the punishment of evildoers, and for the praise of the good."[1]

Duties of servants to their masters.

There is an obligation of fidelity in the duties of a servant towards his master, for a servant, by the fact of entering his service and home, tacitly agrees to promote, as his own, the interests of his employer, neither doing, nor allowing to be done, any wrong to his person, his reputation, his children, nor anything belonging to or concerning him. St. Peter, in addressing himself to dependents of this class,

---

[1] 1 Pet. ii. 13, 14.

says, "Servants, be subject to your masters with all fear; not only to the good and gentle, but also the froward. For this is thanksworthy, if for conscience towards God, a man endure sorrows, suffering wrongfully." [1]

The duties of other inferiors towards superiors, whether of ecclesiastical or civil authority, have a similar bearing. "Whosoever are servants under the yoke, let them count their masters worthy of all honour; lest the name of the Lord and His doctrine be blasphemed." [2] It is also written: "Obey your prelates, and be subject to them. For they watch as being to render an account of your souls; that they may do this with joy, and not with grief. For this is not expedient for you." [3]

Duties of inferiors to superiors.

The duties of masters towards their servants, are to speak with charity and command with gentleness; to feed and keep them in a suitable manner; to have solicitude for them in illness, and not overburden them with harder work than they are able to accomplish: "forbearing threatenings, knowing that the Lord both of them and you is in heaven." [4] We must correct and instruct those who are dependent on us, giving them right teaching, example, and lessons of discipline. "He that rejecteth instruction, despiseth his own soul: but he that yieldeth to reproof, possesseth understanding." [5] We must pay their wages, giving them, with exactitude, the total amount which is their due at the time agreed upon. "Behold, the hire of the labourers, who have reaped down your fields, which by fraud has been kept back by you, crieth; and the cry of them hath entered into the ears of the Lord of sabaoth," [6]

Duties of masters to their servants.

[1] 1 Pet. ii. 18, 19.   [2] 2 Tim. vi. 1.   [3] Heb. xiii. 17.
[4] Eph. vi. 9.   [5] Prov. xv. 32.   [6] Jas. v. 4.

And, " thou shalt not refuse the hire of the needy, and the poor, whether he be thy brother, or a stranger that dwelleth with thee in the land, and is within thy gates." [1]

Duties of superiors to inferiors.
The duties of all other inferiors likewise entail obligations towards them on the part of superiors, duties which may be gathered in consistent proportion from those already cited as binding parents and their children, and masters and their servants.

[1] Deut. xxiv. 14.

CHAPTER XXII.

"Thou shalt not kill." [1]

By the fifth commandment we are forbidden to take away Murder, both physical and spiritual. the life of any human being, either directly by voluntarily committing murder; or indirectly by willingly allowing a death to occur, which it is in our power to prevent, or by permitting anything that might lead to a like crime. "Whosoever shall kill shall be in danger of the judgment." [2] Consequently, not only homicide, and suicide, but duelling, and all injury and abuse of others, frequently leading to violence and loss of life, is against the fifth Commandment; these being most sinful acts of criminal injustice against the Creator and the created. To kill is a sin against God, as supreme and only master of the giving or taking of life; for, "the Lord killeth and maketh alive, He bringeth down to Hell and bringeth back again." [3] And to kill is a sin against man, whose right to live is bestowed by his Creator, and whose murder will be avenged by God. " Whosoever shall shed man's blood, his blood shall be shed: for man was made to the image of God." [4]

Putting to death is lawful, in cases of sentence of Homicide.

[1] Exod. xx. 13.   [2] Matt. v. 21.   [3] 1 Kings ii. 6.   [4] Gen. ix. 6.

condemnation by legitimate authority, this being a power admitted by all people, as necessary for the public good, and recognized also as legal and right by the Church. The ruler of a country is " an avenger to execute wrath upon him that doth evil." [1] To slay is permitted in war, because, although war is in itself deplorable, and must inevitably cause bitter consequences to so many, a just war is regarded as excusable and sometimes indispensable, and has been waged as such in all countries and all ages, uncondemned by the Church.   Of the laws relating to war, it is written : " If at any time thou come to fight against a city, thou shalt first offer it peace.   And if they receive it, and open the gates to thee, all the people that are therein shall be saved, and shall serve thee, paying tribute.   But if they will not make peace, and shall begin war against thee, thou shalt besiege it." [2]   Homicide is also admissible for legitimate defence of ourselves or our neighbour, when it is indispensable for the saving of life, or very valuable property, against an aggressor.

Suicide.   Suicide is a criminal act of injustice against God, because it is a usurpation of the Creator's rights, as giver of life and death ; for we have not greater right to kill ourselves, than to murder another human being.   It is an injustice against civil society, because every one has his part to play in the world, for the benefit, one way or another, of his fellow-creatures.   It is an injustice against domestic society, because we have not the right to dishonour and afflict with sadness any member of the family to which we belong.   It is an injustice against ourselves, because, " they that commit sin and iniquity, are enemies to their own

---

[1] Rom. xiii. iv.   [2] Deut. xx. 10-12.

soul;"[1] and by suicide, unless they repent before dying,
or are actually insane, they die in mortal sin, without
possibility of repentance. There are certain occasions,
however, when we may risk, or even give our lives, that
greater good may come of it, as circumstances render desirable, and even honourable. For instance, in the duties of
a soldier or sailor, who has a place or thing to defend, and
remains at his post, in spite of the death he sees approaching; or when one person dies for another, which our
Saviour speaks of as the highest act of charity, saying,
"Greater love than this no man hath, that a man lay down
his life for his friends."[2]

Duelling is most strictly forbidden by the Church; any Duelling.
one concerned in duelling being guilty of grievous sin, and
those playing the principal part being guilty of a double
crime, by willingly exposing themselves to death, and by
attempting to take the life of another. This is only considered permissible as preventing greater disaster, or as
procuring public welfare, as was the case when David
fought Goliath.[3]

Ill-treatment of our neighbour, forbidden by the fifth Discord and
Commandment, includes all dissension and violence, mis- violence.
chief-making and scandal; for, what creates discord, contention, and hatred, is opposed to the charity we should
feel towards others, and is declared abominable in the
sight of God. "Six things there are, which the Lord
hateth, and the seventh His soul detesteth: Haughty eyes,
a lying tongue, hands that shed innocent blood, a heart
that deviseth wicked plots; feet that are swift to run into
mischief, a deceitful witness that uttereth lies, and him

---

[1] Tobias xii. 10.   [2] John xv. 13.
[3] 1 Kings xvii. 50.

that soweth discord among brethren."[1] A difference of
opinion, and argument consequent thereon, need not produce discord; or if it does, may be but a venial sin, owing
to the unimportance of the matter, or the reluctance or
inadvertence of those concerned. But, "in the quarrels of
the proud is the shedding of blood; and their cursing is a
grievous hearing."[2] In the same manner, ill-treatment of
a violent nature may be venial sin, but more generally
extends to serious outrage. "He that seeketh to revenge
himself, shall find vengeance from the Lord, and He will
surely keep his sins in remembrance."[3] The ill-treatment
of animals is also forbidden by God, who has put them
under the dominion of man, to be employed for our service,
and for our nourishment, and to be destroyed when advisable, but not uselessly tormented or cruelly used. By
doing this we manifest an evil disposition in our own characters; for, "the just man regardeth the lives of his beasts."[4]

Scandal.   As we are forbidden to deprive any human being of
corporeal life, so also are we prohibited spiritual homicide.
That is to say, to cause injury to the life of the soul, directly
or indirectly, by scandal, which means evil suggestion or
example, in word, action or omission; and all else that,
being bad either in reality or in appearance, leads others
into sin; even if the scandal given be not actuated by
a motive of offending God, but is given merely to contribute
to our own pleasure or utility. Scandal is a mortal sin in
itself, for it works detriment to the eternal welfare of another;
but according to circumstances, and the intentions, or dispositions of those concerned, it may frequently be only a
venial sin. Our Lord, in His teaching, said, "Woe to the

[1] Prov. vi. 16–19.   [2] Ecclus. xxvii. 16.   [3] Ecclus. xxviii. 1.
[4] Prov. xii. 10.

world because of scandals! For it must needs be that scandals come; but nevertheless woe to that man by whom the scandal cometh." [1] With our frail nature, however, we are influenced so much by each other, and the giving of scandal is so prevalent, that we should be vigilant in guarding against any recklessness concerning bad example in our words, actions, or omissions, by which we may communicate evil, and be the cause of sin, we know not to how many. When we have had the misfortune to commit such a fault, we ought not only to repent, but to do our utmost to repair the injury.

[1] Matt. xviii. 7.

CHAPTER XXIII.

SIXTH AND NINTH COMMANDMENTS OF GOD.

"Thou shalt not commit adultery."[1]
"Thou shalt not covet thy neighbour's wife."[2]

Impurity.   As the sixth Commandment forbids all sins, of an exterior character, contrary to the virtue of chastity, and the ninth Commandment prohibits all thoughts contrary to this same virtue, the explanation of the two may be combined; for any sin of impurity, whether by act or thought, is of a serious nature, if committed with full understanding and free accord; the gravity of which is fully expressed by many passages of Scripture, relative both to the desire and the accomplishment of such offences. Our Lord, in His Sermon on the Mount, spoke thus: "You have heard that it was said of them of old : Thou shalt not commit adultery. But I say to you, that whosoever shall look on a woman to lust after her, hath already committed adultery with her in his heart."[3]

Impure looks.   Sins against the sixth commandment may be by looks, words, or actions; and against the ninth, by thoughts and desires. Sight provokes imaginations and feelings; and in the eyes we may encounter, only too often, that which

---

[1] Exod. xx. 14.   [2] Deut. v. 21.   [3] Matt. v. 27, 28.

leads the heart astray. We should therefore shun all occasion of sinning against the virtue of chastity, and avoid the temptation of indulging in what is impure, praying to God, in the words of the Psalmist: "Turn away my eyes that they may not behold vanity: quicken me in Thy way."[1] By words, whether in speech or song, we may *Impure words.* stimulate ourselves to wrong-doing, or excite in others temptations to immorality. Words, seeming perhaps harmless to ourselves, will sometimes fall injuriously on other ears, sowing seeds of mischief: and voluptuous poetry, accompanied especially by melody, often works a highly dangerous influence on the imagination. St. Paul writes a recommendation touching this subject, in these terms: "But all uncleanness, let it not be so much as named among you, as becometh saints. Or obscenity, or foolish talking, or scurrility."[2] In our actions, we should *Impure actions.* remember that we are the children of God, placed here on earth to lead an exemplary life in His service, that we may inherit the Kingdom of Heaven. "If any man violate the temple of God, him shall God destroy. For the temple of God is holy, which you are."[3] In thought, *Impure thoughts.* leading to desire, we should preserve purity of mind by assiduous prayer, by employing our time in healthy occupations, both mental and physical, and by being prudent in our choice of associates. "If thou give to thy soul her *Impure desires.* desires, she will make thee a joy to thy enemies. Take no pleasure in riotous assemblies, be they ever so small: for their concertation is continual."[4]

[1] Ps. cxviii. 37. [2] Eph. v. 3, 4.
[3] 1 Cor. iii. 17. [4] Ecclus. xviii. 31, 32.

CHAPTER XXIV.

"Thou shalt not steal." [1]

"Thou shalt not covet thy neighbour's house . . . nor anything that is his." [2]

Stealing and coveting.

THE seventh Commandment forbids us to steal: that is, to possess ourselves, secretly and unjustly, of things that do not belong to us; and the tenth Commandment forbids us to covet: which means, to possess ourselves in desire of things that are the property of our neighbour.

Besides the ordinary or simple pilfering, there are several classes of theft, such as rapine, or stealing by violence, despite the opposition of the proprietor; sacrilegious theft, or the stealing of an object consecrated to God, or of anything on consecrated ground; the unjust detention of what belongs to some one else, consisting in not paying, when it is possible, money that is due, or in retaining, without legitimate reason or permission, what is the property of another. This is equivalent to having appropriated it by thieving in secret. The seventh Commandment also prohibits all frauds and unjust injury to our neighbour's possessions, and prejudice to his reputation; because such injury destroys, or at least damages, his lawful and

---

[1] Exod. xx. 15.   [2] Exod. xx. 17.

legitimate rights to gain money, and consequently is theft; all of which sins are strictly interdicted in Scripture. "The love of our neighbour worketh no evil. Love, therefore, is the fulfilling of the law. . . . The night is past, and the day is at hand. Let us therefore cast off the works of darkness, and put on the armour of light. Let us walk honestly, as in the day." [1]

Stealing is a mortal or a venial sin, according to the intrinsic value of the object, the pecuniary circumstances of the person deprived of it, and the value the proprietor attaches to it. If we have had the misfortune to succumb to temptation in this way, we must make reparation by restoring that which we have taken, or otherwise rectifying the evil done, as far as lies in our power, and as expeditiously as possible; for, until we do this, we are as thieves, and "the unjust shall not possess the Kingdom of God." [2] Until we do penance, we are in danger of death everlasting. "Yea, if I shall say to the just that he shall surely live, and he, trusting in his justice, commit iniquity: all his justices shall be forgotten, and in his iniquity, which he hath committed, in the same shall he die." [3] Where restitution is impracticable, or free remittal is accorded by the person who has the right to grant it, there is dispensation of indemnification. Otherwise it should be made immediately, so as not to cause additional wrong to our neighbour, nor prevent him recovering, as quickly as may be, that which belongs to him, nor expose ourselves to the disaster of dying in sin. If it be impossible to acquit ourselves of the whole obligation, the return of part ought by no means to be delayed. Restitution should be made to the person

---

[1] Rom. xiii. 10, 12, 13.   [2] 1 Cor. vi. 9.   [3] Ezek. xxiii. 13.

stolen from, or, if dead, to his heirs, and, if after proper inquiry it cannot be discovered who is the person wronged, the proceeds should be given to the poor, or to some charitable work—a disposal which could not reasonably offend the rightful owner. Immediate restitution should also be made of anything found, of which the owner is known; and in contracts, whether written or verbal, we should scrupulously adhere to their conditions, never sacrificing conscience to any temporal interest whatever.

Fraud.   Some of the principal modes of fraud or trickery, causing injustice to our neighbour, are: deceiving in trade as to the quality or value of an article, artfully disguising its defects and selling it as perfect; employing wastefully the times of labour due to the person who pays the wages or salary; and cheating at cards or other games. We may also commit wrong towards our neighbour, regarding the seventh Commandment, by participation, advice, command, tacit or active consent in sin, or by keeping silence as to the culprit when an evil act is done. By doing these things we may offend against charity or even justice.

CHAPTER XXV.

" Thou shalt not bear false witness against thy neighbour." [1]

THE eighth Commandment forbids false witness against Untruth.
our neighbour; that is to say, untrue evidence given
before a tribunal of justice, including all lying and
slandering.

False witness is a mortal sin, unless want of free-will or False
knowledge can in any way excuse it; because, ordinarily, testimony.
a witness is called before a court of law, and takes a
solemn oath to speak the truth, and nothing but the truth.
Therefore, keeping silence, and otherwise hiding what is
true, or declaring what is untrue, may result in serious
injury to others, and is a heinous sin; perjury being
a sacrilegious and flagrant crime in the eyes of God and
man. "A false witness shall not be unpunished: and he
that speaketh lies, shall perish." [2]

A lie is that which is written, spoken, or insinuated, by Lying.
word or act, with intention to deceive; whether by assert-
ing as true a thing we believe to be false, or affirming as
false what we believe to be true. For the malice of lying
consists principally in the intention we have to deceive

[1] Exod. xx. 16.   [2] Prov. xix. 9.

our neighbour, not only by hiding the truth, but by leading him into error. There is the jocose lie, told for merriment; the officious lie, told for our own or another person's excuse or defence; and the pernicious lie, told for the injury of one's neighbour. Falsehoods told for some necessary utility to ourselves or others, in no way harming any one, are not grievous, though, strictly speaking, all lying is forbidden, and "the custom thereof is not good."[1]   For we never know when it may lead us, or others, into serious offence, and it is completely opposed to God, who is truth itself, and who has given us the faculty of expressing our thoughts for the end of our salvation. "A thief is better than a man that is always lying: but both of them shall inherit destruction. The manners of lying men are without honour: and their confusion is with them without ceasing."[2]   Lying is pernicious when we have the direct intention or run the evident risk of harming our neighbour; it may therefore be mortal sin, for "the mouth that belieth, killeth the soul."[3]

Mental restrictions.   All mental restriction, equivocation, and prevarication are not permitted when under oath, or whenever the glory of God, or the interest of our neighbour, is concerned. Absolute integrity is indispensable, with reference to truth, for society could not exist if we were allowed to deceive each other. But there are occasions when we are not legitimately called upon to make known the entire truth, and, therefore, where silence or even a certain evasiveness is allowable; for, if we are asked something we are not bound to communicate, or it is very disadvantageous to reveal, we must naturally

[1] Ecclus. vii. 14.   [2] Ecclus. xx. 27, 28.   [3] Wisdom i. 11.

evade the question, or equivocate in our reply; and if our hearer be misled, it is by his own fault or ignorance. Sincerity does not consist in telling out, when not obliged, all we think, or all we know; but only in speaking not contrary to what we think or know; for there are circumstances in which it is most imprudent to make known the whole truth. When we are in possession of a secret told in confidence, discretion requires us to speak and act as if we were ignorant of it; because others have no right to know, and we have no right to make known, by word or act, what has been communicated to us privately. If, therefore, others are deceived by reason of our reticence, in such case it is by their own fault. There are also certain received expressions required by politeness, by which, though they are, in their literal wording, short of the truth, yet is no one deceived, from current usage; as, for example, by a servant saying, when the master does not desire to receive a visit, that his master is " not at home ;" or when we feel the necessity of expressing admiration or a liking for a thing not really to our taste. These are answers that mere civility requires to questions put to us.

Calumny is, correctly speaking, a false and injurious *Calumny and slander.* charge against some one, such as imputing to him habits that he does not possess, or sins which he has not committed. Slander consists in spreading or exaggerating evil reports, unjustly tending to injure our neighbour's reputation; and detraction is the making known, without just cause, the faults in his character. Calumny and slander are, therefore, the most pernicious of lies, because they falsely ruin another's good name; and unless excusable, from ignorance or inadvertence, and other extenuating

M

circumstances, are serious, and may be, mortal sins. "Detractors" also are "hateful to God;"[1] and we should take care of a good name, for it is more lasting "than a thousand treasures precious and great. A good life hath its number of days: but a good name shall continue for ever."[2] The author of any so atrocious injustice as calumny and slander, is bound to retract whatever he has said that is false, and to restore, as fully as may be in his power, the reputation and character he has defamed; repairing the injuries resulting from what has been uttered, and which he might or ought to have foreseen. When there is certainly justifying motive for making known wrong-doings hurtful to our neighbour's reputation, no injustice is done, provided that the reason and purpose are upright, and that the revelation is conveyed only to the persons qualified to receive the information. Further, we are not in fault, or at least not seriously so, when we inform those who are not cognisant of it that the character of a person is exceptionable. We do wrong by listening to, approving of, or encouraging calumny and scandal, and by neglecting any opportunity for preventing or suppressing it; because we are thereby wanting in charity towards the person spoken of, and towards the speaker, and become, ourselves, accomplices and participators in the mischief. "The tale-bearer shall defile his own soul, and shall be hated by all; and he that shall abide with him shall be hateful: the silent and wise man shall be honoured."[3] But we are not culpable in listening, without manifesting disapproval, to calumny or slander, if our motive and intention be just, and in the interest of the calumniated party, or of ourselves, or

[1] Rom. i. 30.   [2] Ecclus. xli. 15, 16.   [3] Ecclus. xxi. 31.

of some friend or person under our charge, or from civility due to a superior, if the one who speaks is in that position. The best course to follow, for the purpose of avoiding all such evil, is to withdraw, when we conveniently can, from the company in which we happen to be; or dexterously to turn the topic of conversation; or show, by our silence, manner, or countenance, the disapproval we feel. " The north wind driveth away rain, as doth a sad countenance a backbiting tongue." [1] Those who are wronged by calumny and scandal should be careful not to overstep the just limits in vindicating their rights, and defending their good name; but would do well to be patient in suffering insult, remembering the example of our Saviour, "who, when He was reviled, did not revile: when He suffered, He threatened not: but delivered Himself to him that judged Him unjustly." [2]

All personal insult, derision, mischief-making, lying and obsequious flattery, rash judgment, unworthy and unwarranted doubt and suspicion, are faults, which may be but venial sins, according to circumstance, intention, and the relative position of persons, but may contribute to the formation of mortal sin in connection with wrongful statements, injurious to the reputation of our neighbour. "Judge not, and you shall not be judged. Condemn not, and you shall not be condemned. Forgive, and you shall be forgiven." [3]

Mischief-making and insult.

Asperity must not be confused with severity in cases where superiors deem sharp correction to be necessary; "for there are many disobedient, vain talkers, and seducers . . . who must be reproved: who subvert whole houses, teaching the things which they ought not. . . .

Reproof and correction.

[1] Prov. xxv. 23.   [2] 1 Pet. ii. 23.   [3] Luke vi. 37.

Wherefore rebuke them sharply, that they may be sound in the faith."[1] Doubts and suspicions must not be confounded with taking prudent measures to prevent evil. These are not only advisable, but often an absolute duty; as in the case of parents, masters, or others who have to watch over their inferiors. "A fool laugheth at the instruction of his father: but he that regardeth reproofs shall become prudent;"[2] and "learning to the prudent is an ornament of gold, and like a bracelet upon his right arm."[3]

Violation of a secret. Another sin in connection with slander, is violation of a secret. First and foremost the confessor is most strictly obliged to keep, in every detail, secrets communicated in the Sacrament of Penance, neither revealing the most trifling sin of a penitent, nor making any use whatever of faults made known in confession. The violation of such secrets is a mortal sin, and a sacrilegious crime, opposed to justice, charity, religion, and the well-being of the faithful. Also any one who has by fault or accident overheard the confession of another person, is bound, as the confessor, for similar reasons, to the like inviolable secrecy, though not under sacrilege. The violation of any secret, known to few and not likely to become public, is sinful, because it is injurious to our neighbour. The violation of a secret, which we have formally promised not to divulge, is a grave sin; and the betrayal of a secret, given and accepted in confidence, whether expressly or tacitly reposed in us, owing to our position as superior, parent, friend, lawyer, or doctor, is a still more grievous sin. A secret ceases to be obligatory when the matter becomes public, or when the glory of God requires it to be disclosed; when its revelation is

[1] Titus i. 10, 11, 13.   [2] Prov. xv. 5.   [3] Ecclus. xxi. 24.

necessary for the public benefit, for the prevention of great evil, either spiritual or temporal, to ourselves, or our neighbour ; because we did not contract the obligation of secrecy with such important and hurtful consequences in prospect. But nothing, under any circumstances, can dispense us from the stringent duty of keeping the sacramental secrecy of confession ; for, we repeat, this is sacred at all times, and guarded by the seal of God.

Those who open or read a letter not addressed to them, easily commit serious sin, because a sealed communication from one person to another, may contain what is very gravely secret, and what should, in any case, be held in respect. There are exceptions, however, that permit, and sometimes demand, as a duty, the opening or reading of private correspondence. As, for instance, when the consent of the person, to whom it is addressed, is tacitly understood, or reasonably presumed to be given ; or when parental or other authority of an equivalent nature, admits of such a proceeding, in carrying out the duty of supervision or guardianship.

Violation of written communications.

" All things that are done, God will bring into judgment for every error, whether it be good or evil:" [1] so we must study to live in obedience to God, and keep His Commandments, striving on earth to merit the eternal life of Heaven : "There the wicked cease from tumult, and there the wearied in strength are at rest." [2] Thus far on the Ten Commandments of God.

[1] Ecclus. xii. 14. [2] Job iii. 17.

CHAPTER XXVI.

THE COMMANDMENTS OF THE CHURCH.

Command-
ments of the
Church.

AMONG the several ecclesiastical ordinances and laws, six come under the heading of general or chief Commandments of the Church. To keep certain appointed days holy; to hear Mass on certain days; to keep certain days of fasting and abstinence; to go to Confession and Communion at least once a year; not to marry within forbidden degrees, or without witnesses, or in penitential seasons with rejoicing.

Sanctification
of holy-days
of obligation.

The first Commandment of the Church ordains that we should sanctify all holy-days of obligation in the same manner as Sunday, by assisting at the Sacrifice of the Mass and abstaining from servile works. This decree has been instituted by ecclesiastical authority in pious commemoration of the principal mysteries of our holy religion, and of religious events appertaining to them. By assisting at the Sacrifice of the Mass must be understood the intention of fulfilling the precept and honouring God. It is more perfect, of course, to join in prayer, and still more perfect to receive Holy Communion—if we can, sacramentally, or, if not, spiritually—that is, in desire.

In England the holy-days of obligation are Christmas, Holy-days of obligation.
the Circumcision, the Epiphany, the Ascension, Corpus
Christi, the Assumption, the feast of St. Peter and St.
Paul, and of All Saints.

The Church ordains that we shall hear Mass on Sundays Obligation of hearing Mass.
and all days of obligation, because Sunday is the day
specially set aside and consecrated to divine worship.
Holy Mass being the highest and most glorious to God
of all sacrifices, it is by assisting in unity at that
religious ceremony, that we can best sanctify Sunday, and
likewise all days of obligation. The Church does not
specify what Mass we must attend, but it may be our
duty to be present at high Mass, if there be a sermon
at that alone. It is mortal sin not to hear Mass on the
days prescribed, unless we have a sufficiently important
reason for our absence—such as illness; the necessity of
remaining with a sick person, or young children; the
enforced duties of a soldier or sailor; the inclement state
of the weather, as in times of heavy falls of rain or snow;
distance from a church or chapel, etc. But where doubt
arises, that disposes us to be under illusion as to our
obligation of attending Mass, the circumstances should be
explained to our confessor, or other priest at hand, and his
sanction obtained as dispensation. We should be present Required dispositions for hearing Mass.
during the whole of the Mass, and devote to it religious
attention. That is to say, keeping our minds occupied
with pious thoughts; following the prayers of the Mass, or
meditating on the Passion of our Lord or the mysteries of
His Incarnation, Life, or Resurrection and Ascension, or
examining our conscience for confession. If we come in
after the Mass is commenced, or leave before its conclusion,

without proper reason, it is sinful, because we are commanded to hear Mass, and not merely a portion of it. It is, therefore, generally considered that we have missed hearing Mass altogether, if we are not present at the Creed, and do not remain until after the communion of the priest. But if we are present before the recital of the Creed and after the priest's communion, there is no mortal sin.

Obligation of fasting and abstinence. The second Commandment of the Church ordains that we should keep the appointed days of fasting and abstinence. Of the former there are the forty days of Lent, the Ember days, certain vigils, and, in England, the Wednesdays and Fridays in Advent; on which it is obligatory for every one over twenty-one years of age to fast, unless, for special reasons, such as sickness, infirmity, old age, over fatigue from necessary causes, there be lawful dispensation.

Fasting mentioned in Scripture. There is mention, both in the Old and New Testaments, of fasting having been practised in ancient times. Our Lord Himself fasted, as an example of penitence, " forty days and forty nights; "[1] and recommended, as requisite against the influence of evil, "prayer and fasting."[2] Our Saviour also spoke of the fasting of His disciples, after He should have left them, saying, "then shall they fast in those days; "[3] which was carried out by them in their ministry, as we read in the Acts of the Apostles, where it is written that St. Paul, accompanied by Barnabas, "prayed with fasting."[4]

The benefits of fasting. Whether as expiation for sin, or to strengthen us against relapse, fasting is a sign of deep sorrow. For when we are

[1] Matt. iv. 2.   [2] Mark ix. 28.
[3] Luke v. 35.   [4] Acts xiv. 22.

in deep affliction we do not think much about gratifying our appetite. It is a means of penance, because it obliges certain privations, and is a safeguard or defence against sin, because it exercises our force of will in mastering or contributing to weaken our evil passions. It is, moreover, a recognition of the punishment we deserve from the just hand of God, shown forth by the compunction of our soul and the mortification of our body. The well-being of the body depends on the soul; and as want of moderation cannot be otherwise than harmful to both, fasting can lessen evil and be of advantage to our eternal welfare. It is certain that physicians are more often called in to heal sickness contracted through lack of moderation, than from any indisposition caused by fasting, and that doctors constantly advocate moderation in the use of food.

Fasting, as ordained by the Church, consists in abstaining from flesh-meat, and in taking during the day only one full ordinary meal, and a light "collation" or refection. The exact limits on the subject of fasting vary in different countries and dioceses: and the alleviations and dispensations accorded, apart from the regularly authorized restrictions concerning this matter, are local. In making a change of residence, whether temporary or not, all must conform to the rules of the diocese in which they happen to be living, unless they have a personal dispensation. This is usually accompanied by the injunction of almsgiving on those who can afford it; or by prayers from those who are too poor to fulfil that obligation. Under all circumstances, when exempt from the obligation of fasting, we should try to make up by abstinence; and in no case are we released from the duty of penance, but should at least offer

Fasting as ordained by the Church.

prayers and good works in accordance with the example shown us by the whole life on earth of our Redeemer.

The fast of Lent. The fast of Lent is from Ash Wednesday until holy Saturday, inclusive, and, excepting the intervening Sundays, is a fast of forty days, instituted in memory of our Lord's fast in the desert. It also commemorates the Passion and Death of our Saviour, and is as a preparation of penitence to worthily celebrate the great feast of Easter.

The fast of Ember-days. The fast of Ember-days, or Four Seasons, occurs four times in the year, on a Wednesday, Friday, and Saturday towards the commencement of each season. This custom was instituted for the purpose of specially praying for the good produce of the earth; and also for the grace of obtaining priests and ministers of the Church, that shall be worthy of their holy office, and zealous in glorifying God by contributing to the salvation and sanctification of souls. The Ember-days occur in spring, the first week of Lent; those of summer, the week immediately preceding Trinity Sunday; those of autumn, the week following the day commemorating the Exaltation of the Cross; and those of winter, the third week of Advent.

The fast of vigils. Fasting on a vigil was specially instituted that we might prepare ourselves to celebrate, in fitting manner, the holy feast of the morrow, thereby to render it more glorious to God, and more beneficial to our own souls. When a vigil occurs on Sunday, the fast is kept on the day previous, because Sunday, being consecrated to the memory of our Lord's Resurrection, is never made a day of penance. There is no vigil for the feast of the Ascension, in recognition presumably of Christ's words: " Can the children of the Bridegroom mourn, as long as the Bridegroom is with them?"[1] The vigils observed in England are the eve of Christmas Day, of St. Peter and St. Paul, of the Assumption, of All Saints, and of Pentecost.

Abstinence is a practice mentioned in Scripture, when "Daniel mourned the days of three weeks, during which flesh entered not into his mouth."[2] By the Church's legislation concerning it, we are, in remembrance of our Saviour's death on the Cross, prohibited from eating the flesh meat of animals on every Friday throughout the year, except that on which Christmas Day may fall. This weekly penance is a reminder of the obligation we have to abjure evil, and habitually cultivate good, for the salvation and sanctification of our souls. Abstinence is also of usual obligation on the Sundays in Lent, but permission to eat meat is granted, though it is forbidden to eat fish and meat at the same meal. All who are over the age of seven years, are bound to abstain, unless by some really grave reason or legitimate dispensation they are exempted. They who are suffering from illness, and the very poor, are free from the obligation. Abstinence is seldom prejudicial to health, especially where abundance of meat and rich living are habitual; and it is assuredly of spiritual benefit in the mortification of our senses. *Abstinence.*

The third Commandment of the Church ordains that we shall, at least once a year, make a Confession of our sins to an authorized priest, and from him receive absolution in the name of our Lord Jesus Christ. *Annual Confession.*

Confession is obligatory on every member of the Church who has attained the age of reason, which of course varies *Obligation of Confession.*

---

[1] Matt. ix. 15. [2] Dan. x. 2.

according as a child's mind may be more or less developed and capable of recognizing the gravity of sin. Children should at an early age be taught to distinguish between right and wrong; they should be instructed in the examination of their conscience; they should be shown their principal faults clearly, but without exaggeration, in a manner that shall excite them to sincere repentance; and they should be inspired with profound respect for the Sacrament of Penance.

Frequent Confession.   The Church exacts only an annual Confession, that we may not increase our sins by disobedience to her divine authority. But by the nature of the case, we should have recourse to the Sacrament of Penance as often as we may feel in imminent danger of falling into mortal sin, and most especially when we have committed mortal sin, which no feeling of shame, however great, should deter us from acknowledging before God. It is written: "Be not ashamed to confess thy sins." [1]

Annual Communion.   Confession must be complete, so that, if in mortal sin, we may, by pardon, re-enter into a state of grace; and although no special time is strictly prescribed on other occasions, it is the precept of the Church to make a yearly Confession at Easter, in conjunction with the Communion of obligation in Paschal time. Any wilful delay beyond the year is a mortal sin, at least if we have any mortal sin to confess.

The fourth Commandment of the Church ordains that we should receive the Blessed Sacrament at least once in the year, and that at Easter or thereabouts, which, strictly speaking, commences in England at the beginning of

[1] Ecclus. iv. 31.

Lent, and ends on Low Sunday, the Sunday following Easter Day.

This is of obligation to all who have attained the age of twelve years, according to St. Aphonsus; though they may be admitted earlier, and as soon as they can "discern the body of our Lord," that is, are capable of understanding the importance and solemnity of the act, and of knowing the requisite dispositions of respect and humility with which all should approach the Blessed Sacrament. "Whosoever shall eat this bread, or drink the chalice of the Lord unworthily, shall be guilty of the Body and the Blood of the Lord."[1] Therefore, "let a man prove himself, and so let him eat of that bread."

Obligation of receiving Communion.

Our Lord Jesus Christ said, "Unless you eat the Flesh of the Son of Man and drink His Blood, you shall not have life in you."[2] Therefore, we can scarcely accomplish this divine precept unless by receiving holy Communion at least once in the year; and indeed, how can we expect to be received by our Saviour into the eternal happiness of Heaven, if we give ourselves so little trouble to receive Him here on earth, and with Him, His promise and pledge of that everlasting life? The time of Easter is of obligation in commemoration of the institution of the most Blessed Sacrament by our Lord Jesus Christ; and to impress us with a vivid remembrance of our Saviour's Passion and death, of which the Holy Eucharist is the perpetual and living memorial, according to Christ's own words as given to us by St. Paul: "As often as you shall eat this bread, and drink the chalice, you shall show the death of the Lord, until He come."[3] It is desirable, but

Frequent Communion.

Easter Communion.

[1] 1 Cor. xi. 27, 28, 29.   [2] John vi. 54.   [3] 1 Cor. xi. 26.

not of obligation, that the Easter Communion should be received in the Church of the parish to which we belong, for, by doing this, we can offer good example one to another; we strengthen the union that should exist between ourselves and the minister of Christ under whose supervision we are placed, by public acknowledgment of his authority; and enable him to recognize those who have acquitted themselves of their duty, that he may try to bring defaulters to repentance.

The fifth Commandment of the Church ordains that we shall contribute to the support of our pastors.

In Catholic countries, people are sometimes obliged by law to do so, and sometimes the State provides for their maintenance. In non-Catholic nations, the support of the Church's ministers depends on the gratuitous offerings of the congregation, which, however, are none the less obligatory.

The sixth Commandment of the Church ordains that we shall not marry within certain degrees of kindred, nor solemnize matrimony at forbidden times.

We are prohibited, by this Commandment, from contracting marriage with persons related by consanguinity in the four degrees of kindred, counted in direct line from the mother and father to whom the parties concerned are united in the same common stock. The alliance is also prohibited between those who are connected with each other by affinity, within the same degrees ; that is to say, between the blood relations of a husband or wife. Both conditions are obligatory under pain of mortal sin, unless a special dispensation is obtained.

The forbidden times for the solemn celebration of

marriage are, from the first Sunday in Advent until after forbidden
the Epiphany ; and from Ash Wednesday until the Sunday times.
after Easter, both inclusive ; because these periods are days
of penance and prayer, when any ceremony of rejoicing
would be inconsistent with the spirit of the Church.

CHAPTER XXVII.

THE GIFT OF GRACE.

Means of keeping the Commandments.

FOR the salvation of our souls we must have faith in all that God has revealed to His Church and must keep the Commandments. But we cannot do this of our own strength alone, nor can we believe those truths, nor obey those precepts that lead us to the glory and happiness of Heaven, without assistance and without means in accordance with that supernatural end—that is, without the help of Divine grace.

The gift of Grace.

Grace is a supernatural and spiritual gift, gratuitously bestowed on us by God alone, through the merits of our Redeemer, to guide us to life everlasting. "God commendeth His charity towards us; . . . for if, when we were enemies, we were reconciled to God by the death of His Son ; much more, being reconciled, shall we be saved by His life. . . . That as sin hath reigned to death, so also grace might reign by justice unto life everlasting, through Jesus Christ our Lord." [1]

Grace, or supernatural gift.

The gift of grace is called " supernatural," because it is of so high a nature that it can only come from God, giving us power to perform actions deserving of Heaven, and

[1] Rom. v. 8, 10, 21.

enabling us to do countless things which we could not accomplish unaided. We cannot obtain grace of our own will, nor deserve to gain it by any ground of claim ; it is something quite distinct from all natural gifts of the body and soul, and is bestowed on us by God, "not according to our works, but according to His own purpose and grace."[1] For instance, the grace of God is made manifest in the conversion which changes our thoughts and ways from error to truth, from vice to virtue, when we would not of our own accord act in opposition to our natural dispositions. Further the grace of God is manifested in striking examples of virtue surpassing the ordinary forces of nature, as in sublime acts of charity, or by the surrender of all earthly comforts for the one purpose of serving God.

The gift of grace is called " spiritual," because it is an inward and invisible bestowal on the soul. It is a gift from God alone, because " Every best gift, and every perfect gift, is from above, coming down from the Father of lights, with whom there is no change, nor shadow of alteration."[2] And it is accorded to us through the merits of our Saviour, because He is our only Redeemer, and the " One Mediator of God and men."[3]

Grace, or spiritual gift.

This gift of God affects our soul in substance and in action ; there are therefore two kinds of grace, namely, habitual grace and actual grace.

---

[1] 2 Tim. i. 9.   [2] Jas. i. 17.   [3] 1 Tim. ii. 5.

CHAPTER XXVIII.

HABITUAL GRACE.

Habitual grace.

HABITUAL grace is a supernatural gift of "justification" which blots out the stain of original sin and communicates divine life to the soul, rendering us worthy of the kingdom of God, transforming our soul, when in a state of sin, to a state of grace. It inheres permanently in the soul, unless we wilfully forfeit it by mortal sin. To keep it, therefore, rests with us; as St. Paul says, "Keep the good thing committed to thy trust by the Holy Ghost, who dwelleth in us."[1]

Sanctifying grace.

Habitual grace is called "sanctifying grace," because it renders the soul supernaturally pure and holy, "by the laver of regeneration, and renovation of the Holy Ghost;"[2] and because, being justified by grace, we become "heirs, according to hope of life everlasting."[3] Habitual grace is also called the "grace of justification," because it elevates the soul from a state of sin to a state of "justice." "As by the offence of one, unto all men to condemnation; so also by the justice of One, unto all men to justification of life."[4]

Habitual grace, a supernatural gift.

We know habitual or sanctifying grace to be a supernatural gift received of God's charity, because it is "not by the works of justice, which we have done, but according to

---

[1] 2 Tim. i. 14.   [2] Titus iii. 5.   [3] Titus iii. 7.   [4] Rom. v. 18.

His mercy He saved us . . . through Jesus Christ our Saviour."[1] We know habitual grace to be our justification from above, blotting out the stain of original sin; for it is written: "Being then freed from sin, we have been made servants of justice."[2] We know, too, that habitual grace communicates divine life to the soul, rendering us inheritors of the Kingdom of Heaven, called "fruit unto sanctification, . . . for the wages of sin is death. But the grace of God, life everlasting, in Christ Jesus our Lord."[3] We also know habitual grace to be a permanent gift that is only forfeited through mortal sin, because "the charity of God is poured forth in our hearts, by the Holy Ghost, who is given to us;"[4] and what God bestows upon us, we cannot lose except through our own fault. Again, we know that our soul loses habitual grace through mortal sin. This is proved from various passages in Scripture—some of which have already been quoted[5]—showing that one mortal sin suffices to place us in opposition to God and deprives us of everlasting life; and making it quite evident that, without habitual grace, we cannot reach the salvation of Heaven. For "there shall not enter into it anything defiled, or that worketh abomination or maketh a lie, but they that are written in the book of life."[6]

It is by the Sacrament of Baptism that children receive, Reception of habitual grace in Baptism. for the first time, habitual grace; and though God may bestow this precious gift on adults before Baptism, any supposition or persuasion that this has been the case in a given person does not dispense from the obligation of receiving the sacrament of regeneration.

---

[1] Titus iii. 5, 6.   [2] Rom. vi. 18.   [3] Rom. vi. 22, 23.   [4] Rom. v. 5.
[5] 1 John iii. 15; Jas. ii. 10; John xv. 6.   [6] Apoc. xxi. 27.

Effect of habitual grace.

With the "sanctification" of habitual grace we are accorded virtues and gifts of the Holy Ghost and the love of God, through the merits of our Saviour, as expressed by St. Paul in the following words: "The grace of our Lord Jesus Christ, and the charity of God, and the communion of the Holy Ghost be with you all. Amen."[1] Habitual grace purifies us from sin and renders us agreeable to God, uniting us to Him by the supernatural bond of love whereby we have the right to call Him our "Father;"[2] and making us participators of that divine life which is a beginning, as it were, of the glory to come. We are "washed . . . sanctified . . . and justified in the name of our Lord Jesus Christ, and the Spirit of our God." Our " bodies are the members of Christ," and our "members are the temple of the Holy Ghost."[3]

Recovery of habitual grace through Penance.

If we have the misfortune to lose habitual grace by mortal sin, there is still a means of recovery. Our heart being full of repentance, and our mind properly disposed, we may make our peace with God through the Sacrament of Penance; or if the Sacrament is by just cause unattainable, then by complete and perfect contrition, accompanied by the earnest desire for Absolution, and the intention and resolution of obtaining it when circumstances permit. We can increase habitual grace by the reception of certain Sacraments, or by actions accomplished for the love of God and for our own progressive advancement towards eternal glory, aided by actual grace. "The path of the just, as a shining light, goeth forwards and increaseth even to perfect day."[4]

Increase of habitual grace.

[1] 2 Cor. xiii. 13.
[2] Rom. viii. 15; 1 John iii. 1.
[3] 1 Cor. vi. 11, 15, 19.
[4] Prov. iv. 18.

CHAPTER XXIX.

ACTUAL GRACE.

ACTUAL grace is a supernatural and occasional movement of grace: a Divine help, which enlightens our understanding, increases our strength, and moves our will from evil, and towards the performance of good actions. Actual grace.

We know that actual grace is a supernatural gift, because it comes direct from God, without any right of claim on our part; making our actions meritorious through the merits of our Saviour, without whom we can do nothing for our own salvation. Our Lord said, "I am the true vine; and My Father is the husbandman. . . . I am the vine; you the branches: he that abideth in Me, and I in him, the same beareth much fruit: for without Me you can do nothing."[1] We know, too, that actual grace is from God, an internal passing movement in the soul, because it is a help accorded for the eliciting some virtuous act, and must therefore pass when the act, needing such supernatural aid, is accomplished. We know also, from the words of the Psalmist, that actual grace is an enlightenment of our understanding and a directing of our will: Actual grace, a supernatural gift.

[1] John xv. 1, 5.

"Give me understanding, and I will search Thy law ; and I will keep it with my whole heart. . . . Direct my steps according to Thy word: and let no iniquity have dominion over me. . . . Help me, and I shall be saved: and I will meditate always on Thy justifications." [1]

Necessity of actual grace.

Actual grace is indispensable for the salvation of adults, as we learn from our Lord's words: "No man can come to Me, except the Father, who hath sent Me, draw him ; and I will raise him up in the last day." [2]

Means of obtaining actual grace.

We should pray that supernatural enlightenment and strength of actual grace be given us as our help in resistance to temptation, or performance of duty, however hard. "Not that we are sufficient to think anything of ourselves, as of ourselves: but our sufficiency is from God." [3] And from Him, if we pray in the right spirit, we shall attain the help of grace; for our Lord said, "If you abide in Me, and My words abide in you, you shall ask whatever you will, and it shall be done unto you." [4] "Therefore I say unto you, all things, whatsoever you ask when ye pray, believe that you shall receive; and they shall come unto you." [5]

Prayer for the help of grace is not only efficacious for the just, but for sinners, because God desires the repentance of evil-doers, and deals patiently with us for our own sake, "not willing that any should perish, but that all should return to penance." [6]

Necessity of praying for actual grace.

The greater our need of actual grace for the resistance of temptation, subjugation of our passions, and patient bearing of trials, the more frequently should we have recourse to

[1] Ps. cxviii. 34, 133, 117.   [2] John vi. 44.   [3] 2 Cor. iii. 5.
[4] John xv. 7.   [5] Mark. xi. 24.   [6] 2 Pet. iii. 9.

prayer for that Divine assistance. Even when we have reason to believe ourselves in a state of grace, we should pray for aid from above, lest we fall; for "he that shall persevere unto the end, shall be saved."[1] Those who know and practise their religion are bound to pray; but God does not deny the help of actual grace to sinners. This He does by lovingly diffusing light into the darkness of their mind, as a warning; by a movement towards good; by some obstacle to the furtherance of their evil designs; by some unlooked-for result, occasioning disgust or remorse; or by an apparently inexplicable pause in wrong-doing: all which may turn the sinner to repentance.

We have always freedom and strength sufficient to resist evil, if we choose to make proper use of it, and strive after the help of grace : " Wherefore he that thinketh himself to stand, let him take heed lest he fall."[2] St. Paul speaks of our sufficiency to resist temptation in these terms : "God is faithful, who will not suffer you to be tempted above that which you are able; but will make also with temptation issue, that you may be able to bear it."[3] Withstanding temptation in general fortifies the soul, just as exercise strengthens the body. It enables us to gain in grace by acts of resignation, patience, mortification, and penitence. It humbles us, lessening our love of independence, and brings us nearer to God in prayer. *Means of increasing actual grace.*

In any case, it is with full liberty that we act, freely accepting or freely rejecting this gift of grace, as is clearly stated by St. Paul, who writes : "By the grace of God, I am what I am; and His grace in me hath not been void, but I *Liberty of action concerning actual grace.*

[1] Matt. x. 22.   [2] 1 Cor. x. 12.   [3] 1 Cor. x. 13.

have laboured more abundantly than all they: yet not I, but the grace of God with me."[1] We are therefore free by the help of grace to do that which pleases God and leads us to salvation; or to expose ourselves, by resistance to grace, to lose the favour of God and eternal recompense; as the Jews, dispersed throughout the universe, have done, of whom our Lord said, " Jerusalem, Jerusalem, that killest the prophets, and stonest them that are sent to thee, how often would I have gathered thy children as the bird doth her brood under her wings, and thou wouldst not ? Behold your home shall be left to you desolate. And I say to you, that you shall not see Me till the time come, when you shall say : Blessed is He that cometh in the name of the Lord."[2] Although resistance to an inspiration of Divine grace is not a sin in itself, yet by opposing it we may fall into sin, and are acting contrary to our own good in this world and our complete happiness in the next. " Every work that is corruptible shall fail in the end : and the worker thereof shall go with it. And every excellent work shall be justified : and the worker thereof shall be honoured therein."[3]

Comparison between habitual and actual grace.

Habitual grace and actual grace are alike supernatural gifts, which God alone can give to help us through this world of temptation and trial to salvation and everlasting happiness. The three differences between these two kinds of grace are, that habitual grace is permanent, so long as we are free from mortal sin; whereas actual grace is a transient help. Habitual grace is not indispensable to the reception of actual grace, which latter is given to those who are in mortal sin; whereas actual grace is absolutely requisite for the recovery of habitual grace.

[1] 1 Cor. xv. 10.   [2] Luke xiii. 34, 35.   [3] Ecclus. xiv. 20, 21.

Also, habitual grace renders us children of God and worthy of the kingdom of Heaven; whereas actual grace is an occasional movement in the soul that helps us in all the varying circumstances of life, but does not of itself give us any right to the inheritance of everlasting life.

CHAPTER XXX.

MERIT.

Merit.   A SUPERNATURAL act of virtue, because performed under
the influence of grace, gives us the right to a supernatural
recompense, which right is called merit. That is to say, an
act of virtue performed by a person in a state of habitual or
sanctifying grace, aided by actual grace, is rewarded with
an increase of habitual grace, and, if that person does not
finally fall away, with increased glory and happiness in
Heaven. We have proof in Scripture of this recompense
of merit. By "doing the truth in charity, we may in all
things grow up in Him who is the head, even Christ." [1]
" He that is just, let him be justified still: and he that is
holy, let him be sanctified still." [2] These two references
show the increase of habitual grace that merit may procure for us ; and the following two quotations point out
the reward of everlasting life to which merit can entitle us.
" Blessed is the man that endureth temptation ; for when
he hath been proved, he shall receive the crown of life,
which God hath promised to them that love Him." [3]
" Blessed are they that wash their robes in the blood of

[1] Eph. iv. 15.   [2] Apoc. xxii. 11.   [3] Jas. i. 12.

the Lamb: that they may have a right to the tree of life, and may enter in by the gates into the city." [1] So also we see that by merit we may gain an increase of glory and happiness in the world to come, through the words of God given in the Revelations of St. John: "Behold I come quickly; and My reward is with Me, to render to every man according to his works." [2] And again, in St. Paul's Epistle to the Corinthians: "I have planted, Apollo watered, but God gave the increase : . . . he that planteth, and he that watereth, are one. And every man shall receive his own reward according to his own labour; . . . every man's work shall be manifest, for the day of the Lord shall declare it." [3]

The merit gained by a soul in a state of habitual grace, with the help of actual grace, through acts of virtue done from a supernatural motive, procures two other rewards, namely, satisfaction and impetration. The merit of "Satisfaction" is obtained by the atonement we make in expiation of the temporal punishment due for sins that have already been pardoned in the Sacrament of Penance. As we can, through our Redeemer, give satisfaction to the justice of God, by voluntary penances, and by those the confessor imposes on us, as well as by patiently enduring any temporal punishment that Providence inflicts upon us, our good works and virtuous actions must, through our Saviour, also become meritorious with reference to temporal punishment due for sin. With our Redeemer, has not God "given us all things ? . . . who is he that shall condemn ? Christ Jesus that died, yea that is risen also again ; who is at the right hand of God, who also maketh intercession for us.

Effects of merit.

---

[1] Apoc. xxii. 4.   [2] Apoc. xxii. 12.   [3] 1 Cor. iii. 8, 13.

Who then shall separate us from the love of Christ?"[1] The merit of Impetration is that by which our virtuous actions and good works ascend towards God, as a claim to the reward of actual graces.   Thus the Angel said to Cornelius the centurion, "Thy prayer is heard, and thy alms are had in remembrance in the sight of God."[2]

Means of gaining merit.   The virtuous actions and good works that procure merit, must all proceed from obedience to the Commandments of God and of the Church, or from some motive taken from the teachings of our faith and accomplished by the help of actual grace: because what is done from a purely earthly motive cannot merit a supernatural recompense.   The more perfect the motive, the more meritorious is the act.   We have entire liberty, and when we co-operate with the gift of actual grace, we freely accept and execute what is desired of us by God, in the manner and by the means He offers, giving us the right to be rewarded according to His promises.   " In doing good, let us not fail.   For in due time we shall reap, not failing. Therefore, whilst we have time, let us work good to all men, but especially to those who are of the household of the faith."[3]   These words teach us that we must acquire merit by our works in this world, for in the next, our actions cannot be meritorious; as is shown by Christ when He said, "The night cometh, when no man can work."[4]   We cannot acquire merit without being in a state of habitual grace aided by grace actual; for our Lord said, "Abide in Me, and I in you.   As the branch cannot bear fruit of itself, unless it abide in the vine, so neither

---

[1] Rom. viii. 32, 34, 35.   [2] Acts x. 31.
[3] Gal. vi. 9, 10.   [4] John ix. 4.

can you, unless you abide in Me."[1] When the soul is not in a state of habitual grace, good works and virtuous actions are not, strictly speaking, deserving of merit, since they give no right to habitual grace or to eternal life. But they are of immeasurable assistance in gaining God's mercy, that we may come forth from a state of sin, and recover sanctifying grace.

One mortal sin suffices for the loss of merit, because by it we lose the divine life of habitual grace, and therefore all privileges attached to that Divine life are necessarily forfeited when it ceases to exist in our souls. As by the effect of mortal sin we are in danger of Hell, we cannot, clearly, preserve any merit for the eternal life of Heaven. " For what participation hath justice with injustice ? or what fellowship hath light with darkness ? "[2] " The justice of the just shall not deliver him, in what day soever he shall sin."[3] But it is a generally admitted opinion that the repentant sinner re-enters into possession of the merits he has lost by mortal sin; and that the iniquities of him who turns from wickedness and is converted, shall not be prejudicial to merits previously gained. " None of his sins, which he hath committed, shall be imputed to him : he hath done judgment and justice, he shall surely live."[4]

Loss of merit.

Recovery of merit.

---

[1] John xv. 4.
[3] Ezek. xxxiii. 12.
[2] 2 Cor. vi. 14.
[4] Ezek. xxxiii. 16.

CHAPTER XXXI.

PREDESTINATION.

Predestination. PREDESTINATION is the prevision and preparation of benefits by which those who are freed from eternal death are most certainly freed. This is the teaching of St. Augustine.

Freedom of action foreseen by God.

Although predestination is a mystery, it is certain that it in no way takes from our entire freedom. In the promised reward of good and punishment of evil, it is evident that we are completely at liberty to merit the recompense of Heaven, by our voluntary co-operation with Divine grace; or to deserve the sufferings of Hell, by doing the wilful and criminal acts we could have avoided. Otherwise, why should our victory over evil be spoken of in Scripture as a "reward,"[1] a "prize,"[2] a "crown,"[3] and our debasement in wickedness as a voluntary "death"[4] to the soul; though God "will have all men to be saved, and to come to the knowledge of the truth;"[5] "not willing that any should perish, but that all should return to penance."[6]

---

[1] Matt. v. 12; Apoc. xxii. 12.   [2] 1 Cor. ix. 24.
[3] 1 Cor. ix. 25; 2 Tim. iv. 8.   [4] Ezek. xxxiii. 11.   [5] 1 Tim. ii. 4.
[6] 2 Pet. iii. 9.

CHAPTER XXXII.

PRAYER.

PRAYER is an uplifting of the soul towards Heaven; a Prayer. raising of the mind and heart to God, by which we worship Him, express our needs, and crave His help. In prayer we offer to God our praise, love, gratitude, and repentance for sin; for we owe to God adoration as to our Creator and Redeemer, as well as contrition for our offences. In prayer, we implore His aid for our spiritual wants in the interest of our future salvation, and of our temporal needs in the interest of our transitory existence here on earth.

The necessity for prayer is founded on the precept and Necessity of prayer. example of our Lord, and on our own nature and its deficiencies. Our Saviour said, " We ought always to pray," [1] and taught His Apostles, saying, " Thus therefore shall you pray;" [2] and again, He said, " Pray, lest ye enter into temptation." [3] St. Paul tells us to be " instant in prayer;" [4] and to " pray without ceasing." [5] Our Lord gave us the example when " He went into a mountain to pray, and He passed the whole night in the prayer of God : " [6]—He, who is " always living to make intercession for us." [7] God, having bestowed on us the gifts of intelligence and will, has thereby made us capable of knowing, loving, and

[1] Luke xviii. 1.   [2] Matt. vi. 9.   [3] Luke xxii. 40.   [4] Rom. xii. 12.
        [5] 1 Thess. v. 17.   [6] Luke vi. 12.   [7] Heb. vii. 25.

obeying Him, and of offering Him the worship of our minds, hearts, and bodies, by an elevation of thought, a recognition of dependence, and a gratitude and confidence, given with all inward feeling, and with all outward sign of reverence and humility, so that we may praise Him and in our ignorance, distress, and sufferings, ask His ever-ready love and help in our perplexities, temptations, and all our moral and physical needs. We do this by interior worship, springing from natural sentiments of homage from the created to the Creator, and from thankfulness from the dependent to the Benefactor; and also by exterior worship, which has its source in a natural desire to outwardly proclaim or manifest with the whole being an intense and irrepressible feeling.

Manner of praying.

We should prepare our souls for prayer, and not be "as a man that tempteth God."[1] We should pray with attention to the words we pronounce, to the sense they express, and to the Presence of God whose hearing and compassion we supplicate; for with wilful disregard to what we say, we show disrespect, and then our prayer becomes worse than worthless. We should try to collect our thoughts, and to pray with our whole heart, not causing voluntary distractions by the deliberate wandering of our eyes, nor permitting casual disorder of our thoughts to obtain the mastery by not checking it with sufficient promptitude and energy; bearing such disorder, however, with calm patience, remembering that we are not worthy of consolation. We should pray with humility, fully realizing that we are but poor sinners, undeserving of God's graces, for "God resisteth the proud, and giveth grace to the humble,"[2] and "the

---

[1] Ecclus. xviii. 23.   [2] Jas. iv. 6.

prayer of him that humbleth himself, shall pierce the clouds."[1] We should pray with fervour and confidence to God, whose truth is infinite, and with whom "all things are possible;"[2] letting our whole soul go forth in the earnestness of supplication, never doubting God's supreme charity, but asking "in faith, nothing wavering; for he that wavereth is like a wave of the sea, which is moved and carried about by the wind."[3] We should pray with perseverance, finding consolation in the patience we may be called upon to exercise, never relaxing our efforts, for in the delay experienced we render greater homage to God, and our prayers become more meritorious. There is "one Mediator of God and man,"[4] and through His merits, and by His name, our prayers will be heard, for He is our Redeemer, who said, "Whatsoever you shall ask the Father in My name, that will I do."[5] We must pray, not only for ourselves, but—in charity towards our neighbour—for "all men:"[6] for the conversion of unbelievers, for the repentance of sinners, for the souls in Purgatory, and even for those that hate us, "for this is good and acceptable in the sight of God our Saviour."[7] Although we may pray for our temporal wants, all that we ask in respect thereof, must be subordinate to our spiritual interests, in no manner detracting from the glory of God or the great object of the salvation of our souls. If we regard our temporal well-being with too high an appreciation, it may prove to the detriment of our eternal welfare, and in gaining worldly comforts and pleasures, we may find that "mourning taketh hold of the end of joy."[8] Our Lord said, "every one that asketh,

[1] Ecclus. xxxv. 21. [2] Matt. xix. 26. [3] Jas. iv. 6. [4] 1 Tim. ii. 5.
[5] John xiv. 13. [6] 1 Tim. ii. 1. [7] 1 Tim. ii. 3. [8] Prov. xiv. 13.

O

receiveth;"[1] but our prayers may be imperfect, and we may "ask amiss;"[2] or our petitions may be prejudicial to the glory of God, or beyond our deserts, or harmful to our spiritual good, and only worthy of refusal by our Lord, who answered "the mother of the sons of Zebedee: . . . you know not what you ask."[3]   We must seek "first the kingdom of God, and His justice, and all these things shall be added;"[4] and we should pray with resignation to God's will, as our Saviour taught us, saying, "Not my will, but Thine be done."[5]

Vocal prayer.   Vocal prayer is often obligatory on those in holy orders, on members of a religious community, or as a penance imposed by the confessor.   Under ordinary circumstances, prayer may be vocal or mental, at will, and in private or in common with other persons.   Among members of a family vocal prayer may be effectual in ensuring punctuality in the performance of this religious duty, in preventing negligence in the discharge of morning and evening prayer, in bringing to bear a wholesome influence on one another, in confirming feelings of piety, and giving a greater spirit of fervour, calling down, by union of souls before God, the blessings of Heaven upon the household.

Public prayer.   Public prayer is that which is offered by a number of people in Church or Chapel.   In it the union of spirit cannot fail to be agreeable to God, and public prayer ascends to Heaven as one fervent supplication, stirring up a feeling of brotherhood in the hearts of those who kneel with one accord, as equals in the sight of God.   The mutual good example, the touching devotion, the melodious chants,

---

[1] Matt. vii. 8.   [2] Jas. iv. 3.   [3] Matt. xx. 20, 22.
[4] Matt. vi. 33.   [5] Luke xxii. 42.

and solemnity of ceremonial, even at times the silence of the House of God, must dispose our soul better for the love and duty we owe to Him and our fellow-creatures. It cannot but render us more calm, patient, and penitent, besides giving comfort, consolation, and strength to the soul, in bringing our thoughts nearer to Heaven. It is written: "Draw nigh to God, and He will draw nigh to you."[1]

Prayer does not depend on a multiplicity of words, but on the spirit with which they are spoken aloud, or offered in silence; for our Lord said, "When you are praying, speak not much, as the heathens. For they think that in their much speaking they may be heard."[2] Therefore, when our hearts would have recourse to prayer, and circumstances afford only the possibility of a momentary elevation of the soul towards God, there is opportunity of what is termed Ejaculatory Prayer; which consists of a few words expressive of love, appeal, faith, or hope. By this means we may pray on all occasions, acquiring the habit of profiting at any instant by ejaculatory prayer, because this is possible at all times and in all places, and does much towards exciting our piety, devotion and confidence, as well as strengthening us in time of temptation. *Ejaculatory prayer.*

Mental prayer is of daily advantage, because, never knowing when our last moment may be at hand, it is well to think, day by day, of the eternal years, to ponder the life of Christ, and render account to God of our souls. Because, further, mental prayer helps us to bear the sorrows and vanquish the temptations of daily existence, making it easier for those to live well who pray well. Mental prayer is commenced by ridding our minds of all wilful *Mental prayer.*

[1] Jas. iv. 8.   [2] Matt. vi. 7.

distractions, and worshipping God with faith and humility, invoking the divine aid of the Holy Spirit that we may pray as we ought, and that our prayers may be heard through the merits of our Lord Jesus Christ. We should spend some fixed time in the meditation, taking for subject one of the great mysteries of our holy religion, or one of the many virtues of our Saviour, and offering affections of praise, love, or gratitude, as the occasion may demand; picturing to our imaginations the scene connected with the subject chosen, to impress it more fully on our minds; and striving that our souls may be filled with salutary thoughts and feelings. We should try to fix our attention upon the matter we have selected for meditation or contemplation, turning over in our minds the reasons which cause us to believe, admire, bless, and praise; studying the practical lessons to be learnt; reflecting upon our own conduct, and considering whether we think, speak, and act in accordance with the teachings inculcated. At the conclusion of the meditation, we elevate our heart and soul to God, in acts of piety and devotion, of desire and supplication, avowing with humility and sorrow our weakness in not having hitherto lived up to the lessons we have derived from the subject of our meditations. We tender expressions of gratitude for the grace vouchsafed, in enabling us to recognize, with full contrition, our misdeeds. We implore assistance in the correction of our faults, the avoidance of wickedness, the practice of Christian virtues, and in our firm resolution of amendment. We ask direction for the way in which we may best serve the glory of God and work out our own sanctification; since it is for the love of God, and not for our own satisfaction, that we should pray with untiring faith and confidence in the merits of our Saviour Jesus Christ. We can, at the same time, apart from the subject of meditation, ask graces for our own personal needs, or those of others; and implore the protection and intercession of the most Blessed Virgin, St. Joseph, our guardian Angel, and patron Saint; making a firm resolve to discontinue some particular fault, or to practise some special virtue. We end all by thanking God, with our whole heart, for the graces He has bestowed on us, asking forgiveness for any negligences of which we may have been guilty, and praying for His blessing on our resolutions, that our thoughts may continually revert, with steadfast purpose, to the resolutions we have formed.

CHAPTER XXXIII.

THE LORD'S PRAYER.

The Lord's Prayer.

THE Lord's Prayer is the most perfect of all prayers, not only because our Saviour is its Author, but also because in its short and simple form, we are taught by Him to manifest all that we should ask of God, as well as the manner and order of our petitions to Him. It is, therefore, in the highest sense of the word a superhuman prayer.

Qualities of the Lord's Prayer.

As the Creed is a summary of all that we must believe, and the Commandments of God and of the Church are an epitome of what we should do, so is the Lord's Prayer a compendium of all that we need ask for, under the form of supplication. It contains the three theological virtues: an act of Faith in God as Creator, Preserver, Redeemer, and Rewarder; an act of Hope in God's providence and fidelity to His promises; an act of Charity towards our neighbours, even our enemies. It is a prayer for all—old and young, rich and poor; and we are told by our Lord Himself to recite it, for He said, " After this manner therefore pray ye;" [1] and it is evident by the wording of the prayer that we are intended to say it every day. The very fact of our Saviour teaching us to pray to God as "our Father,"

[1] Matt. vi. 9.

supposes a tenderness and goodness calculated to inspire us with the utmost love and confidence. He taught us to say, " Our Father," and not " My Father," so that we should not pray for ourselves alone, but in union with all the children of God, thus obliging us to love and pray for our neighbours as ourselves, with Christ Himself at our head; for God "hath subjected all things under His feet, and hath made Him head over all the Church."[1]

The Lord's Prayer is called the "Pater" or the "Paternoster," because these words, in the Latin version, form its commencement: more commonly it is called the "Our Father." This prayer is divided into nine parts; being composed of a preface, or elevation of the soul towards God; seven petitions, which are sub-divided into two parts, the three first concerning God, and the four last concerning ourselves; and a conclusion.

Component parts of the Lord's Prayer.

The words, "Our Father, who art in Heaven," remind us of our creation, redemption, and the eternal happiness for which God destines us. Thus, saying, "Our Father" brings to mind that God is our Father in the order of nature, because "God who created all things . . . of whom all paternity in Heaven and earth is named,"[2] creates out of nothing our soul, and is indirectly the Maker of our body. And He is our Father in supernatural grace, because, by the merits of our Redeemer, we became "sons of God"[3] "and joint-heirs with Christ"[4] through the Sacrament of Baptism. In saying, "who art in Heaven," we not only distinguish our heavenly Father from all others, but are also reminded of the life of joy and glory it is in our

Preface of the Lord's Prayer.

---

[1] Eph. i. 22.   [2] Eph. iii. 9, 15.
[3] 1 John iii. 1.   [4] Rom. viii. 17.

power to gain, through our Saviour, "by whom He hath given us most great and precious promises."[1]

First petition of the Lord's Prayer.   In the first petition, "Hallowed be Thy name," we pray that God may be known, loved, and glorified by all who do not yet acknowledge Him by reason of ignorance; and more completely and excellently still, by those who understand and serve Him but imperfectly. Furthermore, that His name may never be profaned or taken in vain by any approach to blasphemy or irreverence.

Second petition of the Lord's Prayer.   In saying, "Thy kingdom come," we pray that God may reign in our heart by the sanctifying grace given to us, and that we may share in the glories of eternal happiness reigning with the Saints in Heaven. We pray also for the advancement of God's reign on earth, by the spreading, well-being, and development of His holy Church and its teachings.

Third petition of the Lord's Prayer.   In saying, "Thy will be done on earth as it is in Heaven," we pray for grace to accomplish faithfully in all things, God's will on earth as it is unceasingly carried out in Heaven; to obey the Commandments of God and of the Church, and to bear with patience and resignation all sufferings, trials, and temptations, that we may prove ourselves worthy of the kingdom of Heaven.

Our Lord, in His Sermon on the Mount, speaking of this prayer, gave us an outline of our duties towards God, towards others, and towards ourselves; when He said words such as, "Render to God the things that are God's."[2] "All things, therefore, whatsoever you would that men should do to you, do you also to them."[3] "Be you also ready: because at what hour you know not, the Son of Man will come."[4]

[1] 2 Pet. i. 4.   [2] Matt. xxii. 21.   [3] Matt. vii. 12.   [4] Matt. xxiv. 44

In the fourth petition, "Give us this day our daily Fourth petition of the Lord's Prayer. bread," we pray for, all that is necessary for preservation of life; both for the natural life of the body, and the supernatural life of the soul. This is expressed by the words "daily bread," not so much because bread is the principal nourishment of man, and would, if requisite, suffice without other food, but chiefly because, in holy writ, "bread" means any kind of food necessary for our nutrition. The spiritual nourishment also referred to, is the Holy Eucharist; together with the supernatural help of actual grace which is destined to preserve, to increase, and even to recover, when lost, the supernatural life of sanctifying grace. For, "Not in bread alone doth man live, but in every word that proceedeth from the mouth of God;"[1] and "the bread of God is that which cometh down from Heaven, and giveth life to the world."[2]

In saying, "And forgive us our trespasses, as we also Fifth petition of the Lord's Prayer. forgive them that trespass against us," we pray God to pardon our sins, and to remit the punishments they deserve; forgiving us in like manner as we forgive those who sin against us. Therefore we must give our full attention to this demand, which is the only one conditional in the prayer; the result of the supplication we make being dependent, according to the wording of the petition, on our own charity towards others.

In saying, "And lead us not into temptation," the Sixth petition of the Lord's Prayer. word "lead" in no way indicates that God could induce us to do evil; "for God is not a tempter of evils, and He tempteth no man."[3] But we ask God to help us to resist sin; to guard us against any occasions of temptation

---

[1] Matt. iv. 4.   [2] John vi. 33.   [3] Jas. i. 13.

so strong that our weak natures might give way; and to help us to refrain from wickedness by His grace.

Seventh petition of the Lord's Prayer. In saying, "But deliver us from evil," we pray God to preserve us from mortal sin, and also to protect us against the evil one who is ever plotting to thwart our salvation. Bodily sufferings, persecutions, and other like ills may serve us in expiation of past sins; may aid us against indulging too much amid the pleasures of the world; and may attach us more firmly to the service of God. Moreover, we beg Him to deliver us from actual sin, and from all the temporal and spiritual evils that He knows would be the cause or occasion of sin.

Conclusion of the Lord's Prayer. The word "Amen," forming the conclusion, is Hebrew, and signifies, "So be it." It is an assent, an asseveration, a wish. As the conclusion to the Lord's Prayer, the word "Amen" means our affirmation of all the truths contained therein; our assent to all the demands which it contains; and our desire that they should be granted.

CHAPTER XXXIV.

THE ANGELIC SALUTATION.

THE most holy prayer we can address to the Blessed The Angelic Salutation. Virgin, owing to its origin and the circumstances connected with it, is the Ave Maria, or Angelic Salutation. By this we may efficaciously follow up the Lord's Prayer, craving her intercession, that the demands we make may more surely be granted when presented to God through the mediation of her who is our Mother, protectress and most powerful suppliant at the throne of her Divine Son, our Saviour.

This prayer is composed of three parts : the two first, as Component parts of the Angelic Salutation. a preamble to the petition, are formed of the Archangel Gabriel's words to the Blessed Virgin in the Annunciation,[1] —which is the origin of its being called the Angelic Salutation—and of the words of St. Elizabeth at the Visitation of the Blessed Virgin.[2] Her answer was divinely inspired in the sublime Canticle of the Magnificat.[3] The second part is attributed to St. Cyril, and was approved and added by the Church in the year 451.

In this prayer the three greatest names of Christianity Qualities of the Angelic Salutation. are brought together: God, Jesus, and Mary. The name Mary, in Hebrew, may signify Queen, Star, and Bitterness;

[1] Luke i. 28.　　[2] Luke i. 42.　　[3] Luke i. 46-55.

all these are applicable to the sacred Mother of our Lord: as Queen, being nearest to God, above all others; as Star, being the Mother of our Saviour, who is "the light of the world;"[1] as Lady of bitter sorrow, because her sufferings were "as great as the sea."[2]

The first two parts of the Angelic Salutation.

The first two parts of the Angelic Salutation are an expression of the honour and reverence we give to the most Holy Mother of God, on whom was bestowed a plenitude of grace from the time of her Immaculate Conception. For she was preserved by God, not only from sin, but from any imperfection; was united to God by the closest bond in the substantive union of His Son our Lord with our humanity through the mystery of the Incarnation; was blessed with incomparable privileges above all other women; and was declared Mother of Him who was not only Blessed among Men, but the source and cause of all prerogatives and virtues with which His ever-blessed Mother was dowered.

Third part of the Angelic Salutation.

In the third part of the Angelic Salutation, we repeat the name of the Blessed Virgin, in order to dwell upon it with fond respect, confidence, and gratitude towards her, who suffered so deeply for us in conjunction with her Divine Son, our Saviour. We call on the Mother of God, who has such unlimited power to intercede in our favour and obtain for us those graces which the Almighty alone can give; beseeching that she will join her prayers to ours; for even the most just among us are but miserable sinners, never able to make one step towards salvation, without the help of divine grace. The prayer of such a Mother could never be refused by such a Son! We pray for the

[1] John viii. 12.　　　　　[2] Lam. ii. 13.

time present, not knowing what the morrow may bring forth, and being ever subject to temptation when we least think it is near. We pray for the hour of death, as being decisive of our eternity when, in bodily agony or mental suffering, we are enfeebled and pray with more difficulty, or are unable, perhaps, to pray at all.

Conclusion of the Angelic Salutation.

Bossuet remarks that when we recite the Ave Maria, we make an act of faith in the Divinity of Christ; the Divine Maternity of the Blessed Virgin; acknowledge our sinfulness and the power of intercessory prayer, and our great need of our Lady's help at the time of our death.

CHAPTER XXXV.

THE SACRAMENTS.

Definition of the Sacraments.

THE Sacraments are outward and visible "signs," instituted by our Lord Jesus Christ, for the sanctification of our souls by the communication of an inward and spiritual grace. The word "Sacrament" signifies "sacred mystery," and the Sacraments are called "signs," because they are the external indication of an invisible grace conferred on the soul: a material form showing forth a spiritual gift, in accordance with our nature, which is composed of spiritual and material substances. The Sacraments, therefore, consist of matter, form, and the union of the two. "Matter" is the substance used in the outward sign, together with the application thereof to the person who is to receive the Sacrament. "Form" is made up of the sacramental words significant of the grace bestowed; and the "union" of the two is effected by the action of the minister in the administering of the Sacrament. It is certain that the matter and form of each Sacrament were determined by our Saviour; this is undeniably shown in the case of both Baptism and the Holy Eucharist. But as to the others, the time and the circumstances of their institution by our Lord is open to controversy among theologians.

There are seven Sacraments: Baptism, Confirmation, Number of the
Holy Eucharist, Penance, Extreme Unction, Holy Orders, Sacraments.
and Matrimony. The third and sixth were, beyond doubt,
instituted by our Blessed Lord before His Crucifixion, and
the others most probably after His Resurrection. The
number "seven" may be found in connection with many
events mentioned both in the Old and New Testaments.
Among others, the following: "Jacob served seven years
for Rachel,"[1] the daughter of Laban; King Ezechias and
the rulers of the city "went up into the house of the Lord;
and they offered together seven bullocks, and seven rams,
and seven lambs, and seven he-goats for sin;"[2] the
chandelier, or "candlestick" as it was called, in the temple
of Jerusalem had "seven lamps;"[3] the feast of Pentecost
occurred "seven weeks"[4] after the Passover, the Easter of
the old Law, as it does now in the new; our Lord fed the
multitude with "seven loaves,"[5] and afterwards were
gathered up "seven baskets full of what remained of the
fragments;"[6] "seven men of good reputation, full of the
Holy Ghost and wisdom,"[7] were ordained as deacons by
the Apostles; the gifts of the Holy Ghost are "seven"
in number."[8]   There are "seven" corporal and "seven"
spiritual works of mercy, "seven" deadly sins, etc.

Through the Sacraments are conferred "sanctifying" and Effect of the
"sacramental" grace. Sacramental grace is in itself sancti- Sacraments.
fying or habitual grace, attached specially to each Sacrament, and accorded at the time of its reception, in the
measure of our need of it. The "first sanctifying grace"

[1] Gen. xxix. 20.   [2] 2 Paralip. xxix. 20, 21.   [3] Exod. xxv. 37.
    [4] Deut. xvi. 9.   [5] Matt. xv. 36.   [6] Matt. xv. 37.
          [7] Acts vi. 3.   [8] Isa. xi. 2, 3.

reconciles the sinner with God; and what is called "the second sanctifying grace," by which is meant further or additional grace, given to one who is already in a state of grace, increases habitual or justifying grace. The two Sacraments conferring the first sanctifying grace, are Baptism and Penance ; and these are called Sacraments of the " dead," because they are principally for those who have through mortal sin lost the life of sanctifying grace : though it may happen that the catechumens or penitents become justified, through perfect contrition and love of God, before approaching these Sacraments; in which case they receive the second sanctifying grace.   Confirmation, Holy Eucharist, Extreme Unction, Holy Order, and Matrimony, confer the second sanctifying grace, or increase of justifying grace.   These are called the Sacraments of the "living," because they cannot be received with profit and " fruit," unless the soul be already exempt from mortal sin, and therefore in possession of the life of habitual grace, by virtue of the Sacrament of Baptism, or Penance.   It may, however, occur that persons in mortal sin, but thinking themselves in a state of grace, and having at least full attrition for the sin committed, will receive the first sanctifying grace in partaking of the Sacraments of the "living." For it is not so much the sin itself, as affection for sin that is an obstacle to grace entering our souls.   Baptism, Confirmation, and Holy Orders are the three Sacraments that can only be received once, because they impress a Character on the soul—an ineffaceable mark, by which we are consecrated to God, who thereby " hath sealed us, and given the pledge of the Spirit in our hearts." [1]

[1] 2 Cor. i. 22.

For the reception of Baptism by an adult, or the Sacra- ment of Penance, which are the two Sacraments of the " dead," we should be properly disposed with sentiments of faith, hope, love of God, and abhorrence of sin. For receiving the Sacraments of the " living," we ought, in addition, to be in possession of the supernatural life of habitual grace. If we receive any Sacrament in mortal sin we commit thereby a sacrilegious crime.

Baptism may be administered by any one—man or woman—validly in all cases, and licitly also in cases of necessity. Confirmation is, except in rare instances, and then only by special authorization, administered by a Bishop, and the power of conferring the Sacrament of Holy Order belongs quite exclusively to the episcopal dignity. Bishops or any priests are rightful ministers of the other Sacraments, provided they be invested with the requisite authority; as, for instance, of the Sacrament of Penance. For the validity of any Sacrament, it is absolutely indispensable that there should be "the intention" to do at least what the Church prescribes; and for adults, their "consent," express or tacit, is necessary. The collation of a Sacrament does not depend on the faith or holiness of him who administers it, but on the visible sign, being coupled, in the manner required, with the form pronounced by the Minister. If an authorized priest or minister were wicked enough not to believe in some or any part of what he was doing, or were to administer a Sacrament in grievous sin, he would still confer it, provided he had the intention of bestowing what is regarded by the Church as a Sacrament.

There are certain ceremonies connected with the

P

administration of the Sacraments, which are not abso-

administration
of the
Sacraments.

lutely necessary, but do add to their solemn and impressive effect, making us more fully realize their efficacy and holiness, and vividly exciting our devotion and respect.

CHAPTER XXXVI.

SACRAMENTALS.

"SACRAMENTALS" are rites possessing some outward re- _{Sacramentals.} semblance to the Sacraments, and which, though not of divine institution, are initiated or approved by the Church. The "Sacraments" were instituted by our Lord, and communicate infallibly the supernatural gift of Divine grace, if their efficacy be not hindered by any evil disposition in the soul; whereas the "Sacramentals" were instituted by the Church, and remit venial sins, not in themselves, but by reason of the pious dispositions they excite;—namely, increased movements of fear and love of God, of detestation of sin, and other liftings of the heart towards God.

The principal Sacramentals, enumerated by devout ^{Principal}_{Sacramentals.} writers, are the repeating of the "Pater Noster" or of the "Confiteor," especially in conjunction with the priest at Holy Mass; the "blessing" given by bishop or priest, more particularly at the altar; the Benediction given with the Holy Sacrament; blessed bread; the kiss of peace; the pious use of various objects blessed by the Church, such as Holy Water, the Crucifix, etc.; or good works executed in the name of the Church, such as teaching the Catechism to the ignorant, contributing towards the propagation of the Gospel, etc.

Effect of
Sacramentals.

It should be fully understood that Sacramentals do not remit venial sins by a power given them by God over and above the good dispositions with which they are used; but either by the suffrages of the Church, or by the effect of the devout prayers of those who use them, they draw down upon the soul the remission of venial sin and of temporal punishment due for such sin. The Sacramentals have a special efficacy from the blessing of prayer, through which, for example, when a person takes holy water, accompanying the outward act with the desire that God may cleanse the heart, the prayer of the Church becomes joined to his own.

CHAPTER XXXVII.

THE SACRAMENT OF BAPTISM.

BAPTISM is first in order of the Sacraments, because, without Baptism. it we can be admitted to none other; and if we were to participate in any other Sacrament, it would remain void, and we, knowingly and wilfully unbaptized, would commit a sacrilegious sin. God might accord persons so acting sanctifying grace, but it would not be conferred through the bestowal of the Sacrament.

The word "baptism" is a Greek word which signifies "ablution" or "immersion." This was the manner of baptizing in the primitive Church, symbolizing purification, and expressive of the spiritual effect of this Sacrament. Although St. John baptized, his was but the figure of the real Baptism; the sign of heartfelt penitence, in preparation for receiving the grace of the remission of sins; but it neither contained nor conferred that grace.

According to some theologians, our Lord instituted the Institution of the Sacrament of Baptism. Sacrament of Baptism on receiving from St. John the figurative baptism. In the opinion of others, it was after the Resurrection of our Saviour, when He said to His Apostles, "Teach ye all nations, baptizing them in the name of the Father, and of the Son, and of the Holy Ghost." [1]

[1] Matt. xxviii. 19.

Effect of
Baptism.

In the Sacrament of Baptism instituted by our Lord Jesus Christ, He effaces the stain of original sin, and communicates to our souls the supernatural life of sanctifying or habitual grace, rendering us Christians, children of God, members of His Church, and inheritors of the kingdom of Heaven. Baptism imprints, as before stated, an ineffaceable Character on the soul, as St. Paul explains by saying, "Grieve not the Holy Spirit of God, whereby you are sealed unto the day of redemption."[1] In adults, having the necessary dispositions, the grace conferred by the Sacrament of Baptism effaces "actual" sin as well as "original" sin, and remits the temporal punishment due for sin. St. Paul affirms this in exhorting sinners to contrition and Baptism, in these words : "Be penitent, therefore, and be converted, that your sins may be blotted out."[2] "Do penance, and be baptized, every one of you, in the name of Jesus Christ, for the remission of your sins : and you shall receive the gift of the Holy Ghost."[3] To those who sin after Baptism, but who do not die in mortal sin, there remains expiation of purgation in this world, or of Purgatory in the next, for there is "no condemnation to them that are in Christ Jesus, who walk not according to the flesh."[4] Those who die undefiled by any kind of sin, are numbered among the just, and immediately enter Heaven. By Baptism we are made Christians, for those who "have been baptized in Christ have put on Christ."[5] We are "children of God by faith in Christ Jesus ;"[6] and members of His Church, having entered by Baptism that great religious society established by our Lord, and being designated in Scripture as "believing."[7]

[1] Eph. iv. 30.   [2] Acts iii. 19.   [3] Acts ii. 38.   [4] Rom. viii. 1.
[5] Gal. iii. 27.   [6] Gal. iii. 26.   [7] 1 Cor. vii. 14.

We are inheritors of the Kingdom of Heaven, "for the Spirit Himself giveth testimony to our spirit, that we are the sons of God. And if sons, heirs also ; heirs indeed of God, and joint heirs with Christ : yet so, if we suffer with Him."[1] Although Baptism blots out the stain of sin, it does not absolve us from the temporal consequences of original sin, but leaves us ever subject to suffering, ignorance, concupiscence, and death. This is in order to prove our virtue and steadfastness towards God, to afford us opportunities of expiating our own faults by resistance to temptation, and by patience and forbearance, thereby giving us occasions for increasing sanctifying grace in our souls, and of gaining new merits wherewith to add to our heavenly glory and happiness.

In cases of necessity, when ecclesiastical administration of the Sacrament of Baptism cannot be procured, any person anywhere of either sex, of any age or religion, may baptize. Indeed, it is obligatory so to baptize, when an unbaptized child or adult is in danger of death, and no priest is at hand; but otherwise it is not permissible under pain of sin. In any case, the omitted ceremonies must, as soon as convenient, be supplied by a priest, and the Baptism itself must be renewed, conditionally, if there be any doubt as to its having been validly administered. *Minister of the Sacrament of Baptism.*

To baptize validly, water must be poured on the forehead, while the person baptizing says at the same time, with the intention of carrying out the precept of the Church : "I baptize thee in the name of the Father, and of the Son, and of the Holy Ghost." Great care should be taken, while pronouncing these words, that the water *Manner of administering Baptism.*

[1] Rom. viii. 16, 17.

should be poured on the forehead three times, forming the sign of the cross at each pouring; to bring more clearly to mind the Sacrifice of our Saviour, the source of baptismal grace, and the Holy Trinity, named while conferring this Sacrament. If there be any doubt whether the person has been already baptized, and dangerous illness affords not time to make proper inquiries, the Baptism must be made "conditional," by the person who administers it, saying: "If thou art not baptized, I baptize thee," etc. In the same manner, if there be doubt as to whether the person be still alive, the words should be in a conditional form: "If thou art living, I baptize thee," etc.

Necessity of Baptism.

Baptism is absolutely necessary for salvation, for our Lord said, "Unless a man be born again of water and the Holy Ghost, he cannot enter into the Kingdom of God."[1] "He that believeth and is baptized, shall be saved: but he that believeth not shall be condemned."[2]

Baptism of Desire.

But when the Baptism of Water cannot possibly be effected, it may be supplied by the Baptism of Desire; "for whosoever shall call upon the name of the Lord, shall be saved."[3] This, however, neither gives the Character of the true Baptism, nor the right of participating in the other Sacraments of the Church; and will remit temporal punishment due to sin, together with eternal punishment, only when the desire and devotion are sufficiently ardent. The Baptism of desire is the perfect love of God, with the strong resolve of obedience to all that God has commanded, including the desire for Baptism. But after the passing away of the circumstances that have called forth

[1] John iii. 5.   [2] Mark xvi. 16.   [3] Rom. x. 13.

the desire, Baptism must voluntarily be sought for on the first available opportunity, and be administered according to the rites of the Church; otherwise, by the clear evidence of the desire having ceased to exist, a grievous sin is committed.

The Baptism of Water may also be supplied by the Baptism of Blood, or martyrdom; which, properly speaking, is death endured in the name of our Lord, to preserve faith, chastity, or some other Christian virtue. This Baptism of Blood, in which a man or woman manifests the greatest proof of love for the Creator, remits all punishment due to sin, as in ordinary Baptism. This is distinctly so explained in the sense of the words of Christ, "He that shall lose his life for My sake, shall save it."[1] But if the martyrdom is a torture that does not result in death, Baptism of Water must be administered as soon as procurable, as in the case of the Baptism of Desire, to ratify, and increase the gifts received.

Baptism of blood.

No avoidable delay is admissible in the Baptism of a child; and parents are greatly and sometimes grievously at fault in thus exposing a soul to exclusion from Heaven; for it is written: "There shall not enter into it anything defiled."[2] It is therefore according to faith, that every child, though of itself sinless, so far as actual sin is concerned, is deprived, if dying unbaptized, of the sight of God and glory of Heaven. In the opinion of some theologians, they are taken to the place called Limbo, where the souls of the just went, who died before our Saviour's coming on earth. It is evident, that by the justice of God, these children enjoy a great degree of happiness, though how far their

Urgency of administering Baptism.

[1] Luke ix. 24.　　■　　[2] Apoc. xxi. 27.

exclusion from Heaven is realized by them, to the tempering of that happiness, is unknown.   Probably not at all.

Dispositions for the reception of Baptism.   For the Baptism of children who have not attained the age of reason, or of adults who have always been deprived of that faculty, or who have lost the use of it before being baptized, any disposition for the reception of the Sacrament is necessarily dispensed with, because they are incapable of judging for themselves on such matters, and consequently cannot oppose the grace of God working in the Sacrament. But for the Baptism of adults in possession of reason, their full consent is indispensable for its validity.   They should also have sufficient knowledge of the principal truths of religion, and adequate feelings of faith, hope, love of God, and sincere repentance of sin, at least from the motive of attrition.   With consent, but without the necessary dispositions, Baptism would be valid, but would not efface the stain of original and actual sin, nor give sanctifying grace to the soul until such time as the requisite knowledge and fitting dispositions should drive away all obstacle to the full reception of sanctifying grace.

Promises in Baptism.   The promises, solemn, sacred, and irrevocable, exacted by the Church, from the catechumen, or from the godfather or godmother in the name of the infant to be baptized, are the renouncing of Satan, his pomps and his works.   That is to say, the embracing the law of our Saviour, and declaring adherence henceforth to God and His holy will; and the rejecting the vanities of the world, overindulgence in outward show, and flattering deceptions of pride, which can be of little avail in this life, and are compromising to the interests of our eternal happiness. Further, the repudiating the wicked and false maxims of the world, combining all that selfish love of luxuries and all those worldly dispositions so totally opposed to the doctrines and examples of our Lord. It is important for parents or godparents to explain to children, as soon as they are capable of understanding them, the value and consequences of the promises that have been made in their name, the grace that has been accorded to them by God, the privileges with which they have been endowed in having been made members of the Holy Catholic Church, and the necessity for their remembering in whose service they are to pass their lives. They should teach children to celebrate worthily the anniversary of that day on which they received the life of sanctifying grace through the Sacrament of Baptism; instructing them to ask pardon, with all sincerity of heart, for sins meanwhile committed, and to renew, with ardent fervour, the solemn pledges given in Baptism, praying for the help of Divine grace in carrying out their resolutions.

For the solemn administration of the Sacrament of Baptism, the godfather or godmother may, if necessary, be "represented" by some one else, who, however, contracts none of the obligations of the godparents. The Church exacts that every child to be baptized should have a sponsor to act in her name in making the required promises, and to see to the due carrying out of the same by the child who receives this Sacrament. Godparents must at least have attained the age of discretion, and be in full possession of the use of reason. They must be Catholics, because the Church admits none but her followers to assume this position. They must be of good faith and morals, and adequately versed in the knowledge of our

Godparents necessary in Baptism.

holy religion, that their teaching may be pure, and their instruction sufficient for those entrusted to their spiritual direction. Of course neither the father nor the mother of the child to be baptized can act as sponsor. According to the laws of the Church, the godparent contracts a spiritual affinity with the child, preventing marriage either with the child or with its mother or father in case of the death of either. This spiritual alliance, however, is only formed in the solemn administration of the Sacrament of Baptism, and not in connection with ceremonies of the Church performed for a Baptism that has already been conferred without the ceremonies prescribed.

Duties of godparents and godchildren.

The duty of godparents is to love their godchildren in a spiritual manner to teach them, or have them taught, in default of their natural parents, the principles of the Christian faith, and to remind them of the serious and sacred promises and obligations contracted 'on their behalf before Holy Church. The duty of godchildren is to respect and to love, in a spiritual manner, their godparents, and receive, with gentleness and grateful recognition, their good counsel and charitable corrections.

CHAPTER XXXVIII.

THE SACRAMENT OF CONFIRMATION.

CONFIRMATION is a Sacrament coming next in order after Baptism, and being as it were its completion. By it we receive, in more especial manner than in that Sacrament, the Holy Ghost, and are enriched with gifts and graces fortifying our souls and making us perfect Christians, steadfast in our faith and the service of our Saviour, even at the peril of our lives.

The first instance recorded in Scripture of the administration of Confirmation is of several Samaritans, who, having been baptized, were confirmed by St. Peter and St. John. These "laid their hands upon them, and they received the Holy Ghost." [1] St. Paul also, when establishing the Church at Ephesus, found certain of St. John's disciples, and "they were baptized in the name of the Lord Jesus. And when Paul had imposed his hands on them, the Holy Ghost came upon them, and they spoke with tongues and prophesied." [2]

The constant Tradition of the Church witnesses to the use of Holy Chrism in the administration of the Sacrament of Confirmation. Although there is but one mention of it in Scripture, where St. Paul says, "Now He that confirmeth

---

[1] Acts viii. 17.   [2] Acts xix. 5, 6.

us with you in Christ and that hath anointed us, is God;" [1] yet our Lord, in commanding His Apostles to instruct all nations, added: "teaching them to observe all things whatsoever I have commanded you." [2] Therefore, Tradition, coming direct from the Apostles; gives us the knowledge of many things sometimes unwritten in Scripture. The Holy Chrism used in Confirmation, and composed of balm, or balsam, and olive-oil, is blessed on Holy Thursday by bishops, who alone have the right of giving this blessing.

Effect of Confirmation.

The Sacrament of Confirmation, as already stated, gives an indelible Character to the soul, as expressed by St. Paul, who says, "God hath sealed us, and given the pledge of the Spirit in our hearts." [3] It increases the grace received at our Baptism, and since time lessened, bringing us to a state of greater spiritual perfection and the fulness of the Holy Spirit; giving us courage to combat and endure hardships like good soldiers of our Lord Jesus Christ. But although the Character is unalterable, the other effects are apportioned according to the purity of conscience and disposition of each individual, and are not vouchsafed to any one in mortal sin. Confirmation bestows on those who are worthily disposed the seven gifts of the Holy Ghost, which are supernatural virtues of "wisdom, understanding, counsel, fortitude, knowledge, godliness, and fear of the Lord." [4] These virtues beautify our souls and dispose them to follow the inspirations of the Holy Ghost, and to profit by the fruits of the Spirit: "charity, joy, peace, patience, benignity, goodness, longanimity, mildness, faith, modesty, continency, and

[1] 2 Cor. i. 21.
[2] Mark xxviii. 20.
[3] 2 Cor. i. 22.
[4] Isa. xi. 2, 3.

chastity."[1]   As is seen in Scripture, the gifts of the Holy
Ghost were manifested in an external manner through the
power of speaking in different tongues, prophesying, and
various other outward and miraculous effects.[2]   This was for
the purpose of showing by visible signs the divinity and
efficacity of this Sacrament, for the authorization, establishment, and propagation of the Gospel and Christian Church ;
though the invisible and essential effects were the same
then as they are to this day.

The gift of "wisdom" gives us a more correct judgment   Gifts of the
Holy Spirit.
of worldly interests from which we should more and more
detach ourselves, and a deeper appreciation of godly things,
raising our soul to a greater love and truer estimate of
all that makes for our eternal welfare.

The gift of "understanding" develops our intelligence
concerning the revealed truths of our holy religion, leading
us to discover ever fresh beauties in its divine realities.

The gift of "counsel" enables us to have the power of
discerning whatever shall best guide us in acting for the
glory of God, the spiritual interest of our neighbour, and
our own sanctification.

The gift of "fortitude" moves us to throw off fear of
threats and punishments, and to bear, with unfailing
patience and courage, all that may be for the glory of God,
and our own salvation.

The gift of "knowledge" brings us to a clearer vision
of all that we owe to God ; and of the grandeur and bliss-
fulness of the heaven-born destiny that awaits us.

The gift of "godliness" inspires us to practise, with
devout and tender feelings of piety, not only the obligatory

---

[1] Gal. v. 22, 23   [2] Acts xix. 6.

duties of our religion, but all that is fitting in the service of our Saviour, and agreeable to Him.

The gift of "fear" infuses into our souls a sense of profound respect and filial devotion, so that we may mortify ourselves in the pleasures of this life, and be able at all times to present them before God in purity.

Fruits of the Holy Spirit. Of the fruits of the Holy Spirit, "Charity" is the first and greatest, because it is the true love of God and our neighbour shed abroad in our hearts and made manifest in our actions.

"Joy" expresses the happy disposition of a soul, rejoicing always in a clear conscience before God.

"Peace" is that sentiment of harmony and tranquillity which disposes us to be on good terms with others, even at the cost of trouble and humiliation to ourselves.

"Patience" is the calm resignation that helps us to bear mental and physical sufferings uncomplainingly.

"Benignity" moves us to be indulgent toward the faults of others, putting up with them, and making all allowance for them, in gentleness and forbearance.

"Goodness" is that kindly feeling that prompts us to abstain from giving pain to others, and to inconvenience ourselves, if necessary, in order to render them a service.

"Long-suffering" is the patient restraint in word and action, that causes us to be never precipitate, but to await favourable moments for doing good or correcting evil, even allowing a lesser evil to have its way for the avoidance of a greater.

"Mildness" is a generous feeling by which we restrain our own tempers and evince a kindly treatment of others who may annoy us.

· "Faith" or Faithfulness, is that conscientiousness which renders us exact in all engagements, and strictly loyal to all promises.

"Modesty" induces us to be moderate in the use of all things that are allowable, and never to be exaggerated in our words or acts, nor unduly inclined to make known our good works.

"Continency" gives us self-command in the indulging of our sensual passions, preventing us from going beyond what is legitimate in the satisfaction of our senses.

"Chastity" causes us to avoid all occasions and circumstances likely to prove dangerous, even to the practice of self-imposed privations and mortifications, to ensure the jealous preservation of that most delicate virtue.

The Sacrament of Confirmation should be received after attaining the age of reason, and may then be received at any convenient time. Although it is not indispensable for salvation, those who wilfully neglect to benefit by this Sacrament, when they have the facility for doing so, become, according to circumstances, more or less culpable. The fact of our Lord having established it for the good of our souls, is in itself an obligation for us to receive it, and to profit by the gifts of the Holy Ghost. Failing to seek it is a sign of indifference, unquestionably blameworthy. *Obligation of receiving Confirmation.*

The Sacrament of Confirmation is administered by bishops only, except under special conditions when recourse cannot be had to a bishop, but then only by virtue of delegation of powers from the Pope. It being shown by Tradition and Scripture that the Apostles alone had the right of administering this Sacrament, it is clear that bishops only, as possessing the plenitude of the Sacerdotal *Minister of the Sacrament of Confirmation.*

Q

office, have the power of conferring the plenitude of the Christian character.

Dispositions
for the
reception of
Confirmation.

The name of a Saint is taken in Confirmation, at choice, and must be taken, if by some exceptional chance such name have not already been given in Baptism. Rightly to receive the Sacrament of Confirmation we must be in a state of grace, and sufficiently instructed in the principal truths and mysteries of our holy religion, including, of course, an adequate knowledge of the meaning and value of the Sacrament itself. In order the better to profit by the descent of the Holy Spirit into our soul, we should prepare ourselves by quiet meditation, prayer, and ardent desire for this Sacrament, as did the Apostles before the coming of the Holy Ghost on the day of Pentecost. " All these were persevering with one mind in prayer, with the women, and Mary the Mother of Jesus, and with His brethren."[1] Those who approach this Sacrament unworthily commit a sacrilegious sin. They receive the ineffaceable Character of Confirmation, but none of the gifts of the Holy Spirit, until such time as the heart being fully contrite, and confession made, absolution shall purify the soul from obstacles voluntarily hindering the right reception of the Sacrament.

[1] Acts i. 14.

CHAPTER XXXIX.

THE SACRAMENT AND SACRIFICE OF THE HOLY EUCHARIST.

THE Sacrament of the Holy Eucharist contains the true Body, Blood, Soul, and Divinity of our Lord Jesus Christ, under the outward appearances of bread and wine. It is called the "Eucharist," because this word, in the original Greek, means "thanksgiving." It is called the Sacred " Host," which word signifies " Victim," because in it our Saviour is really renewing the Sacrifice of Himself for us day by day. It is called the "Blessed Sacrament of the altar," because the consecration and mystery of transubstantiation take place nowhere lawfully but on the consecrated stone of the altar; also because the Holy Sacrament is kept in the tabernacle over the altar, that we may worship our Redeemer under the veil or outward appearance of Bread, just as He was adored, when on earth in the form of Man, though His divinity was hidden under the veil or appearance of humanity. The Holy Eucharist is the central mystery of Catholic worship, towards which all the ceremonial service of the Church converges. It contains the essential principle of Christianity, and is the very soul of our religion.

Institution of the Holy Eucharist.

Our Saviour instituted the Blessed Sacrament of the Eucharist, as the great means of communicating grace to our souls, in the closest union of Himself with us through the miracle of transubstantiation. This was on the eve of His Passion, when He " took bread, and blessed, and broke: and gave to His disciples and said: Take ye, and eat: This is My Body. And taking the chalice He gave thanks, and gave to them, saying: Drink ye all of this. For this is My Blood of the new testament, which shall be shed for many unto remission of sins." [1] In establishing the Sacrament of the Eucharist, our Lord commanded His Apostles to act in accordance with His words, and gave them power to do that which He Himself had done, by saying, " Do this for a commemoration of Me." [2] Therefore His meaning clearly was that they, His Apostles and priests, were to give thanks, consecrate, break, eat, and distribute to others in the same manner that He had done. It is quite certain that our Lord, knowing the inmost thoughts of His disciples, would not have allowed them to rest under a misunderstanding of His words or the power given them by Him; and thus not only be misled themselves, but mislead all those who should follow their teaching. Both the belief of our Saviour's Apostles in His real Presence, and their distinct grasp of the authority given them by Him, is plainly demonstrated by St. Paul's words : " The chalice of benediction, which we bless, is it not the communion of the Blood of Christ ? and the bread, which we break, is it not the partaking of the Body of the Lord ? " [3] It is, consequently, an incontestable fact that this most Holy Sacrament contains the real Body and Blood of our Saviour, together

Real presence of our Lord Jesus Christ in the Eucharist.

---

[1] Matt. xxvi. 26–28.   [2] Luke xxii. 19.   [3] 1 Cor. x. 16.

with His Soul and Divinity united inseparably to them.
His words were absolute, and admit of no other interpretation than that given by His Apostles, which He
sanctioned them to retain, and was made more obvious by
the fact that, in the languages used in the New Testament,
the word " this," employed by our Saviour in saying, " This
is my Body," is neuter, and therefore could not have referred
to the bread as merely bread, which word in those tongues
is of the masculine gender. There is, accordingly, no reason
whatever for doubting that our Lord intended us to understand that the substance of bread and wine held in
His Sacred Hands on this most memorable occasion was, by
a miracle of His almighty power, really and truly changed
into His precious Blood and Body. If the Presence of our
Saviour in the Blessed Sacrament were only figurative,
and had been accepted only as such in the beginning,
it is more than improbable that during so many ages, the
true followers of Christ would have abandoned this
simple belief for one so infinitely beyond our reasoning
powers. It is, therefore, impossible that our Lord should
have taught His Apostles to regard His Presence in the
Holy Eucharist as merely typical. It is also impossible
that in past ages, when the faculties of the mind were as
keen as they are now, the members of His true Church
should have adopted the belief in the real Presence of
Christ, had His teaching, and the teaching of His Apostles
after Him, been of a presence figurative. Moreover, there
has never been found any trace of a change in the
belief of the Faithful, that He is really present in the
Sacrament of the most Holy Eucharist; although it was
no doubt easy for vast numbers, even with good intentions,

to read and explain the Scriptures according to their own fancy, while authoritative and rightful teaching is rejected for private interpretation.

Our Lord's references to His real Presence in the Eucharist before its institution.

Before the institution of the Holy Eucharist, our Lord clearly announced its future establishment as a Sacrament for the communication of grace through His Sacred Body and Blood, by saying, "I am the bread of life . . . I am the living bread which came down from Heaven. If any man eat of this bread, he shall live for ever; and the bread that I will give, is My Flesh, for the life of the world." [1] He furthermore confirmed the true meaning of His words in the sense already explained, by reiterating the reality of His Presence in the Sacrament of the Holy Eucharist, in His answer to the Jews, who asked, "How can this man give us his flesh to eat ? Then Jesus said to them : Amen, Amen, I say unto you : except you eat the Flesh of the Son of Man, and drink His Blood, you shall not have life in you. He that eateth My Flesh, and drinketh My Blood, hath everlasting life : and I will raise him up at the last day. For My Flesh is meat indeed : and My Blood is drink indeed." [2] In all this, our Saviour's words were absolute in declaring His future real Presence in the Sacrament He was about to establish, and never once referred to the bread as a figurative representation of Himself, nor spoke of it in the light of a spiritual presence superinduced by faith alone.

Evidences of our Lord's real Presence in the Eucharist.

There is a constant record in successive periods up to a comparatively late date, of even miraculous proofs of the reality of the Divine Presence in the Blessed Sacrament. Simply countless are the instances we may see or experience,

---

[1] John vi. 48, 51, 52.   [2] John vi. 53–56.

of the ineffable benefit to the soul, derived from Holy Communion, affording a perceptible increase of virtue both in feeling and action. Whether these are always very enduring or not, which depends on the disposition of the persons receiving the Holy Sacrament, they effectually prove a supernatural grace inseparable from the real Presence of our Lord Jesus Christ in this sacred mystery of the Eucharist.

The words of our Redeemer, repeated by the priest at the moment of consecration, effect the transubstantiation *Consecration and Transubstantiation.* of the bread and wine into the Body and Blood, Soul and Divinity of our Lord Jesus Christ. By this God works a miracle of instantaneous change of substances, calling forth utmost admiration, devotion, and gratitude, and giving occasion for manifesting our entire faith in the word of our Lord and confidence in His power, by the acceptance of a miracle appealing to our spiritual perceptions only. Those who refuse to believe in this miracle of God, discredit thereby His omnipotence. For, having faith in God's omnipotence, what prevents belief in His ability to transfer the power of working, through the ministry of His priests, a most wondrous miracle in Transubstantiation ? Our faith is on this account the more meritorious, that we believe what we cannot see; and, as we believe in God whom we have not seen, why should we not place unhesitating faith in the veracity and power of God, to whom the miracle of transubstantiation, performed daily in our presence, is no greater than those wonders that are seen with the eyes of our body ? For example: the changing of water into wine at the marriage feast at Cana in Galilee; the immediate healing of the sick and infirm, so frequently recorded in Scripture; the marvellous cures effected in our own times, through faith in the God we have never seen, yet still believe in; and, though not miraculous, the continual change and conversion of substances, such as of the different grains that become leaves, flowers, fruit; and of the aliments we consume, whose nourishing properties are transmuted into our flesh and blood.

After consecration.
After the transubstantiation worked through the words of consecration, there remains nothing of the bread and wine but the outward semblance. Our Lord's Body and Blood, Soul and Divinity, are in each species because, being living and immortal, His Body and Blood are inseparable from each other, and equally inseparable from His Soul and Divinity. Though the consecrated Host be divided, though it be broken up into many parts, our Lord remains whole and entire in each drop of the consecrated wine, in each particle of the consecrated Host, as a reflection—by way of illustration—of some object is entire in every fragment of a broken mirror. It is a mistake to argue against the real Presence from the indignities sometimes practised on the Consecrated Host. The Sacred Body and Blood of our Saviour in the Holy Eucharist remain impassible and intangible after being united to us through the medium of the Host, and are proof also against the effects of exterior accidents or acts of impiety; the sacred Presence of our Lord Jesus Christ ceasing to exist as soon as the outward semblances have changed. Had our Saviour constituted an alteration in the appearance, touch, smell, or taste of the Holy Eucharist in the miracle of transubstantiation, the miracle would scarcely have been augmented, but our merit of faith in the veracity of God would have been considerably

diminished by such manifestation to our bodily senses, of the actual Presence of our Redeemer.

Our Saviour is everywhere as God, but as God and Man He is simultaneously present in Heaven and in the Holy Eucharist. Hence the Body, Blood, Soul, and Divinity of our Lord Jesus Christ being contained in the Blessed Sacrament of the altar, call for a visible sign of recognition and adoration, shown in the genuflection it is our express duty to make on passing before a tabernacle containing the Holy Sacrament, and in devoutly kneeling on both knees when passing the Sacrament exposed. This act is the most eminently religious by which we can give outward demonstration of the pious respect we owe to our Lord in the Sacrament of the altar. It is an affirmative expression of the Catholic faith in the reality of His Presence in the Holy Eucharist; an efficacious prayer even, if the genuflection is accompanied by a feeling of piety and devotion. For kneeling has ever been considered a most religious posture, and is mentioned in connection with prayer in the Old and New Testaments.[1] We also have an example from our Lord Himself, who went to the Mount of Olives, "and kneeling down, He prayed."[2]

Genuflection before the Sacrament of the altar.

Our Saviour instituted the Holy Eucharist to give Himself to us in a manner that might, by means of Holy Communion, be perceptible to us, and by which we might, through our good dispositions, reap most consolatory and beneficial effects, in health and in sickness. To be, further, our solace and encouragement here on earth, the comforter of our griefs, the receiver of our devotion and expression of

Reasons for which our Saviour instituted the Eucharist.

[1] Paralip. vi. 13; Acts ix. 40, xx. 36.   [2] Luke xxii. 41.

spiritual and temporal needs, our refuge of consolation, ever awaiting our visit at any and every hour.

Reasons for which our Lord gave Himself under the appearance of bread and wine.

According to some theologians, the reason why our Lord gave Himself to us here on earth in the form of nourishment is, that sin, having been brought into the world through the eating of a forbidden fruit for the satisfaction of the body and gratification of the senses; therefore an aliment, which with us is the closest means of union, should become a source of sanctification to our souls, consisting of the Humanity as well as the Divinity of the Saviour of mankind. Bread was chosen by our Lord for our Communion in the Holy Eucharist, being most suitable to be kept, divided, distributed, and received by all, whether in sickness or in health. As bread is the form of nutriment most generally considered necessary in everyday life, so is the bread of the Blessed Sacrament the most essential spiritual nourishment. The wine, consecrated at the altar, reminds us of the Crucifixion of our Lord, whereby His precious Blood was shed for us; and, further, as wine gives strength and vigour to the body, so, in the Eucharist, it signifies the strength and vigour imparted to our souls by participation in the Blessed Sacrament.

Obligation of receiving Communion.

Communion is of obligation for all members of Christ's Church who have attained an age when they fully possess the requisite dispositions, alluded to in the ecclesiastical precept, to receive Communion annually, " at Easter or thereabouts." Wilful disregard of this Commandment is a mortal sin. It was our Lord Himself who established Communion as a means necessary for our salvation, when He said, " Except you eat the Flesh of the Son of Man, and drink His Blood, you shall not have life in you."[1] However, Communion

---

[1] John vi. 54.

in one kind was shown by Him to be sufficient, when Communion of one kind. He said, "If any man eat of this bread, he shall live for ever . . . he that eateth Me, the same also shall live by Me."[1] And again when, after His Resurrection, He was with His disciples, "and it came to pass, whilst He was at table with them, He took bread, and blessed, and brake, and gave to them."[2] The Apostles also continued to distribute one kind "in the communion of the breaking of bread."[3] When saying, "Drink ye all of this,"[4] our Lord addressed Himself to His Apostles personally, in reference to their act of consecration in the Sacrifice of the Mass. The injunction, "Do this,"[5] was given to them only; and no mention is made in Scripture of our Saviour's express command relating to the distribution of the Blessed Sacrament to the laity, as to whether it should be under both kinds, or one kind alone. It is written: "Whosoever shall eat this bread, or drink the chalice of the Lord unworthily, shall be guilty of the Body and of the Blood of the Lord."[6] If, therefore, it be certain that persons can be guilty both of the Body and Blood of our Lord, in receiving Communion under one kind, it is equally positive that, in partaking of one kind, they receive the whole Sacrament, both of the Body and Blood of our Redeemer. The priest partakes of both kinds whenever he says Mass; but when not celebrating the Holy Sacrifice, priests of every grade receive Communion in the same manner as the laity.

In the yearly Communion of obligation, we merely Necessity of Communion. execute the Commandment of the Church to the letter, to enter, however, into the full spirit of the Church, and

---

[1] John vi. 52, 58. [2] Luke xxiv. 30. [3] Acts ii. 42.
[4] Matt. xxvi. 27. [5] Luke xxii. 19. [6] 1 Cor. xi. 27.

reap the abundant fruit of this union with our Saviour, Communion should be as frequent as ordered or allowed by our confessor, who is best able to judge of our spiritual

Effects of Communion. needs and the disposition of our souls. The constant union with our Lord in Holy Communion weakens our evil tendencies, and helps us to triumph in time of temptation, and to gain a victory over ourselves in the battle of life. "For the flesh lusteth against the spirit, and the spirit against the flesh."[1] It produces a gradual amelioration in our nature; an increase of spirituality and goodness, making us "partakers of the Divine nature,"[2] according to the promise of our Saviour, who said, "He that eateth My Flesh and drinketh My Blood, abideth in Me, and I in him."[3] It increases sanctifying grace in the soul; effaces venial sin of which we are truly repentant; and is a preparation for the eternal union with God that shall be ours in the glory and happiness of Heaven.

Dispositions for receiving Communion. As the Holy Eucharist is a Sacrament of the living, the necessary dispositions for rightly receiving Communion, consist in being in a state of grace, that is, in the conscience being entirely free from mortal sin. Otherwise we should commit a sacrilege, and expose ourselves to severe spiritual and temporal physical punishments. For, according to the words of St. Paul, "Whosoever shall eat this bread, or drink the chalice of the Lord unworthily, shall be guilty of the Body and of the Blood of the Lord. . . . For he that eateth and drinketh unworthily, eateth and drinketh judgment to himself, not discerning the Body of the Lord."[4] Dispositions, not strictly obligatory, but nevertheless most

---

[1] Gal. v. 17.   [2] 2 Pet. i. 4.
[3] John vi. 57   [4] 1 Cor. xi. 27, 29.

expedient, are the purifying of the soul from venial sins with a strong desire to avoid falling into temptation, and the making serious effort to correct ourselves of faults displeasing to God, and to adorn our souls with holy thoughts, firm resolves of good, and the meritorious actions performed in the strength of Faith, the confidence of Hope, the generous love of Charity, as well as other virtues springing from these three theological virtues. As to the requisite dispositions of our bodies, it is absolutely essential that we should fast from midnight, scrupulously avoiding to eat or drink anything whatsoever, either by intention or inadvertence; leaving no possible chance of violating the precept not to swallow any substance that has entered the mouth from without. Our outward behaviour should be such as is suitable, and should be eminently consistent with reserve, propriety, modesty, and purity, both in our attire and manner. We should approach the altar-rail with the utmost gravity of demeanour, receiving the Holy Host from the hand of the priest, without unnecessary contact of the lips or teeth, and retiring, without precipitation, to quiet meditation, adoration, and other prayer, in which we should spend some length of time, say, a quarter of an hour. For what moment can be so propitious for the supplications we have to make, and for offering grateful recognition of the favours we have received, as when we are temporarily the living Tabernacles of our Lord Jesus Christ? We should express to Him the worship and gratitude of our whole hearts, imploring aid for our own spiritual and temporal needs, for those of the living and the dead who share our prayers, and for all the faithful of holy Church; making good resolutions for our future conduct, and asking help of grace in the accomplishment of our desires and resolves. It is furthermore well to keep, throughout the day, a devout remembrance of the inestimable favour received, and even a pious recollection of our first Communion.

Communion of Viaticum.

The one occasion when the Holy Sacrament is allowed, and even commanded, to be received without obligation of fasting, is in the case of dangerous illness. Communion is then called "Viaticum," which word signifies, "food for the journey;" because the sick person is receiving the Holy Host on the outset of his voyage from this world, to meet the supreme moment decisive of eternity. It is not only as an obligation, but as an invaluable blessing that our Saviour thus deigns to come as our consolation and spiritual support in the last struggle of life. We should, therefore, while we have health and strength, frequent the Holy Sacrament as often as possible; ever preparing ourselves for that last moment of our existence here below, and praying that we may piously receive our Saviour in the Communion of Viaticum, at the hour of our death, with dispositions of Faith, Hope, and Charity, so that He may receive us into eternal glory and everlasting happiness.

The Holy Eucharist as a Sacrifice.

When instituting the Holy Eucharist, our Lord meant it also to be a means of continually offering Himself in Sacrifice for us : sacrifice being the highest act of religion ; the most solemn and sublime kind of worship. As the sacrifices of the Old Law, with the shedding of blood, were figurative of the Sacrifice offered by our Saviour on Mount Calvary; so were the sacrifices of the Old Law, without the shedding of blood, typical of the Sacrifice of the New Law, mentioned in Scripture as "a clean oblation." [1] The

[1] Mal. i. 11.

Holy Eucharist is then, not only a Sacrament, but also a Sacrifice instituted by our Saviour—a Sacrifice of the Body and Blood of our Redeemer, offered to God through the instrumentality of the priest, under the appearance of bread and wine, for applying to the faithful individually the merits of the Sacrifice on the Cross, which is applied to the world at large. The consecration first of the bread singly, and then of the wine singly, in Holy Mass, is a symbolical separation or severance of the Body and Blood of our Lord. The nature, then, of this Sacrifice is a mystical death, or notable change representing death, of the real living Victim, our Lord Jesus Christ, whose Body and Blood, Soul and Divinity remain inseparable in both kinds, and in each part of each kind; because we know Christ "dieth now no more."[1] The total change of the elements which constitutes the Sacrifice shows that God, being Creator and omnipotent Master of life and death, has no need of our offerings. It is also symbolical of our entire dependence on Him.

We know that our Lord, in instituting the Holy Eucharist, would have it to be a Sacrifice as well as a Sacrament, because when saying to His Apostles, "Do this for a commemoration of Me,"[2] He gave them power to perform that miracle which He Himself had accomplished, bestowing on them, on their legitimate successors, and those whom they lawfully ordained, the right of consecrating and addressing Himself exclusively to them. And His words undoubtedly signified, that they were to offer sacrifice, in the "clean oblation," under the appearance of bread and wine, renewing unceasingly, in a bloodless manner, the

---

[1] Rom. vi. 9.   [2] Luke xxii. 19.

Sacrifice of His Body and Blood in the Sacrifice of the Cross. And that this was thoroughly understood by the Apostles, is testified by St. Paul's words: "As often as you shall eat this bread, and drink the chalice, you shall show the death of the Lord, until He come."[1] Furthermore, if our Saviour had intended the Holy Eucharist to be a Sacrament only, by which we might receive His sacred Body and Blood in Communion, His Ministers could have partaken of them under the species of bread alone without any necessity for the two kinds. These were, therefore, evidently needed to show the separation of the Body and Blood, and create an unbloody Sacrifice that should bring perpetually before our memory the great bloody Sacrifice offered up by our Redeemer for the salvation of the world.

It is a mystery most capable of exciting our gratitude and love; a means of adoration, expiation, reparation, praise, and thanksgiving, offered to God through the merits of our Redeemer; and a method of bestowing the grace of His merits on all mankind, especially on those assisting at the Sacrifice of the Mass. Holy Mass may also be celebrated for the dead, because those in Purgatory are in a state of grace, and are consequently living members of the Church, and by virtue of the Communion of Saints, can participate in the fruit of this holy Sacrifice, particularly on the anniversary of death. This is an article of faith handed down from very ancient Tradition as coming from the Apostles. But as the application of the fruit depends on God's judgment concerning the dead, we know not how soon our prayers may be efficacious in delivering a soul from Purgatory.

The Sacrifice of the Mass offered for the dead.

[1] 1 Cor. xi. 26.

CHAPTER XL.

THE SACRAMENT OF PENANCE.

PENANCE is a Sacrament instituted by the infinite mercy Penance of our Lord Jesus Christ, for the remission of sins committed after Baptism, through Contrition, Confession, Satisfaction, and Absolution, wherein the penitent is forgiven by God through the agency of His minister, the priest, acting on the authority of our Saviour. The forgiveness of sin, by perfect contrition, was brought about before the coming of our Lord, much less easily and effectually than by means of the Sacrament of Penance. Perfect contrition is, however, still sufficient for the remission of eternal punishment due for sin, whenever the Sacrament of Penance be not procurable and is earnestly desired.

Our Lord instituted the Sacrament of Penance and gave Institution of the Sacrament of Penance. to His Apostles, to their legitimate successors, and to those authorized by them, power, in His Name, to pardon sins or to retain them according to their judgment of the dispositions of the penitent. This He did when He said to His disciples: "Peace be unto you. As the Father hath sent Me, I also send you . . . whose sins you shall forgive, they shall be forgiven them; and whose sins you shall

R

retain, they shall be retained."[1] The Confession of sins
alluded to by St. James, who says, "Confess therefore
your sins one to another;"[2]—so often misunderstood by
Protestants,—concerns the Sacrament of Extreme Unction,
as may clearly be seen from the context, which expressly
mentions the administration of that Sacrament by "the
priests of the Church."[3] These are naturally signified,
in the previous quotation, as the authorized receivers of
Confession.

Necessity of Penance.

By the remission of sins Sanctifying grace is communicated to the soul, whereof the act of absolution is the outward sign. This Sacrament is therefore necessary for the
salvation of those who have committed mortal sin after
Baptism, a truth defined by the Catholic Church to be
an Article of Faith. The matter of this Sacrament is
commonly thought to consist in the Contrition, Confession,
and "Satisfaction" of the penitent; and the form, in the
action and words of the priest in Absolution. The words
"penitence" and "penance" are derived from the Latin,
and signify "repentance" and "punishment." Penitence is
a supernatural virtue; its principle springing from divine
grace, and its motive from sincere regret for having acted
contrary to the will of God; and it is a virtue absolutely
necessary at all times for obtaining the pardon of mortal
sin. Contrition, Confession, and Absolution are indispensable for the validity of the Sacrament of Penance, for
God cannot pardon sins that are not entirely repented of;
and Absolution given by the priest, in the name of our
Saviour, depends on a full self-accusation on the part of
the penitent.

---

[1] John xx. 21, 23.   [2] Jas. v. 16.   [3] Jas. v. 14.

Contrition is a deep regret and detestation of the sin Contrition.
perpetrated, with a firm purpose not to repeat the same, and
a general resolve to correct the error of our ways. Thus,
contrition includes two acts: heartfelt repentant grief, and
a sincere resolution to avoid sinful habits in the future.
There are two kinds of contrition, the one called perfect
contrition, and the other attrition, or imperfect contrition;
differing from each other by the motives inspiring them,
and by the effects they produce. Perfect contrition has Perfect
but one motive, consisting in love of God and a consequent contrition.
horror of sin, as displeasing to God. This arises from
absolute appreciation of His infinite goodness, the benefits
received from Him, and the perfect love He has bestowed
upon us through our Redeemer Jesus Christ. By perfect
contrition, which also includes the implicit desire for Confession and Absolution, as we have before stated, the stain
of sin is effaced, and we re-enter a state of grace and
reconciliation with God, even before receiving the Sacrament of Penance. Imperfect contrition, though prompted Imperfect
by supernatural motives, is of an inferior quality, self contrition.
largely entering into it in the fear of eternal punishment,
and a desire for everlasting happiness, but does not include
a horror of venial sin. Imperfect contrition does not of
itself reconcile us with God, but disposes us for the reception
of forgiveness in the Sacrament of Penance. Though perfect
contrition is undoubtedly the more efficacious means of
avoiding sin and gaining in grace, imperfect contrition
suffices for the reception of the Sacrament, provided that it
be free from willingness and desire to sin if the torments
of Hell and joys of Heaven had no existence, and that it
also includes a commencement at least of love for God.

Necessary
qualities of
contrition.

There are four qualities indispensable to contrition for sin. It must be internal, supernatural, sovereign, and universal. It must come from the heart in earnestness and sincerity of repentance; inspiring an act of will contrary to that which had induced sin, a detestation for any evil that may have separated us from God, and a firm purpose of amendment, not merely as spoken with the lips, but as coming from the inmost depths of the soul. It must be supernatural in its principle, through the help of divine grace, and supernatural in its motive, the wish to please God and gain our eternal salvation, through love of our Creator, Benefactor, and Redeemer, and hopeful desire for pardon. It must be supreme; that is, the love of God and abhorrence of evil must predominate over all other feeling; mortal sin involving our greatest punishment here and greatest losses in eternity. It has the triple character of irreligion towards our Creator, ingratitude towards our Redeemer, and want of sorrow for such irreligion and ingratitude, so long as not effaced by sincere repentance. It must be universal for all mortal sins without exception, for there cannot be entire sincerity of contrition if we have sorrow for some grievous sins, and still maintain affection for others as grievous; nor can there be partial absolution, forgiving one mortal sin and retaining another. Contrition of such a kind would be a profanation of the Sacrament of Penance. As venial sin is not incompatible with sanctifying grace, it follows that some may be pardoned, while we have not contrition for others; but if we consciously withhold all sorrow for venial sins, Absolution given for them alone would be invalid. Again, should we honestly think we have sufficient contrition without really possessing it, the Absolution would be invalid. The firm determination and resolution of will which must accompany contrition is completely indispensable, being inseparable from true repentance. Otherwise Confession would be useless, and furthermore a new sin would be committed by our insincerity of purpose in asking God's pardon for sins which we had no intention of trying to overcome, and would be liable to repeat upon the slightest provocation. We must not only have the strong desire to resist sin, but must carry out our resolution to conquer it by making serious effort to correct deliberate venial sins, so frequently the forerunners of mortal sins; taking vigilant precautions against the gratification of our evil inclinations, and avoiding all occasions of temptation to which we should probably yield. Hence, the penitent who neglects Confession and Communion, knowing from experience that those Sacraments are a necessary safeguard against his evil ways, has not the firm purpose needful in contrition.

(margin: Purpose of amendment accompanying contrition.)

Confession is the self-accusation made to a duly authorized priest of all grievous sins committed since Baptism, or since the last Confession. Our Lord instituted Confession when giving power to His Apostles for the remission of sins: the necessity for Confession being implicitly included in the words: "Whose sins you shall forgive, they are forgiven them; and whose sins you shall retain, they are retained."[1] The priest, acting in God's name, can only judge from what the penitent makes known to him whether a sinner is worthy or unworthy of Absolution; and can forgive or retain only those sins of which he is given full knowledge. Therefore he cannot fulfil his office except through means of a penitent's self-accusation in Confession.

(margin: Confession.)

In the Catholic Church it has always been understood that

[1] John xx. 23.

Institution
of Confession.

our Lord Jesus Christ Himself instituted Confession for the remission or retention of sins through the instrumentality of His ministers. It is evident that through so many ages, this practice, so naturally repugnant to human sensibilities, would not have been followed had it not been certainly instituted by our Saviour, who, in His infinite goodness, gave us this means of healing the wounds of venial sin and of curing the more malignant injuries of mortal sin. Con-

Obligation of
Confession.

fession is, according to the regulations of the Church, strictly obligatory once a year, and before receiving any Sacrament of " the living," when one has had the misfortune to commit a mortal sin. It is more in accordance, however, with the spirit of the Church's teaching to confess any mortal sin without delay, so that we neglect not an indispensable means of salvation by voluntarily risking death while a crime rendering us at enmity with God is upon our conscience. " The beginning of the pride of man, is to fall off from God,"[1] and Confession humbles that pride which " is the beginning of all sin."[2] Humility before God in the self-accusation of our sins to a minister of Christ's Church brings honour to the soul; for a humble avowal of sin and sincere repentance is always deserving of a feeling of esteem for the penitent sinner. " Before destruction, the heart of a man is exalted; and before he be glorified, it is

Advantages of
Confession.

humbled."[3] Confession improves the character, redoubling our energy in the correction of our faults, so as not to have the shame of acknowledging our weakness by falling anew into the same sin; and that we may persevere in a state of grace, beginning a new life in peace with God and man. It comforts the heart, soothes the conscience,

[1] Ecclus. x. 14.   [2] Ecclus. x. 15.   [3] Prov. xviii. 12.

infuses new hope, and relaxes the burden of sin that weighed down our souls and rendered us more ready to yield to fresh temptations. The confessor instructs us in our ignorance; enlightens us in our doubts, scruples, or illusions; calms our remorse or desolation; counsels us in temptation or apprehension of danger; encourages us to bear our trials with patience, and with willingness to incur sacrifices that make for our sanctification and eternal salvation.

A sincere Confession should be marked with completeness, humility, prudence, and simplicity.

Necessary qualities of Confession.

A Confession to be complete, in the sense required by the Church, consists in an exact self-accusation of all the mortal sins, if any, committed since the last were absolved; the number of times they have been repeated; and the circumstances aggravating them, by which the nature of the sin is changed. Of all these things the confessor must necessarily be made fully cognisant, for the purpose of judging justly of the penitent and his actions. By voluntarily omitting a mortal sin in Confession, we not only do not receive pardon, but commit a sacrilege, which act of profanation, together with the sins concealed and confessed, must be made known in the tribunal of Penance, with true repentance for the double crime, whether to the same or to another priest, for Absolution. A mortal sin, omitted unwittingly, should be declared in the next Confession, but Absolution cannot be received without this full avowal of the sin. "He that hideth his sins, shall not prosper; but he that shall confess and forsake them, shall obtain mercy."[1] When tempted to withhold a mortal sin in the Sacrament of Penance, we should bear in mind

Completeness of Confession.

[1] Prov. xxviii. 13.

three considerations. First—that our attempted deceit as regards mortal sin adds yet another grievous offence against God, from whom no secret is hid; "for the Lord searcheth all hearts, and understandeth all the thoughts of minds;"[1] and at the last day, will lay bare, before all, those sins which have remained unforgiven. Secondly—that a priest, by virtue of his ecclesiastical vows, is under the strictest possible obligation of secrecy; and is bound to make no use whatsoever of a Confession, since the avowal of a penitent is a secret belonging to God, whose place the priest takes in the tribunal of Penance, and who is so far from ignoring the weaknesses of human nature and sinfulness in the world, that he feels for the sinner the sympathy of sincere and fatherly charity. Thirdly—that we are not craving this spiritual remedy with any uncertainty of cure, as we might the aid of a physician, but are seeking the infallible restorative of sanctifying grace that gives life to the soul stricken unto death by sin.

Humility in Confession.

For a Confession to be humble, outward distraction should be avoided by the penitent, whose manner should be modest and devout, both on entering the tribunal of Penance and during Confession; whose tone and attitude should be meek and unassuming; whose self-condemnation should be fully significant of the abasement that sincere contrition brings into the heart; and whose attention should be firmly fixed with religious reverence on the words of admonition, counsel, or encouragement, spoken by the priest, whom we should not regard as an ordinary man, but as the representative of our Saviour, when administering this Sacrament.

[1] 1 Paralip. xxviii. 9.

A Confession, to be prudent, must be made in terms as Prudence in
respectful and pure as the subject admits of; the penitent Confession.
asking the confessor's aid in any perplexity as to mode of
expression; telling just so much of the character of another
person, who may be implicated in the sin, as shall be
necessary for the full understanding of it; in such case,
if possible, choosing a confessor to whom the accomplice is
unknown; never mentioning the faults or sins of others
without proper reason for doing so; and under no provocation revealing the name of another person.

A Confession, to be simple, should be declared without Simplicity of
exaggeration, toning down, or excuse, but in plain language, Confession.
unadulterated with purposeless and profuse phrases, and
without the obscurity of meaning that often leads us, though
not intentionally, to a misrepresentation of facts we desire
to communicate, thereby deceiving the confessor in his
judgment of us whether favourable or unfavourable.

To prepare for the Sacrament of Penance—which is Preparation
for the
one of the most important acts of our lives, concern- Sacrament of
Penance.
ing, as it does, our eternal salvation—we must make an
examination of conscience, and dispose ourselves to obtain
sincere contrition for the sins we are about to confess, and
for the steadfast purpose of amendment we intend making.
We must pray devoutly for enlightenment in the understanding of our faults and the full realization of our
unworthiness, devoutly imploring God's grace for the
complete repentance of our sins, and strength of resolution
to avoid future evil temptations. The examination of Examination
of conscience.
conscience required varies according to the way of life and
position of each individual, and according to the frequency
of Confession. But in all cases, it should be made seriously

and with method, examining ourselves in reference to the Commandments of God and of the Church, and the seven capital sins, and with regard to the performance of the duties demanded by the position we occupy in life, as well as the occasions of sin most likely to lead to a fall. At the same time, we should avoid being too long in our preparation, or unduly scrupulous in our examination, which would result in confusion of ideas and exaggeration. A daily examination of conscience is very useful in helping us to realize the faults or temptations to which we are most inclined, and to remember those we may have committed day by day; though, with over-scrupulous minds, it may be detrimental in causing delusions or excessive and unfounded alarm. With others, the constant recollection of certain sins may be equally injurious, if carried too far, by allowing our thoughts to dwell upon occasions and circumstances connected with sins more advantageously dismissed from the imagination. We must excite contrition and a resolution of amendment, in whatever ways are best calculated to appeal to us individually. By the reading of pious books inducing sentiments of devotion; by meditating on the everlasting punishments of hell we may incur, and the eternal happiness and glory of Heaven we may be denied; by contemplating the sufferings, borne in infinite love for us by our Saviour, who "appeared for the destruction of sin by the sacrifice of Himself:"[1] again, by considering sin in itself, as an act of ingratitude, contempt, and injustice towards God, who is ever beneficent, merciful, almighty, and all-wise, striving to understand in fitting degree that indulgence of the senses in this

[1] Heb. ix. 26.

transitory life brings about sharp penalties in the future, and "that the sufferings of this time are not worthy to be compared with the glory to come."[1]

The minister of the Sacrament of Penance is a priest duly authorized. That is to say, although the power for the remission of sins is inherent in the sacerdotal character, and conferred on all priests at their ordination, they must, before exercising it, be given by episcopal approbation power of jurisdiction. As all priests have not the same aptitude for the requisite spiritual direction of souls, and even the most holy and intelligent of them may not be able to adapt themselves to all sorts and conditions of people, the choice of a confessor is very important. We should pray for Divine light in our selection, and generally allow ourselves to be guided by the inspirations of Providence in this serious matter, on which an influence so salutary and precious to the soul greatly depends. The Church leaves absolute freedom in the selection of any priest duly authorized for hearing Confessions, and those having control over children and others, possess no right to impose any restrictions concerning the choice of a confessor. They should advise or direct them with interest in their good, but leave them entire liberty to select without interference, or to change their spiritual director, unless such choice or change evidently arise from caprice or some equally unworthy and unreasonable motive. We should open out our hearts unreservedly to our confessor, affording him unrestrained liberty to counsel us, or administer charitable reprimand, with outspoken frankness as to our general conduct, unprejudiced by human respect. This

Minister of the Sacrament of Penance.

Choice of a confessor.

---

[1] Rom. viii. 18.

is a service that no one else is so qualified to offer, and one we should accept with unshrinking confidence and manifest gratitude. "For we have not a high priest who cannot have compassion on our infirmities : but one tempted in all things like as we are, without sin. Let us go therefore with confidence to the throne of grace: that we may obtain mercy, and find grace in seasonable aid"[1]—words that in their measure apply to Christ's priests.

Satisfaction.   Satisfaction is a penance imposed on us by the confessor, including restoration of stolen property, and reparation of scandal. Although Absolution wipes out the guilt of mortal sin, delivering us from eternal punishment, there usually remains a temporal punishment due for evil deeds, unless the penitent's dispositions are of such perfection that, by the Divine mercy of God, even that debt is cancelled. The penance enjoined by the confessor is not always equal to the offence committed, which may still have to be expiated more fully by further punishment, whether in this world or in Purgatory. It is an act of atonement towards God and our neighbour, for in the Sacrament of Penance the mercy of our Lord is extended to us by the remission of eternal chastisement, and justice is compassionately enforced upon us by means of temporal punishment in commutation of the everlasting penalties we have deserved. The Church exacts fulfilment of the satisfaction imposed, under pain of sin, the penance being more or less severe according to the gravity of the offence confessed, except when it is either impossible or too difficult of accomplishment, in which case it is our duty to make this known to the confessor, respectfully begging that the

[1] Heb. iv. 15, 16.

penance may be changed. Another priest will commonly object to alter the penance unless the penitent can give legitimate reasons for not being able to apply to the same confessor ; and, even under this condition, some will have it that a repetition of the preceding Confession would be necessary. The penance imposed should be carried out with exactitude as the time, place, and manner of execution demanded by Christ's minister, and with devout sentiments of piety and fervour, united to sincere repentance of the sins for which atonement is being offered.

Absolution is that sentence of forgiveness so consoling Absolution. and reassuring to a repentant conscience, pronounced by the priest in the name of our Lord Jesus Christ, by the authority He gave in the words already quoted.[1] When the penitent is properly disposed, absolution gives remission of guilt and eternal punishment, a restoring of merit and sanctifying grace, consolation and a return of quiet to mind and heart. There are reserved cases where the enormity of crime, or affiliation with certain secret societies, etc., does not admit of a confessor granting Absolution without special permission. It has been decreed as a dogma of faith that the Pope, as concerning the Church at large, and bishops, as regarding their respective dioceses, have the right to limit the power of administering Absolution ; but in cases of necessity, where there is danger of death, all priests can give absolution wherever and whoever they may be. Absolution from sin is one of the most solemnly happy moments of our existence, when " we know that we have passed from death to life." [2] It is a purifying of the soul that gives back the right to Heaven previously

---

[1] John xx. 21–23.   [2] 1 John iii. 14.

possessed but withheld from us by mortal sin ; for "the justice of the just shall not deliver him, in what day soever he shall sin : and the wickedness of the wicked shall not hurt him, in what day soever he shall turn from his wicked-

Effects of absolution.

ness." [1] The Sacrament of Penance bestows on us a supernatural strength and grace that fortifies the soul and produces a progressive improvement of character in those who persevere in practices bringing them nearer to God. At the moment of Absolution, we should offer up a humble act of contrition, renewing it even after leaving the tribunal of Penance, with sincere expressions of gratitude, love, and obedience, mingled with regret for the past and a strong resolution to avoid, by the help of divine grace, future sin, and to merit the inestimable mercy to be received in this Sacrament.

[1] Ezek. xxxiii. 12.

CHAPTER XLI.

INDULGENCES.

FAR from resting content with the penance enjoined by Non-sacramental satisfaction. our confessor in the tribunal of Penance—which is so frequently inadequate to that deserved, and known to God alone—we should try to render further satisfaction to our Lord by self-imposed acts of penitence, good works, and the gaining of Indulgences, in remission of the punishment which we have hereafter to bear in expiation. Penance may be voluntarily inflicted by all kinds of acts, moral and physical, referring to God, our neighbour, or ourselves, offered in reparation for sins committed, and accepted for at least part payment of the debt of temporal punishment we have contracted. Instances may be patient resignation in the sufferings or trials that come to us; help or service rendered to a fellow-creature; and any mortification of the mind, heart, or body. For true repentance includes regret for the past, resolute will of amendment in the future, and proportionate atonement, whether towards the Divine Justice or towards our neighbour—when the offence requires practicable reparation—or towards ourselves, by undergoing the punishments we have merited, without delay, and removing obstacles to speedy and perfect union with God.

Indulgences.   The name "Indulgence" is derived from a Latin word meaning "pardon." An Indulgence is an act of mercy exercised by the Church, apart from the Sacrament of Penance, by which we may gain partial or plenary remission, through the merits of our Saviour, of the temporal punishment remaining due for sin; the guilt and eternal punishment having been already remitted in absolution. Through an Indulgence is gained the cancelling of temporal punishment due for sin, equivalent, as some hold, though mistakenly, to that canonical or public penance inflicted on sinners according to an ancient discipline of the Church. A partial Indulgence, in like manner, is supposed by some to forgive a limited portion of the temporal punishment, represented by a certain number of days or years equal to the chastisement enforced by the Church in the early ages of Christianity, which would have lasted that space of time. Such views have been condemned, or are now exploded. A plenary Indulgence is not the entire remission of the penalty that would have been imposed at the time of canonical penances, but a remission of all penalty due on account of sin, to the end of time.

Power of the Church to grant Indulgences.   It is an article of faith that the Church has power to grant Indulgences by authority of our Lord, who gave that right to His Apostles when he said, "Amen, I say to you, whatsoever you shall bind upon earth, shall be bound also in Heaven; and whatsoever you shall loose upon earth, shall be loosed also in Heaven. Again I say to you, that if two of you shall consent upon earth, concerning anything whatsoever they shall ask, it shall be done to them by My Father who is in Heaven."[1] The use of this power may be

[1] Matt. xviii. 18, 19.

seen in Scripture where St. Paul absolved the sinner, whom he had before excommunicated, on his doing penance, saying, " To him that is such an one, this rebuke is sufficient, that is given by many : so that contrariwise, you should rather pardon and comfort him, lest perhaps such an one be swallowed up with over-much sorrow. For which cause I beseech you, that you would confirm your charity towards him. . . . And to whom you have pardoned anything, I also. For what I have pardoned, if I have pardoned anything, for your sakes have I done it in the person of Christ." [1]

Bishops may in their respective dioceses accord a partial Indulgence of forty days, or of one year, on the day a new Church is consecrated ; but the plenary power of granting Indulgences pertains exclusively to the Pope.

Authorization of Indulgences.

The virtue of Indulgences outflows from the infinite merits of our Lord Jesus Christ, and the abundant merits of the ever Blessed and Immaculate Virgin ; as also from the merits of Saints, whose merits, being superfluous in their own offering of the satisfaction due to divine justice, have remained in the spiritual and common treasury of the Church. Indulgences remit not either the guilt or the eternal punishment of sin, and a most wicked calumny it is to assert that they are permissions to commit sin. They remit, under given conditions, a part or the whole of the temporary punishment due to sin. They apply directly to those who gain them, and are rendered profitable to those to whom they are made over. They can be applied to the dead, yet benefit them only by way of suffrage.

Source and meaning of Indulgences.

To gain an Indulgence we must not only have the *Dispositions*

---

[1] 2 Cor. ii. 6–8, 10.

S

for gaining
Indulgences.

intention to do so, either actually at the moment, or virtually by reason of an intention previously fixed upon, but we must be in a state of grace at least when carrying out the ultimate condition to which the Indulgence is attached, and fully discharge all the other conditions prescribed. To gain a plenary Indulgence it is further necessary to be exempt from deliberate affection even to venial sin. It is not out of place to remark, in reference to plenary Indulgences, that Communion when prescribed may be received in any Church whatsoever, provided that a contrary ordinance be not otherwise attached. No prayers of ordinary obligation can serve for the gaining of an Indulgence, unless such be declared permissible in the edict connected therewith. As no Indulgence can be obtained when there is sin unforgiven in the soul, it follows that the desire to obtain an Indulgence for ourselves or others is a most powerful incentive to repentance. It should be added that the Council of Trent pronounces anathema against those who assert that Indulgences are useless, or who deny that the power to grant them abides in the Church.

Advantages of
Indulgences.

Indulgences are in no way compulsory, but we should regard the gaining of them as tantamount to the amassing of untold wealth—a fortune that dies not with us, but is of inestimable value in the future. We, who have such a natural repugnance for all suffering in this world, should unquestionably strain every effort to mitigate or perhaps exempt ourselves from those immeasurably more intense sufferings in the life to come. Of greater merit it undoubtedly is to gain Indulgences for the dead than for ourselves, because charity is most pleasing to God, in whose sight we acquire higher favour by self-abnegation in the heroic act of offering all our deeds of satisfaction and the suffrages that may be applied to us after death, to the Blessed Virgin, that she may, at will, distribute and bestow such favours on souls in Purgatory. This offering, or donation, called "The Heroic Act," accords us certain very great privileges applicable to the dead, and does not prevent priests from offering the Holy Sacrifice of the Mass for other intentions, nor the laity from praying for whom they will, or from gaining other merit by other and further acts of virtue.

CHAPTER XLII.

THE SACRAMENT OF EXTREME UNCTION.

Extreme Unction.

EXTREME Unction is a Sacrament instituted by our Lord Jesus Christ, for the spiritual comfort and bodily relief of the sick. This Sacrament is called " Extreme Unction " because it is administered when persons are thought to be near the close of their existence in this world, that they may by it receive grace and strength for the conflict with death, even as in Confirmation they have received grace and strength for the battle of life. This Unction is made of olive oil blessed by a bishop on Holy Thursday, is consecrated to the use of this Sacrament, and is the outward " sign " productive of an inward and spiritual grace, thus constituting a true Sacrament and ever held to be such by the Catholic Church.

Institution of the Sacrament of Extreme Unction.

When this Sacrament was instituted by our Lord is not defined in Scripture, but it is clearly shown to have been of Divine institution, and practised by the Apostles according to our Saviour's instructions, when " they preached that men should do penance: . . . and anointed with oil many that were sick." [1]   Again it is referred to in more decided terms by St. James, who confirms the teaching that Extreme Unction is a Sacrament, by attributing a super-

[1] Mark vi. 12, 13.

natural virtue of grace and remission of sins to the sign of anointing the sick with oil, when he says, "Is any man sick among you? Let him bring in the priests of the Church, and let them pray over him, anointing him with oil in the name of the Lord. And the prayer of faith shall save the sick man: and the Lord shall raise him up: and if he be in sins, they shall be forgiven him."[1]

For the due reception of the Sacrament of Extreme Unction we must be in a state of grace, and accept it with sentiments of contrition for sin, and resignation to the will of God. Extreme Unction effaces venial sin, part or all of the temporal punishment due to sin, and mortal sin sometimes, according to the dispositions of the person anointed. But in the case last-named only under condition that full attrition has been felt for the evil committed since last receiving Absolution, and through involuntary omission, as for example, when by reason of illness, Confession has been deferred. Or, when having received absolution with good will, yet insufficient sorrow—by which absolution has been rendered void—full repentance and strong desire for well-doing are in the soul at the time Extreme Unction is administered. This Sacrament alleviates bodily sufferings, and gives back health to those whom God wills should continue to live. For "the prayer of faith shall save the sick man; and the Lord shall raise him up."[2] It renews our spiritual forces in the most decisive moment of our existence, giving us strength to fight against the enemy of our salvation; fortifying us against the terror of death, and against temptations to impatience, despair, and distrust; soothing our troubles, and giving us

Dispositions for receiving Extreme Unction.

Effects of Extreme Unction.

[1] Jas. v. 14, 15.   [2] Jas. v. 15.

courage to say with confidence and love, "Father, into Thy hands I commend My spirit."[1]

Obligation of receiving Extreme Unction.

All members of the Church, who have by Baptism become entitled to participate in the other Sacraments, should, when dangerously ill, receive Extreme Unction; excepting the case of children who have not attained the age of reason, or of adults who have never had the use of reason. This Sacrament may be received several times during life when there is peril of death, yet not twice in the same illness, unless there have been an interval of convalescence. It is, in all charity, the duty of those attending sick persons to call to their mind, and even urge upon them the reception of a Sacrament so salutary alike to soul and body; to send for a priest without awaiting the last extremity, before consciousness may have lapsed, or death come on unawares. Culpable, more or less, do we become through any voluntary neglect in obtaining so great a benefit and consolation, tendered to us by our Saviour in our last moments. For the reception of the supernatural grace given us for recovering health in this life, or for passing away from it to eternal life in a better world, we should carefully dispose our consciences and prepare our souls.

[1] Luke xxiii. 46.

CHAPTER XLIII.

THE SACRAMENT OF HOLY ORDER.

HOLY Order is a Sacrament instituted by our Lord Jesus   Holy Order.
Christ, giving power and authority for the consecration of
the Eucharist, the administration of that and other Sacraments, and the accomplishment of all ecclesiastical functions proper to the privileges of priesthood. Ordination
consists of a visible "sign" in the imposition of hands,
accompanied by certain prayers productive of an inward
and spiritual grace, thus constituting a true Sacrament.
This is an article of faith in the Catholic Church; and is
spoken of by St. Paul, in these words: "Neglect not the
grace that is in thee, which was given thee by prophecy,
with the imposition of the hands of the priesthood." [1]

Though Scripture does not state in positive terms when   Institution of
                                                          the Sacrament
our Saviour established this Sacrament, it is recognized by   of Holy Order.
the Church to have been established at the institution of
the Holy Eucharist and Sacrifice of the Mass, when He
gave His Apostles power to consecrate the Bread and Wine,
saying, "Do this for a commemoration of Me." [2] We see
Ordination practised by the disciples, when they appointed
"seven men of good reputation, full of the Holy Ghost and
wisdom ; . . . these they set before the Apostles; and they,

[1] 1 Tim. iv. 14.   [2] Luke xxii. 19: 1 Cor. xi. 24.

praying, imposed hands upon them."[1] Again, Ordination is referred to in Scripture, when the Apostles, "praying, and imposing their hands,[2] . . . ordained to them priests in every church."[3] And the different grades of priesthood are expressly mentioned by St. Paul, who quotes our Lord thus: "He gave some apostles, and some prophets, and other some evangelists, and other some pastors and doctors, for the perfecting of the saints, for the work of the ministry, for the edifying of the body of Christ."[4]

Major and minor grades in the Church.   There are four classes of "minor" orders, namely, door-keeper, reader, exorcist, and acolyte. These were instituted in the first ages of the Church's establishment, and without being a Sacrament or irretrievably binding, serve successively to prepare for the reception of Holy Orders. Of the "major" orders, there are subdeacons, deacons, and priests, irrevocably consecrated to the service of the Church. The tonsure is not an order, but merely an ecclesiastical ceremony, in which a bishop officiates. It is as a kind of noviciate for those preparing to receive the Sacrament of Holy Order. The tonsure, however, gives the right of wearing the surplice and usual ecclesiastical costume. Holy Order provides us spiritual rulers, instructors, and advisers, who are sound in their teaching and sure in their jurisdiction; devoted and charitable in their administration of reproof or counsel; assiduous in all their parochial labours; rejoicing with those who are happy, and lamenting with those who weep. Women are entirely excluded from all sacerdotal ministry, it being written: "Let women keep silence in the Churches: for it is not permitted them to speak."[5]

---

[1] Acts vi. 3, 6.   [2] Acts xiii. 3.   [3] Acts xiv. 22.
[4] Eph. iv. 11, 12; 1 Cor. xii. 28.   [5] 1 Cor. xiv. 34.

The necessary conditions for receiving the Sacrament of Holy Order are : that a man should have been baptized, without which the reception of any of the Sacraments is invalid; that he should be in a state of grace, Holy Order being a Sacrament of the living; that he should have a divine vocation or calling for what he undertakes; that he should have been confirmed, and therefore have learnt the principal truths of religion. He should also be of the required age, and have gone through the requisite instruction to give him thorough knowledge of the duties he has to fulfil, and the teaching he has to expound; he should be of a virtuous disposition, in order to keep the vow of chastity he is obliged to make, the morality of his life being tested by the publication of the banns relating to the Sacrament of Holy Orders. This vow of chastity is most binding, because it is a solemn promise made to God, and continency is very necessary in the priesthood. St. Paul writes what may be applied to the vow of celibacy, " I would have you to be without solicitude. He that is without a wife, is solicitous for the things that belong to the Lord, how he may please God. But he that is with a wife, is solicitous for the things of the world, how he may please his wife. . . . And this I speak for your profit; not to cast a snare upon you; but for that which is decent, and which may give you power to attend upon the Lord, without impediment."[1] "He that is called by God,"[2] may know his vocation from his inward and calm conviction, his liking and fitness for the purity of a life consecrated to the service of our Blessed Lord. Parents or others in authority, or possessing influence, have no right to oppose, under any pretext whatever, such a

[1] 1 Cor. vii. 32, 33, 35.   [2] Heb. v. 4.

vocation, that may procure for the Church a good priest, contributing to the salvation of very many.

Effects of Ordination.

Although there are degrees in Ordination, there is only one Sacrament of Holy Order, the administration of which belongs essentially to the episcopal rank of pastors. Ordination imparts an indelible character and increase of sanctifying grace to the soul, with actual graces for the worthy fulfilment of ecclesiastical duties, to the greater glory of God, and the salvation of men.

Privileges of different degrees of ecclesiastics.

The order of Subdeacon gives the right of serving the deacon at the altar, of touching the sacred vessels and linen that come in contact with the Holy Eucharist, and of chanting the Epistle at High Mass. It also imposes two obligations common to the priesthood : those of perpetual chastity and the daily recitation of the holy office. The order of Deacon accords the right of immediately serving the priest at High Mass, and of chanting the Gospel. A deacon can further, with permission from the bishop, preach, and administer solemnly the Sacrament of Baptism and even that of the Holy Eucharist. The order of Priesthood confers the power of consecration at the Holy Sacrifice of the Mass; the right of dispensing Absolution for the remission of sins ; of administering all Sacraments, with the exception of Holy Order and Confirmation; and of carrying out generally the several sacerdotal functions. A Bishop having received the plenitude of sacerdotal power possesses rights superior to those of ordinary priests ; whereby he is the administrator of the Sacraments of Holy Order and Confirmation, ruler of the priests of his diocese, and judge, in the first instance, of faith and morals touching those under his supervision, and ruler also of all the faithful, conjointly with the other bishops and his Holiness the Pope, who alone has the right by his approval or censure to give definitive decisions. St. Paul refers to this class of pastors, saying, "Take heed to yourselves and to the whole flock, wherein the Holy Ghost hath placed you bishops to rule the Church of God, which He hath purchased with His own Blood."[1] The other titles of ecclesiastical dignity, such as Archbishop or Cardinal, are accompanied by certain privileges, but are merely honorary ranks, instituted by the Church, and conferred by the Pope, who alone is the one bishop above all others, occupying, as direct successor of St. Peter, the episcopal see of Rome, possessing the authority given to that Apostle by our Lord Jesus Christ, with the prerogative of infallibility when, as Head of the entire Church, he decides any point of faith or morals.

Our duty towards our pastors is to pray that they may labour zealously for the glory of God and our spiritual direction; to respect their sacred calling as the ministers of Christ; to excuse their faults or shortcomings, since, being but human, the Sacrament of Holy Order has not rendered them impeccable. We should furthermore treat all ecclesiastics, not only with courtesy, but with veneration and consideration, according to their grades of office. St. Paul commends them to our esteem, saying, "Remember your prelates who have spoken the word of God to you; whose faith follow, considering the end of their conversation, Jesus Christ, yesterday, and to-day, and the same for ever . . . obey your prelates, and be subject to them. For they watch as being to render an account of your

Duties of the laity towards ecclesiastics.

---

[1] Acts xx. 28.

souls; that they may do this with joy, and not with grief, for this is not expedient for you."[1]   And St. John writes: "We are of God.   He that knoweth God, heareth us.   He that is not of God, heareth us not.   By this we know the spirit of truth, and the spirit of error."[2]

[1] Heb. xiii. 7, 8, 17.   [2] 1 John iv. 6.

CHAPTER XLIV.

THE SACRAMENT OF MARRIAGE.

MARRIAGE was instituted by God at the beginning of the world, when He joined together our first parents, Adam and his wife.[1] It was elevated to the dignity of a Sacrament by our Lord Jesus Christ, to sanctify the union of the sexes. Marriage is the legitimate alliance of man and woman, by their mutual and free consent, contracted according to the laws of the Church. It is a Sacrament by the contract of the two parties in holy union, which is the outward sign productive of grace. St. Paul speaks of it as being " a great Sacrament." [2] Husbands and wives are recommended to love each other in matrimony " as Christ also loved the Church, and delivered Himself up for it, that He might sanctify it, cleansing it by the laver of water in the word of life." [3] Marriage is defined, as an article of faith by the Church, to be a Sacrament.

Matrimony.

When our Lord instituted the Sacrament of matrimony is not exactly expressed in Scripture, but possibly, when He restored Marriage to its original institution, He conferred upon it the dignity and grace of a Sacrament.[4]

Institution of matrimony as a Sacrament.

The Church exacts a publication of matrimonial banns before celebrating the nuptial rites, in order that obstacles,

Impediments to matrimony.

[1] Gen. ii. 25.   [2] Eph. v. 32.   [3] Eph. v. 25, 26.   [4] Matt. xix. 6.

if any, may be discovered; it being the duty of every one who is cognisant of an impediment to make it known to ecclesiastical authority. Christians, free of all impediments, and having attained the age specified by the Church, can receive this Sacrament; but those finding themselves bound by restrictions before entering the matrimonial state, can only be released by special dispensation proceeding from ecclesiastical authority. Prohibitive impediments render a marriage illicit and sinful, but not void; diriment impediments, however, nullify a marriage. The principal prohibitive impediments are: solemnizing marriage at certain times of the year forbidden by the Church, that is to say, during Advent and Lent; difference of religion between Catholics and heretics; a simple vow of chastity, etc. The principal diriment impediments are: clandestine marriage, that is, without the presence of the authorized priest and two witnesses—although in England and some other places clandestine marriages are admitted as valid;—lack of reason or proper age; the solemn vow of chastity implicitly contained in the reception of the Subdiaconate, Diaconate, and Priesthood, and taken by members of religious orders; proximity of relationship; disparity of religion between a Catholic and an infidel; absence of free consent, that is, when marriage is forced on any one by violence or unjust menace of a serious nature, fraud, error, etc. Those persons who are married only by civil law, and not before God, in presence of the proper pastor of the parish, or other priest deputed to replace him, and two witnesses, are declared by the Church to be living in mortal sin, and their marriage is void, by virtue of the right our Lord gave His Church, in the promise He made to His ministers : "Whatsoever you shall bind upon earth, shall be bound also in Heaven; and whatsoever you shall loose upon earth, shall be loosed also in Heaven." [1]

For the right reception of the Sacrament of matrimony, we must be in a state of grace, having so disposed our souls by pious participation in the Sacraments of Penance and the Holy Eucharist, that we may obtain the graces so necessary for the just fulfilment of obligations, and patient bearing of trials incidental to, or necessarily accompanying, the matrimonial state. Confession is strongly recommended before marriage, but is not obligatory if the contracting persons are in a state of grace. Those who, in mortal sin, present themselves for the reception of this Sacrament, not only do not receive the grace of the Sacrament, but are guilty of a sacrilegious sin, and expose themselves to the malediction of Heaven. Moreover, it is written, " Every best gift, and every perfect gift, is from above, coming down from the Father of lights." [2] Those who marry should therefore pray to God for the gift of understanding in the choice of that person to whom they are to be united until death, and on whom their happiness in this world shall so much depend. They should consult their parents and their confessor; they should take every possible precaution to know correctly the person's heart, mind, religious principles, and character generally; having also a care as to suitability of age, condition, and fortune. For disproportionate alliances of any kind are often unhappy ones. They should approach the holy state of matrimony with a firm intention to regard sacredly those reasons for which God established it, and pass the marriage day in a sinless manner.

Dispositions for the reception of matrimony.

Obligations resulting from matrimony.

[1] Matt. xviii. 18.   [2] Jas. i. 17.

They should give mutual protection and companionship through the trials and sufferings of life, supporting, comforting, and sanctifying each other by the supernatural influence of this Sacrament; working together in unity of spirit for eternal salvation; loving one another with an attachment subordinate only to their love for God, and bringing to Him, through baptism in the Church, the children He has committed to their charge, educating them in a Christian manner to love and serve Him faithfully and obtain everlasting life.

Indissolubility of marriage.

Marriage contracted under the requisite conditions is absolutely binding till death, our Lord having so established it, when saying, "Those whom God hath joined together, let no man put asunder."[1]   Dissolution of

Inadmissibility of divorce.

marriage by means of divorce, even though tolerated by civil law, is in no way countenanced by the Church, being a criminal violation of the Divine law and of the Sacrament of marriage instituted by our Lord, who said, " Whosoever shall put away his wife and marry another, committeth adultery against her.   And if the wife shall put away her husband and be married to another, she committeth adultery."[2]   St. Paul writes : " To them that are married, not I but the Lord commandeth, that the wife depart not from her husband . . . and let not the husband put away his wife."[3]   Were divorce permitted, it would subserve to disturb the peace of conjugal happiness, and engender capriciousness, inconstancy, despotism and immorality ; exposing the woman, more especially, to all those embarrassments and afflictions attending so calamitous and false a position.   It would deprive the children of the

[1] Matt. xix. 6.   [2] Mark x. 11, 12.   [3] 1 Cor. vii. 10, 11.

example and education that, under the twofold influence of paternal and maternal affection, should be theirs; besides causing scandalous lawsuits, and difficulties trenching on interests pecuniary.

The Church holds, and has ever held, religious celibacy Celibacy. to be a more perfect state than marriage. According to St. Paul's teaching: "He that is without a wife, is solicitous for the things that belong to the Lord, how he may please God . . . and the unmarried woman and the virgin thinketh on the things of the Lord, that she may be holy both in body and in spirit . . . I say to the unmarried, and to the widows: It is good for them if they so continue."[1] But if we are tempted to incontinency, "it is better to marry than to be burnt,"[2] namely, with the fire of concupiscence. Christian virginity is worthy of the utmost honour and respect, but unfortunately it does not follow that all who renounce marriage are the more saintly on that account.

[1] 1 Cor. vii. 32, 34, 8.   [2] 1 Cor. vii. 9.

CHAPTER XLV.

RELIGIOUS CEREMONIES, SYMBOLISMS, AND DEVOTIONS.

Ceremonies, symbolisms, and devotions. FOR a requisite understanding and estimate of the pious practices and ceremonies peculiar to the Catholic Church, and their full bearing on the essentials of true religion, it is necessary we should possess a correct knowledge of their import. By this means we shall realize more clearly the significance of all those symbolisms that meet the eye, and which, instead of passing by us unnoticed, may appeal to our intelligence with greater insight and to our feelings with greater force. For, nothing that to the ignorant appears as mere show or ornament, is without a religious meaning in the Holy Catholic Church of our Lord Jesus Christ; and the signs and external forms connected with our holy religion are a language speaking to our senses in a manner calculated to quicken emotions of reverent feeling and devotion.

Many there are of different religious denominations, who take exception to the rich vestments, profusion of lights, floral and other ornaments used in the Catholic Church; but even those who are the most simple in their form of worship, and the most rigorous concerning the non-decoration of their religious edifices, are frequently the most rigid regarding the ceremonies and dress they have

adopted. As, for example, the Quakers, who make themselves thus conspicuous, even in everyday life. Yet, there
is certainly no reason for supposing prayers to be in the
sight of God more meritorious when offered up in an
edifice unadorned, and under a scheme of worship devoid
of all ceremonial.

Faith and Religion, as we have already recognized, have
existed since the beginning of the world; and we are
bound to acknowledge that they were in all times manifested by outward demonstrations under the form of public
worship, which was ever accompanied by certain ceremonies,
recorded in the Old Testament to have been instituted
by God Himself. Unquestionably God does not give us
to understand that He has any preference for strict
simplicity; but, on the contrary, that He is pleased with
all that is replete with beauty and variety. His Temple,
which Solomon was engaged in erecting during the space
of seven years, is described as of unequalled grandeur,
elaborate in delicate design and enriched with plenteous
decoration. "There was nothing in the Temple that was
not covered with gold: And all the walls of the Temple
round about he carved with divers figures and carvings:
and he made in them cherubims and palm trees, and divers
representations, as it were standing out, and coming forth
from the wall. And the floor of the house he also overlaid
with gold within and without."[1] With such an example
of splendour, and the many instances we have before our
eyes in daily life amongst things of God's creation, should
we not take the work and obvious will of God as our
pattern, for the accessories connected with the worship of

Ceremonies of divine institution.

[1] 2 Kings vi. 22, 29, 30.

Him who said, "Heaven is My throne, and the earth My footstool"?[1]

In the New Testament we read how our Lord Himself followed the practices of the Mosaic Law, and complied with the religious observances in force among the Jews, evincing thereby His approval of them ; and then, in establishing the realities of our religion, substituted other ceremonies, of which the preceding were simply figurative These external rites were strictly adhered to by the Apostles, and have been progressively developed in succeeding ages by the Church, whose forms of worship leave nothing for individual determination or private interpretation, but offer a series of striking ceremonies and symbolisms, in harmony with the Unity and Catholicity of the true Church. The ceremonies themselves, however, are not everywhere quite alike, several differences existing in those of the Oriental Churches in communion with the Holy See.

Ritual.   Ritual greatly aids to excite feelings of reverence and piety; so much so, indeed, that where outward marks of respect are dispensed with, the feeling itself is apt to disappear or to become at least diminished from too great familiarity. The ceremonial and decoration of the Church serve to instruct the mind, as well as appeal to the heart, and very often work a far greater effect on the devotional feelings and imagination—more especially of the less educated class —than where ritual is wholly dispensed with. Thus, as we so often offend God through our senses, so do we wisely utilize them to draw us towards Him and to bring us aid in our worship. But, although ceremony is desirable in religion, the earnestness or truth of worship is by no means

[1] Isa. lxvi. 1.

dependent upon ritual, as may easily be seen by comparison between the devotion prevailing among the poor in country chapels, and that displayed in the most magnificent of our Cathedrals. The lights, flowers, pictures, and precious stones which adorn our altars, as also the movements, the intonations of voice of those ministering in the Sanctuary, and the varied forms of melodious sounds made use of in Church music, result from a natural desire to show all possible homage and honour due to the sacred Presence of our Lord and Saviour in the Blessed Sacrament of the altar. But ritual is a matter which cannot be fashioned according to private judgment. It must be consistent with and subservient to doctrine, and be carried out under authority of the Church. Were ceremony to go beyond doctrine—as is the case in certain ritualistic Anglican Churches, where the real Presence (which to the Catholic way of thinking means a real absence) is insinuated by the form of ceremony adopted—ritual would become worse than meaningless, it would be misleading.

The symbolic meanings which became by degrees annexed to ceremonies, vestments, etc., are not always or not wholly the historical reasons for them; and are even not unfrequently pious ideas originating from the inventive devotion of Catholics after the practices themselves had grown into custom. They are, however, very efficacious to help us to realize the intrinsic worth of our surroundings, and to feel with deeper emotion, the import of all we see and hear in the observances of our religion.

We ought further to have some idea of the religious associations which are daily recalled to our minds ; for no season or time passes that may not remind us of some more

Division of the Liturgical year.

or less striking event connected with our holy religion. Thus the Liturgical year, beginning with the first Sunday in Advent, is divided into four sections, which are commemorative of the principal mysteries and incidents in the life of our Saviour, and afford matter for constant meditation.

Advent, in which occurs the feast of the Immaculate Conception, is a preparation for the celebration of Christmas; reminding us of those ages of waiting and suspense, passed by the Patriarchs and Prophets, before the birth of our Saviour, when the figurative events of the primitive religion smoothed the way for the coming of Christ. Christmas and the Epiphany, including the feast of the Circumcision, relate to the infancy and hidden life of our Lord, and to very many of the most important mysteries of our religion.

The time of Septuagesima—during, or just before, which is the feast of the Purification—represents our Lord's public life spent in preaching the Gospel and performing miracles. It is a preparation for Lent, which commences on Ash Wednesday, and brings to memory the days of our Saviour's Passion and death. With Passion and Palm Sunday, Lent brings us to Easter. The feast of the Annunciation also occurs about this time.

From the day we celebrate the great mystery of our Redeemer's Resurrection, throughout Paschal-time, and the feast of the Ascension, we have brought before us our Lord's glorious life, when He showed Himself, living, to His Apostles, and confirmed their faith.

At Pentecost we are reminded of the descent of the Holy Ghost on the Apostles, their preaching of the Gospel, and the establishment of the Church. In the time that follows, are included the feasts of Holy Trinity, Corpus Christi, the Assumption, and All Saints. We approach the termination of the ecclesiastical year by a day consecrated to prayers for the dead, and remembrance of the last judgment; death and judgment being the inevitable ending of our existence in this world.

Every day in the year is religiously observed by the Church; some holy days being of Obligation to the faithful, and others of Devotion, to celebrate, in rejoicing or in penance, different anniversaries connected with our holy religion. But, aside from these more particular circumstances of annual note, each day of the week brings with it some pious reflection to the hearts of Christians. *Recollections for every day in the year.*

On Sundays we are reminded of the birth and glorious Resurrection of our Saviour, of the descent of the Holy Ghost on the Apostles, and of God the Father, who rested from the work of creation on the seventh day, and sanctified it. Thus with the former mention of the Son and the Holy Ghost, is brought to our minds the mystery of the Blessed Trinity, to whose honour Sundays are specially consecrated.

On Mondays our memory may naturally turn towards the dead, and our prayers may be chiefly said for their speedy delivery from cleansing fires. It is also a day chosen for the homage owed to God's Angels, and particularly to our guardian Angel.

Tuesdays are by many dedicated to the Apostles.

Wednesdays are commonly set aside in memory of St. Joseph.

On Thursdays we offer special devotion to the Holy Eucharist, in remembrance of the day on which our Blessed

Lord gave Himself to us in perpetuity in this Holy Sacrament.

Fridays are consecrated to the Passion and death of our Saviour; the first Friday of the month being specifically dedicated to the Sacred Heart.

Saturdays are devoted to the ever-blessed Mother of God, whose poignant grief, after our Lord's agony and death on the Cross, should quicken in our hearts a tender remembrance of and intense esteem for the Mother of our Redeemer.

CHAPTER XLVI.

THE SIGN OF THE CROSS.

ONE of the first pious acts of our holy religion, taught us *The sign of the Cross.* from very infancy, is the sign of the Cross. Tradition declares it to have been in use from the time of the Apostles. To this practice, accompanied with the use of holy water, is attached an Indulgence. The sign of the *Manner of forming the* Cross is a profession of Christianity and of adherence to *sign of the Cross.* the Catholic faith. It is made with the right hand from forehead to breast and from left to right shoulder, while the words: "In the name of the Father, and of the Son, and of the Holy Ghost, Amen," are being uttered. It signifies our belief in the mystery of the Blessed Trinity, indicated by the words we pronounce; and also our faith in the mystery of the Redemption, by the cross we form on ourselves, which necessarily includes the mystery of the Incarnation. The conclusion, "Amen," is a ratification of the preceding words, being expressive of desire that our invocation may be heard. The sign of the Cross made with the thumb on forehead, mouth, and heart, signifies that we believe, profess, and love the truth of the Catholic faith. The priest makes the sign of the Cross in the name of the Holy Trinity, with his right hand, when blessing the faithful, or any object he is consecrating to religious use, also in the administration of the Sacraments, and in all ceremonies of the Church. We should make the sign of the Cross, with deliberation and respect, at the beginning and ending of each day; at the commencement and closing of our prayers; and in temptation or bodily danger. A true Christian should never be ashamed of the sign of the Cross; for, as St. Peter tells us: "If you be reproached for the name of Christ, you shall be blessed;"[1] and St. Paul warns us that we should glory in naught "save in the Cross of our Lord Jesus Christ."[2]

[1] 1 Pet. iv. 14.   [2] Gal. vi. 14.

CHAPTER XLVII.

HOLY WATER.

THE use of holy water is an act of piety instituted by the Holy Water. Church, common amongst the faithful, and employed in all religious ceremonies. Holy water is used to drive away all that is evil and impure, and to draw down divine aid upon us, whether for the good of our soul or body. That holy water is productive of these effects we know from the prayers of the Church while blessing it, which ask of God all that is beneficial to the bodies and souls of those who make use of it, and the banishment of what is foul and corrupt. These prayers are efficacious from the pro- mises made in favour of faith, and the power given to the Church. We also know that holy water avails to procure the remission of sins, if those who employ it are rightly disposed, as explained already in its use as a " Sacramental." It is a customary practice to make the sign of the Cross with holy water on entering or quitting a church; and at home in illness, temptation, or danger; a practice we should ever keep up in a spirit of faith and penitence, that we may derive therefrom all the salutary effects it is meant to produce. Holy water is also used by the priest in the sprinkling of the altar, and of the faithful, whether living or dead, and of any object of piety blessed by the Church.

CHAPTER XLVIII.

THE WAY OF THE CROSS.

Origin of the Way of the Cross.

THE " Way of the Cross," in Latin the " Via Crucis," is a devotional exercise instituted by the Church, to which are attached abundant Indulgences. The fourteen pictures or images ranged round churches, and called "Stations of the Cross," represent fourteen scenes of our Lord's Passion, from the palace of Pilate to the summit of Mount Calvary and to the tomb. Before each of these the faithful kneel in prayer and pious meditation ; a practice of devotion in memory of the path trodden by our Saviour when going to His Crucifixion. The origin of this custom, as Tradition tells us, is that the Blessed Virgin, after the death of Christ, frequently followed the road sanctified by His Passion and cruel Death. Her example was followed by the faithful of Palestine, and afterwards by numberless devout pilgrims

The Way of the Cross in Churches.

from all parts of the world. To encourage this act of piety, the Church had accorded Indulgences to such as prayed devoutly at the scenes of Christ's sufferings and death ; but as the favour did not extend to those unable to visit the Holy Land, the Devotion known as the Way of the Cross was permitted, having the like Indulgences annexed to this pious exercise as those accorded to the visiting of the actual scenes of our Lord's Passion. Persons who are sick, infirm, or otherwise incapacitated from praying at the

different Stations of the Cross in churches, may gain the _{The Way of}
Indulgences of the Via Crucis by using a Crucifix, to
which the blessing of these Indulgences is attached for
their personal use only, by some one specially authorized.

The Way of the Cross is a devotion calculated to enlighten
our minds, and place most vividly before them the sufferings our Lord voluntarily underwent for the salvation
of mankind. For "God spared not even His own Son, but
delivered Him up for us all."[1] It should appeal to our
understandings, showing us how worthless are the interests
of this world as compared with those of eternity, which
alone ought to be our most important thought throughout
life, both for our own sakes and in justice to the Sacrifice
our Redeemer made for us by His Passion and Death on
the Cross. It should excite our full repentance for sins
committed, and sorrow for any surviving affection for evil,
when we contemplate the humiliations and agonies of mind
and body undergone by our Saviour, in expiation of sin,
"that whosoever believeth in Him, may not perish, but
may have life everlasting."[2] It should stimulate our
gratitude and love for Him who, by the "exceeding charity
wherewith He loved us,"[3] constituted Himself a Victim
in our stead, to save us from damnation, and entitle us,
through His merits, to the eternal joys of Heaven. It
should strengthen us in temptation and encourage us to
bear our crosses in life, and to accept, with resignation, the
death that awaits us, which is the beginning of the true
life we all should strive to gain, as St. Peter exhorts us,
saying, "Christ also suffered for us, leaving you an example
that you should follow His steps."[4] It should afford us

The Way of the Cross as practised with a Crucifix.

What may be · gained by practising the Way of the Cross.

[1] Rom. viii. 32.   [2] John iii. 16.   [3] Eph. ii. 4.   [4] 1 Pet. ii. 21.

consolation to meditate on the work of our salvation wrought by Him who has manifested for us the tenderest sympathy and most compassionate mercy. We should realize that by bearing the miseries and trials of our life here below, in patience, humility, and love of our Saviour, we make them meritorious for happiness and glory in the world to come, with Christ who suffered for us, "so to enter into His glory."[1] We should also reflect that by the gaining of Indulgences attached to the Way of the Cross, we may pay a debt to Divine justice for ourselves and others to whom we would apply them; losing not merit ourselves while thus offering a work of charity for the dead, but profiting by the promised recompense of our Lord, who said, "As long as you did it to one of these My least brethren, you did it to Me."[2]

Manner of practising the Way of the Cross.

The customary manner of following the Way of the Cross is to kneel at each of the fourteen stations, and meditate upon the subject represented, saying a Pater, Ave, and Gloria, after each meditation; and at the end, five Paters, Aves, and Glorias, for the intentions of his Holiness the Pope; or six, if the person be a member of the third order of St. Francis of Assisi. Prayers for the Pope are not essential, except when the Way of the Cross is being said with the aid only of a Crucifix. For those who are incapable of concentrating their attention sufficiently to meditate at length, a thought in affectionate and grateful remembrance of the circumstance they are contemplating, suffices. To gain Indulgences, some inclination at least should be made towards the different Stations in turn, none of them being omitted, nor any interruption of long duration allowed.

[1] Luke xxiv. 26.   [2] Matt. xxv. 40.

CHAPTER XLIX.

THE ROSARY.

THE method by which Catholics most generally manifest The Rosary. a particular devotion towards the Blessed Virgin, is the holy Rosary; a religious exercise consisting chiefly of the prayer most acceptable to the Mother of our Lord. It is related that the Blessed Virgin herself made known the Rosary to St. Dominic in the thirteenth century, since when it has been generally accepted and honoured by the Church. The Rosary was also in prominence in the appari- tions of the Blessed Virgin to Bernadette at Lourdes in the year 1858.[1] Many Indulgences have been attached to the reciting of it, provided that the Rosary used is blessed for the person who possesses it, and has the Indulgences attached to it by a Dominican or other priest who has authority to communicate them.

The Rosary is composed of fifteen mysteries; all, with Component parts of the Rosary. the exception of the two last, expressly spoken of in Scripture, and referring to the fundamental truths and principal mysteries of our holy religion. It is divided into fifteen decades, the mysteries being arranged in three sets of five each, corresponding to the three great

[1] See " N. D. de Lourdes," by Henri Lasserre.

divisions of our Lord's life: His infancy and youth; His Passion and death; and His Resurrection and glory. The words of the Rosary are nearly all inspired, being made up of the Creed, the Lord's Prayer, and the Doxology, so frequently used in the Liturgy of the Church.

Manner of saying the Rosary.   To say the Rosary, we make the sign of the Cross in the name of the Father, and of the Son, and of the Holy Ghost. Many then recite the Creed, and three Hail Marys in memory of the Holy Trinity; afterwards, the Lord's Prayer is said at the beginning of each mystery, followed by ten Hail Marys recited during or after meditation upon them. At the end of every decade we repeat, "Glory be to the Father, etc."

The mysteries of the Rosary, and what they teach.   In the joyful mysteries, the Annunciation teaches us humility and abnegation of self; the Visitation, charity towards our neighbour; the Nativity, detachment from the luxuries and vanity of this world; the Presentation, purity and the spirit of obedience; the finding in the Temple, a desire to know God and serve Him. In the Sorrowful Mysteries, the Agony and Prayer in the garden of Olives, teach us prayer and resignation to the will of God; the Scourging, practice of physical mortification, and patience in bodily sufferings; the Crowning with thorns, humbling of our pride, and indifference for worldly praise; the carrying of the Cross, courage, fortitude, and endurance in bearing all the trials of life; the Crucifixion, self-sacrifice, prayer for the conversion of sinners, the perseverance of the just, and help and consolation to souls in Purgatory. In the Glorious Mysteries, the Resurrection teaches us in faith and hope and love to arise from sin with a firm purpose of leading a better life; the

Ascension, hope and desire of Heaven, and love for heavenly things; the descent of the Holy Ghost; the love of God above all things, and advance in grace by the practice of Christian virtues; the Assumption, devotion to the Blessed Virgin, and to live in readiness for death; the Coronation of the Blessed Virgin, perseverance in good, and the hope of eternal happiness, there where the Mother of God reigns as Queen of Heaven.

U

CHAPTER L.

CHURCH SYMBOLISMS AND ECCLESIASTICAL DECORATIONS.

Architectural symbolisms of a Church.

A CHURCH is usually constructed in shape of a Cross, and is generally situated facing east : the principal reason given being, that our Saviour was crucified in the east. Therefore many, when praying, love to turn towards the scene of His immolation and look towards Him who is "the Light of the world," and of Whom the rising sun that illuminates our earth from east to west is, in a certain sense, typical.

The high-vaulted roof, and the pinnacles or towers above the sacred edifice, are symbolical of the desire we should feel to detach our thoughts and wishes from things of earth, and to raise our hearts to God. The sculptured gurgoyles in Gothic Churches, frequently grotesque in shape, are emblematic of the evil spirits that tempt us through life.

The altar.

The altar represents our Redeemer, who is the Foundation Stone of the Church. It is a table of stone, with five crosses carved thereon in remembrance of the five wounds in our Saviour's hands, feet, and side. The altar contains certain relics of Martyrs, because in the primitive ages, Mass was said in the catacombs above the bodies of Martyrs ; and also to denote the intimate union of our Lord with His Saints.

The three linen cloths upon the altar are in memory of those wherein our Lord was wrapped in the tomb; and the Crucifix above the tabernacle is figurative of His Sacrifice on Mount Calvary.

The lamp ever burning before the Blessed Sacrament is to indicate the Sacred Presence of our Saviour in the Holy Eucharist, and to remind us of the feelings of reverence and devotion we should exhibit towards Him who, in the search after truth, lightens our darkness with the gift of illuminating grace. Seven lamps—in frequent use—signify the seven Sacraments. The candles of white wax, always burning during Holy Mass, are expressive of the purity of our Lord; and the light signifies His Divinity and our faith. As the candles are consumed in shedding light, so was our Lord sacrificed in illuminating our understanding by the Redemption of the world.

Illumination of the Church.

Concerning the symbolical meanings of the different colours employed in ecclesiastical vestments and altar decorations, we may note that the only authorized liturgical colours are white, red, green, violet, black, and rose colour. These must predominate in any design of mixed colours, except where gold is very largely used. White symbolizes innocence, faith, and the glory of Heaven: it is in use on the feast of Holy Trinity; on most of the festivals of our Blessed Lord; on Sundays during Paschal time; on feast days dedicated to the Blessed Virgin, the Angels, and those Saints who were not martyred. Red, from its resemblance to fire and blood, is significant of ardent love, and is used on the Feast of Pentecost, when the Holy Ghost descended on the Apostles in the form of tongues of fire; on the days set aside in memory of different martyrs who shed their

Ecclesiastical colours and how used.

blood for love of our Saviour; and on festivals commemorative of the various implements of torture by which our Lord suffered. Green signifies hope, fecundity, and immortality: it is in use on Sundays between the Epiphany and Septuagesima, and. from the third Sunday after Pentecost to Advent. Thus it is employed as a general rule, except during Paschal time, on days of penance, and the Sundays already mentioned. Violet is expressive of mortification and penitence: it is used during Advent and Lent; on Ember days, except in the week of Pentecost; on Rogation days and days of penance; for the administration of the Sacraments of Penance and Extreme Unction; at many processions, and at the Sacrament of Baptism before the pouring of the baptismal water. Black is a sign of mourning and grief: it is used on Good Friday at the Mass of the presanctified; in burial services, and Masses for the dead. Rose colour is only used at Solemn Mass on the third Sunday in Advent and the fourth Sunday in Lent.

Sacred vessels and their appurtenances. Of the sacred vessels used in connection with the Holy Sacrament at the Sacrifice of the Mass, the chalice takes its origin from the cup employed by our Saviour in the institution of the Eucharist, and is said to represent His tomb. The paten, meant to receive the Host, and placed over the Chalice, may likewise be considered typical of the stone that barred the entrance to His holy sepulchre. The cruets serve for the wine and water to be used in the Sacrifice of the Mass. The Ciborium is a covered vase destined for the reception of the consecrated Hosts reserved for Communion. The Monstrance is a shrine of silver or silver gilt, sometimes ornamented with precious stones, in which the sacred Host is placed at Benediction during Exposition of the Blessed Sacrament. The Lunette is the crescent-shaped gold or silver clasp, holding the Sacred Host, which is deposited within the crystal centre of the Monstrance. The Thurible or censer is a metal vase, suspended by chains for the burning of incense, which incense is kept in a boat-shaped receptacle, and transferred to the censer by means of a scoop. The Aspersorium is a portable vessel for holy water, sprinkled by the priest with a brush, called the aspergillum.

The Burse is a flat square case of cardboard, covered with silk, which serves at the Sacrifice of the Mass to hold the Corporal, when it is not in actual use. The Veil is a square of silk, covering the chalice and paten at the commencement and termination of Holy Mass. Both are of like colour with the chasuble and other vestments in use for the day.

The Corporal is a square of white linen with a cross worked near the centre of its outer edge. It is placed by the priest on the altar, under the Host and Chalice, and is figurative of the shroud that covered the sacred Body of our Saviour in the tomb. The Pall is a small square of folds of white linen used to cover the paten and chalice. The Purificator is a piece of white linen with a cross in the centre, folded lengthways in three folds, and used by the priest to wipe the chalice, as well as his lips, after the Communion. The Lavabo towel is the linen cloth with which the priest wipes his hands at the Sacrifice of the Mass. It is placed with the cruets, and handed to the officiating priest by the assistants. It is usual to employ three altar cloths of fine linen, the upper and most prominent one often being edged with lace or embroidery.

Ecclesiastical vestments and ornaments.

The vestments and ordinary garments worn by ecclesiastics are as follows: The Cassock—the long, closely-buttoned garb common to ecclesiastics of every grade—is of black, signifying humility and penitence; violet denotes the episcopal dignity; red is worn by Cardinals; and white is exclusively the costume of the Pope. The Biretta is a cap with three and sometimes four projecting corners, worn by priests, deacons, and subdeacons during the less solemn portions of High Mass. The Amice is a piece of white linen, oblong in shape, with a cross near the centre, worn by the priest over his shoulders under the alb. It is symbolical of the cloth bound over the face of our Saviour when the Jews struck Him, bidding Him prophesy who had dealt the blows. The Alb is a long loose garment of white linen frequently bordered with lace or embroidery, signifying innocence and sanctity; and is emblematic of the robe in which our Redeemer was clothed when He appeared before Herod. The alb is worn by the celebrant at Holy Mass, and also by the deacon and subdeacon at solemn High Mass. The Rochet is a much shorter vestment than the alb, and is distinguished from the surplice by the close-fitting sleeves reaching to the hands. It is worn by bishops and abbots, and also by some other dignitaries of the Church, as, for instance, some Canons by virtue of privilege. The lace on the cuffs is turned over black, violet, or scarlet, according to the distinction of the wearer. The Cincture is a girdle fastened round the waist, binding the alb. It represents the ropes used in the Passion of our Lord, and is emblematic of chastity. The surplice is a short white linen garment worn over the cassock in choir and in the administration of the Sacraments. It is symbolical of the new life of our Lord, which should radiate from His ministers in acts outflowing from holiness and all Christian virtues.

The Chasuble is the vestment of a priest celebrating the Sacrifice of the Mass. It is usually of precious material, reaching to about the knees in front, a little lower at the back, and is open at the sides. It represents the purple robe in which our Saviour was derisively arrayed by Pilate's soldiers, and is expressive of the charity and perfect patience with which He bore those indignities for us. The Cross on the back represents our Redeemer's Passion, and the sufferings that preceded it. The Stole is a narrow vestment, often of costly stuff, and of the same texture as the chasuble used at Mass. It is about four inches wide, with a cross embroidered at each end and one in the centre. The stole is worn by the priest round his neck and across his breast, during Mass, and whenever the alb is used, being kept in place by the girdle; otherwise it is allowed to hang straight down. A deacon is privileged to wear it, but only over his left shoulder, fastened at the right side. When a bishop wears it, both ends remain pendant without crossing, since he has already on his breast the pectoral cross. The Pope always wears it. The stole indicates the right of administering the Sacraments, and signifies the innocence and immortality lost through the sin of Adam and restored by the merits of our Blessed Lord. The Maniple is a piece of material of the same colour and quality as the stole and chasuble, with a cross embroidered on the centre and at each end: it is worn at High Mass only, by the priest, deacon, and subdeacon, on the left arm, hanging at equal length on both sides. It represents the cords which tied the hands of our Saviour, and signifies the fruit of good works laboriously accomplished. The Dalmatic worn by deacons, and the Tunic or Tunicle worn by subdeacons, are vestments of the same colour and texture as the officiating priest's chasuble, and differ little from each other in shape. They symbolize justice and joy, and the strength that is given by grace and the practice of good works. The Humeral veil is a long scarf of the same material as the vestments, worn by the subdeacon over his shoulders from the " Offertory " to the " Pater," while he holds the paten in assisting at High Mass. It is also worn by the Priest when giving Benediction, and in processions of the Blessed Sacrament, and when the Blessed Sacrament is removed from one place to another : the humeral veil then used being always white. The Cope is a long loose vestment in shape like a cloak, descending nearly to the feet, open in front and fastened at the neck by a clasp. It is of white silk when worn during the Asperging before Mass, and at Benediction, because presumed to be symbolical of a glorious immortality; and is of black, violet, or red on different other occasions.

Distinctive ecclesiastical ornaments.

In addition to the foregoing, there are certain distinctive pontifical ornaments, proper to the use of the highest dignitaries of the Church. Those common to the Pope, Cardinals, and bishops are eight in number. For example: the pectoral Cross is of gold, hanging by a chain round the neck of a Cardinal or bishop, as a sign of constant protection by the Cross of our Saviour, and worn in continual remembrance of His Passion. The episcopal ring symbolizes unvarying fidelity to our holy religion, and is kissed by the faithful as a token of their adherence and submission to the authority of the Church before receiving the Sacred Host, and at least in public receptions. The Crozier signifies power to govern with gentleness and to administer correction within the limits of the holder's jurisdiction. The bishop's mitre has two points, that may be considered figurative of the Old and New Testaments strengthening his mind and will against the adversaries of the Church. It is always white, or white and gold, signifying the chastity that should preserve the senses having their chief seat in the head, from any impurity. The Pope also uses the mitre in religious cere-monies; but when acting as supreme head of the Church, he wears the Tiara, which is a triple crown, significant of his threefold authority over the Church militant, the Church suffering, and the Church triumphant.

The Liturgy used in the West is always in the Latin language, so that the various ceremonies may be identical, in conformity with the Unity and Catholicity of the Church. Further, because Latin is more suited to the Mass than a language changeable and common to the multitude, being used chiefly by scholars in all branches of science, and by theologians. But the full meaning of the Latin prayers should be taught to the faithful by their pastors, and can be generally understood and followed through the trans-lation given in the vernacular. Some few words of Greek and Hebrew are introduced into the liturgy, helping to denote union of nations in the Catholic Church, and as a token of homage to the liturgical languages employed by the Apostles—a kind of recognition that the Sacrifice of our days is identical with that offered by the Apostles

Liturgical use of the Latin language.

themselves in the Churches founded by them. This uniting of the three languages, used in the Liturgy of the Mass, dates back even to the inscription on the cross of our Blessed Lord, written in Hebrew, Greek, and Latin.

Liturgical books.   The Missal, used by the priest, contains all the prayers and ceremonies of Holy Mass, proper for the different days throughout the year. The Ritual is a book of prayers and ceremonies for the administration of the Sacraments, benedictions, funeral services, processions, etc. The Pontifical is a volume of ecclesiastical rites and prayers, relating to the special functions of a bishop. The Ceremonial of bishops is a book containing in detail the ceremonies connected with solemn and important occasions on which a bishop officiates. The Martyrology is a register of the names of Saints and Martyrs honoured by the Church. The Breviary is an abbreviation of the ancient office, comprising a summary of the principal portions of Scripture, especially the Psalms; also the lives of the greatest of the Saints, and some most beautiful prayers of the Church, for the daily use of ecclesiastics in Major Orders.

CHAPTER LI.

THE HOLY SACRIFICE OF THE MASS.

BEFORE the celebration of High Mass on Sundays and certain other days, the priest administers the "Asperges," or sprinkling of holy water, by way of preparation through purification for the great Sacrifice that is about to be offered, and to drive away evil spirits. This blessing we should receive in faith and humility, praying with contrite heart that God may cleanse us from our sins, and purify our thoughts and intentions, through the merits of our Lord Jesus Christ. *Aspersion of holy water.*

The ceremonies of Holy Mass may be divided into three principal sections. The first part extends to the "Offertory," and recalls the time of waiting, from the fall of our first parents to the triumphal entry of our Saviour into Jerusalem. The second part is from the "Offertory" to the "Agnus Dei," and represents our Saviour's Passion and Death on the Cross; and the third part is figurative of our Lord's descent into Limbo, the time He passed among His Apostles after His Resurrection, and the last blessing He gave them at His Ascension. *Ceremonies and constituent parts of the Mass.*

At the commencement of Holy Mass, the celebrant bows towards the Crucifix with profound humility, in *Before the altar, at the commencement of the Mass.*

remembrance of the first offering made by our Saviour of Himself to God the Father, for the Redemption of the world. Then, standing below the first step of the altar, he and the people with him make the sign of the Cross, saying, "In nomine Patris, et Filii, et Spiritus Sancti, Amen," in memory of the Sacrifice on Mount Calvary, and because the priest, by the authority of God and the power of the Holy Spirit, is about to offer the same Victim, Jesus Christ.

"Judica me Deus."

The celebrant then assumes the attitude of a repentant sinner, and, with hands joined, recites the psalm, "Judica me Deus," expressive of his desire to ascend to the altar, and of his confidence in God. This psalm is omitted in Masses for the dead, and from Passion Sunday to Good Friday inclusively, on account of the words "quare tristis es anima mea et quare conturbas me?" "Why art thou sad, O my soul, and why dost thou disquiet me?"

"Confiteor."

Bending down in great humility and contrition, the priest says the "Confiteor," striking his breast three times at the words, "mea culpa, mea culpa, mea maxima culpa," in token of sorrow, imploring the intercession of the Blessed Virgin and the saints, and the prayers of the faithful, that God may be disposed to forgive the sins thus confessed before men to Him. The assistants repeat the "Confiteor," and the people in like manner silently avouch their sins to God, calling upon the priest for the aid of his prayers. After which a mutual appeal is made to God for absolution and remission of sins.

The priest kisses the altar.

The priest ascends the altar steps while praying, kisses, and then, at High Mass, incenses the altar. Such kiss is given nine times during the course of the Mass, as a mark of honour and veneration towards the Saints, some of whose relics have been there placed by the bishop at the consecration of the altar, and whose lives have been devoted to God, and further as a token of filial devotion to our Saviour, represented by the consecrated stone. The nine occasions referred to occur before the "Introit," before the "Collect," before the "Offertory," at the "Orate fratres," at the "Te igitur," at the "Supplices," before and after the "Post Communion," and before the "Benediction."

The priest reads the "Introit" of the day at the right The "Introit." side of the altar. The name of this prayer in itself signifies entry in close proximity to the tabernacle. It was sung originally by the Clerus, or the Clergy, as they entered the choir. A portion of this prayer generally recalls the desires of the Prophets and Patriarchs, for the coming of the Messias.

The "Kyrie Eleison" is begun by the priest, as he stands " Kyrie Eleison." facing the Cross, and by the assistants alternately, being in conjunction with the "Christe Eleison," repeated nine times, to remind us that we cannot too often implore our Saviour's mercy for all our sins and the necessities of life. These invocations are in Greek.

" The Gloria in excelsis Deo " is a canticle of admiration, "Gloria in excelsis Deo." praise, gratitude, and joy, recalling the nativity of our Saviour and the hymn of praise sung by the Angels at Bethlehem. At High Mass, the priest intones the first few words, raising his hands, to indicate that we should elevate our hearts to God, then joining them immediately, as if to grasp the "peace" that is promised "to men of good will," while the chant is continued by the choir. An inclination of the head is made at the name "Jesu Christe," and again during the words, "suscipe deprecationem nostram." The "Gloria in excelsis Deo" is omitted in Masses for the dead, during Advent and Lent, and on the three Rogation days, because it is not suitable to sing of joy when our hearts are filled with sadness, both on account of the souls in Purgatory and for our own sins.

" Dominus vobiscum."   The celebrant then turns and addresses the people with the words, "Dominus Vobiscum." This salutation is made by him eight times during the course of the Mass, praying, in common with those assembled, that the grace of our Saviour's Redemption may be always with the faithful, and that by this Redemption the prayers of the faithful may be favourably heard. The answer, "Et cum spiritu tuo," is the same wish reiterated towards the priest as mediator between the faithful and God, showing a unity of heart between the prayers of the people and those of the celebrant—a unity which belongs to the very soul of the Christian religion. At this point in the Mass, a bishop substitutes "Pax vobiscum" for the words of the ordinary priest, because our Lord thus addressed His disciples after His Resurrection, and a bishop more particularly impersonates our Saviour.

The "Collects."   Before reading the "Collects"—signifying "summary of devotions" or "assembling of the faithful" (both interpretations being admitted by grave authors)—the celebrant says, "Oremus." This exhortation to pray, which constantly recurs in the Mass, is meant to stimulate our feelings of piety and to concentrate our attention in prayer that the supplications of those assembled may be heard. The priest then recites the Collects of the day, with his hands extended, in imitation of the Saviour of mankind, who prayed for us with His arms outstretched on the Cross.

The response, "Amen" given here, and again frequently "Amen. occurring throughout the liturgy of the Church, is a Hebrew word, signifying "truly," "certainly," meaning that the foregoing prayer of the priest contains the thoughts and intentions of the people, which they ratify by this simple reply of consent and confirmation.

The "Epistle" is an instruction taken from Scripture, The and recited by the priest standing on the right-hand side of "Epistle." the altar, and chanted, in solemn High Mass, by the sub-deacon. Its origin is, that before the coming of our Lord, the Jews read from the Books of the Law and the Prophets, in their reunions of the Sabbath. This was a custom adhered to by the Apostles, who read portions of the Old Testament relating chiefly to the Holy Eucharist, instituted in the new Law by our Lord Jesus Christ. The Epistle further signifies all that was as a preparation for the advent of our Saviour and His founding of the new Law. The response of the assistants, " Deo gratias," is an exclamation of thanks to God for the means of knowledge He has to us afforded by His teaching.

The "Gradual," made up of some verses of a psalm, or The "Gradual." an anthem, taken from Holy Scripture, is not said during Paschal time, and is omitted in Lent, and during the octave of Pentecost. The reason of this is variously explained by different authors.

The word, "Alleluia," chanted after the "Gradual," The "Alleluia." is a Hebrew word, and is an expression of joy signifying praise to the Lord. It is omitted on days of penance or mourning.

The "Tract," in substitution of the " Alleluia," is sung The "Tract." at High Mass with slow solemnity ; and in certain Masses, the "Alleluia" is followed by what is called the "Prose" or "Sequence," which is only rarely used.

"Munda cor meum." The priest, standing near the centre of the altar, bows his head profoundly, praying God to purify his heart and his lips as a preparation for the reading of the Gospel ; and by a second supplication, appeals for God's blessing, that he may read the Gospel worthily. Or, if a deacon is assisting at High Mass, he recites the first prayer, "Munda cor meum," and the celebrant says the second in his name, giving a blessing.

The "Gospel." The priest passes to the further side of the altar when the "Gospel" is recited, to symbolize the preaching of the Gospel, rejected by the Jews and then accepted by the Gentiles. At High Mass the deacon in like manner. A sign of the Cross is made on the Missal, signifying that in it is written the life of Christ crucified ; then on the forehead, mouth, and heart, meaning that we should never be ashamed to believe in the Cross of our Saviour, but remain constant in our belief and profession of loyalty to it, that we may reap the reward of justice and faith. The Gospel is chanted by the priest or deacon, and listened to by the people, standing, thus proclaiming our readiness to obey the dictates of our Master and be devoted to His service even at the peril of our lives. The assistants, at the end, say, "Laus Tibi Christe," in praise of Him we serve; and, in conclusion, the priest kisses the book, saying, "Per evangelica dicta deleantur nostra delicta;" "By the words of the Gospel may our sins be blotted out," except in Masses for the dead, when the Gospel has not been read directly for the salvation of those who listen. At this point a sermon is preached—if High Mass is being celebrated, at least—or some pastoral letter read; in accordance with the commands of our Saviour, that His pastors should give instruction, as He Himself did when teaching in the Synagogue, and elsewhere.

The "Nicene Creed" is a profession of faith sung on The "Credo." Sundays and on certain feast days, by the choir, and said in silence by the people. The first words, "Credo in unum Deum," are intoned by the priest, who extends and raises his hands, indicative that the grace of faith comes from God, from whom descends every good and perfect gift. During the words, "Et incarnatus est de Spiritu Sancto ex Maria Virgine, et homo factus est," the congregation, together with the celebrant, kneel, in adoration of our Saviour, and reverence towards the great mysteries of the Incarnation and Redemption.

The "Offertory" follows, during which a collection is The "Offertory." commonly made in support of the clergy. This offering, in former ages, consisted in presentation of bread, wine, and other gifts for the needs of the Church, the pastors, and the poor.

The celebrant, facing the centre of the altar, lifts his Oblation of the Host. eyes towards Heaven, and then offers in his own name and that of all the faithful, both living and dead, the bread placed on the paten, to God the Father Eternal. After pronouncing the last words of the prayer, "Suscipe, sancte Pater," he makes a sign of the Cross with the paten and host about to be consecrated, above the corporal and over the centre cross of the altar stone, because our Saviour's Sacrifice of Himself was accomplished on the Cross, and to show, by this movement towards the different parts of the earth, that the oblation is made for the salvation of all.

Oblation of the chalice.

The priest next pours wine into the chalice, and adding a small quantity of water, prays that, by the mystery of this wine and water, we may become partakers of the Divinity of our Saviour, and then offers the chalice to Almighty God. In solemn High Mass the deacon offers it together with the celebrant. Then, making a sign of the Cross with the chalice, he replaces it on the corporal, and again makes a sign of the Cross with his hand over the chalice and the Host, while saying, " Veni, sanctificator omnipotens, æterne Deus; et benedic hoc sacrificium tuo sancto nomini præparatum."

The reason why water is mixed with the wine.

Water is mixed with the wine, because Tradition asserts that our Lord did this in accordance with the Jewish custom, during the feast of azymes, as the drinking of pure wine was considered too luxurious for such an occasion, the wine of Palestine being very strong. Water is also mixed with the wine in memory of the Blood and water that flowed from our Saviour's side, when pierced by the soldier's lance after His crucifixion ; to show, moreover, the union of the Humanity of our Lord with His Divinity, and furthermore the union of the faithful with their Redeemer, represented by the inseparable blending of the wine and water.

The Host for consecration.

The Host used for consecration in the Sacrifice of the Mass, is of bread unleavened, because our Lord, in cele-brating the feast of the Passover, and conforming to the Mosaic Law in the use of unleavened bread, employed it in instituting the Holy Eucharist ; but, according to Tradition, did not make it obligatory in the consecration at the altar.

The quality of the matter used for consecration.

If any different substance were used for consecration than unleavened or leavened bread, it would render the consecration null; and as azyme bread is commanded by the Church, a priest would commit mortal sin by employing leavened bread, though the consecration would be valid. The wine must be made from the unadulterated juice of the grape; and neither the bread nor the wine is to be consecrated singly, the "matter" of the Sacrament being both bread and wine. If one species were consecrated without the other, the act would be valid but sacrilegious; and if the officiating priest, having consecrated the bread, were unable, through sudden indisposition, to continue the Sacrifice, another priest should finish the Mass, even had he already broken his fast.

In solemn High Mass, incense is blessed by the celebrant, who then incenses the bread and wine and the altar, while praying that the mercy of God may descend on us, as the incense ascends towards Heaven; repeating the words of the Psalmist, "Dirigatur Domine oratio mea," and praying that our hearts may not incline our lips to speak evil in seeking excuse for our sins. Incense, being a symbol of the fragrance of charity and love, he adds, "Accendat in nobis Dominus ignem sui amoris, et flammam æternæ caritatis. Amen." *The incensing and accompanying prayers.*

The priest then moves to the Epistle side of the altar and washes the index finger and the thumb of both hands, since these have to touch the consecrated Host. At the same time he recites part of the twenty-fifth Psalm, beginning at the words, "Lavabo inter innocentes manus meas," adding the "Gloria Patri," which, however, is omitted in Masses for the dead, and from Passion Sunday until the day before Holy Thursday, inclusively. This ablution signifies that our souls should be purified more *"Lavabo."*

and more from fault and imperfection, as we journey through life and approach the day of union with our Saviour.

"Suscipe Sancta Trinitas." Standing before the centre of the altar, and with head bowed down, the priest says, "Suscipe Sancta Trinitas," praying that the Sacrifice offered in memory of the Passion and Resurrection of our Redeemer, and in honour of the Blessed Virgin and Saints, may be received by God; and that they, whose glory has its source in the merits of our Lord, may deign to intercede on our behalf.

"'Orate fratres." After having implored the help of Heaven, the priest turns to the faithful with the words, "Orate fratres," asking their prayers in favour of the oblation he is making for them as well as for himself. He extends his hands and re-unites them to symbolize the charity that should fill the heart of him who offers the Sacrifice, and which should be a bond of union among the people. Their answer, "Suscipiat Dominus," is a supplication that the Sacrifice may be accepted from the hands of the celebrant for the glory and honour of our Lord, and for the benefit of His holy Church; to which the priest responds, "Amen," as in confirmation of the desire expressed.

The "Secret." In a low but to others inaudible voice, the celebrant now recites a prayer changing with the day, called the "Secret," on account of the silence that prevails around; inspiring those present to dismiss all worldly considerations from their minds and concentrate their thoughts in prayer.

The "Preface." Then in a loud voice the priest recites, or at High Mass chants, the "Preface," exhorting the people to raise their hearts to God, and give thanks to the Lord. To this invitation they answer in assent. The "Preface" of the day is proceeded with, and at the words "Sanctus, sanctus, sanctus," the faithful all kneel at sound of the bell.

Immediately after the "Sanctus," commences the "Canon" of the Mass, so named because this portion is practically the same always, the word Canon meaning "fixed rule." It once was strictly forbidden to translate into the vernacular this most solemn portion of the Mass. The Canon, or fixed rite, is divided into three principal parts, forming the prayers before, during, and after the consecration, accompanied by many signs of the Cross, made by the priest in memory of our Lord's Passion and Crucifixion. Thus are we reminded, that the consecration of the Sacred species, the acceptance of the Sacrifice by God, and the fruit we therefrom derive, proceed from the Cross of our Lord Jesus Christ. The celebrant prays in silence during this part of the Mass, in remembrance of the three hours our Saviour passed on the Cross in prayer, when no word from Him broke the stillness, except His seven memorable last words, handed down to us in the Gospels. Not without interest is it to bear in mind that the priest raises his voice seven times between the "Offertory" and the "Communion;" namely, at the "Orate fratres," the "Preface," the "Nobis quoque peccatoribus," the "Paternoster," the "Pax Domini," the "Agnus Dei," and the "Domine non sum dignus."

The first part of the Canon begins by the words, "Te igitur, clementissime Pater," in which the priest prays for the whole of the Catholic Church, for its peace and unity, for the Pope, for the diocesan bishop, and for all orthodox believers in the true faith. The three signs of the Cross made by the priest at the words, "Benedicas haec dona,

The "Canon" of the Mass.

"Te igitur."

haec munera, haec sancta sacrificia illibata," when calling down the blessing of God on the holy Sacrifice, may recall how our Saviour was given up by God, by Judas, and by the Jews. But such interpretations are fanciful.

The "Memento" for the living. In the "Memento" for the living, the celebrant prays for the living members of the Church, naming those for whom he wishes to offer special supplication.

"Hanc igitur." In the prayer, "Hanc igitur oblationem," when the bell rings and the second part of the Canon commences, the priest spreads his hands over the Host and Chalice, signifying that he and the people with him offer themselves in sacrifice to the Eternal Father. The celebrant meanwhile implores God to have mercy on himself and all the faithful who are present; to deign to give them peace in this life, to preserve them from eternal condemnation, and to receive them among the elect of Heaven.

"Quam oblationem." Finally, in the prayer, "Quam oblationem," the celebrant prays God to bless the offering of the Sacrifice, that it may be acceptable in His sight; making the sign of the Cross three times at the words, "Benedictam, adscriptam, ratam, rationabilem, acceptabilemque facere digneris," to remind us, some have capriciously imagined, that our Lord was sold to the priests, the scribes, and the pharisees. He supplicates the Almighty to work the miracle of Transubstantiation, adding two signs of the Cross, at the words, "Ut nobis corpus et sanguis fiat dilectissimi Filii tui Domini nostri Jesu Christi," to designate Judas the traitor and Jesus whom he sold. Another arbitrary notion.

Consecration of the Host. Just before the first words of the Consecration, at the "Qui, pridie quam pateretur," the celebrant takes the Host in his hands, impersonating our Lord at the Last

Supper, who announced the sufferings He was so shortly
to undergo. In remembrance of these, the priest makes the
sign of the Cross at the consecration of the bread, and again
at the consecration of the wine, calling down God's blessing
just before pronouncing the words effecting the transubstantiation. At this moment Christ the Supreme Priest
speaks through the intermediary of His minister, who says,
"Hoc est enim Corpus Meum," after which he genuflects,
adores, and elevates the Sacred Host in sight of the people,
while the bell rings to give warning that the Holy Act
is being or has been fulfilled. Having repeated the words
of consecration, "Hic est enim calix Sanguinis Mei," he Consecration
of the chalice.
does the same with the Chalice, as with the Host, then
replaces it on the corporal, while the bell is once more rung.

During the Elevation, as previously at the incensing of the
altar, the assistant lifts the border of the priest's chasuble,
conformably to a custom prevalent in bygone times, when
this vestment was of a more voluminous and unwieldy
shape, interfering with the easy movements of the
celebrant.

The third part of the "Canon" commences with the "Unde et
memores."
words, "Unde et memores," declaring the actual Presence
of the Victim sacrificed on the altar, expressing grateful
recognition of the Passion, Resurrection, and Ascension of
our Lord, and a supplication that the eternal Father may,
in propitiation for our sins, accept the Body and Blood
of His Divine Son, as a Sacrifice holy and immaculate. In representation of the five wounds of our Saviour,
the priest makes a sign of the Cross five times while
offering the Sacred Host and Chalice of eternal life to God
the Father, saying, "Hostiam puram, Hostiam sanctam,

312 CATHOLIC DOCTRINE AND DISCIPLINE.

Hostiam immaculatam, Panem sanctum vitæ aeternæ, et Calicem salutis perpetuæ."

"Supplices." The outstretching of our Lord's Body on the Cross, the flowing forth of His precious Blood, and the fruit of His Passion are represented by the two signs of the Cross the priest makes over the Holy Eucharist, and that made on himself, in the prayer, "Supplices Te rogamus;" while entreating the blessing and grace of Heaven for all those who receive the Body and Blood of our Saviour: "Ut quotquot, ex hac altaris participatione, sacrosanctum Filii Tui Corpus et Sanguinem sumpserimus, omni benedictione cœlesti et gratia repleamur."

The "Memento" for the dead. Then follows the "Memento" for the dead, imploring the deliverance of the souls from Purgatory, of those who have gone before us with profession of faith, and sleep the sleep of peace.

"Nobis quoque peccatoribus." At the "Nobis quoque peccatoribus," which concludes the "Canon," the celebrant strikes his breast in recognition of his own sinfulness and that of the congregation, at the same time expressing hope and confidence in the divine mercy of God, that we may participate in the glories of Heaven; not by the merit of our own works, but by the merits of our Redeemer, assisted by the intercession of the Saints. At the words, "Sanctificas, vivificas, benedicis," the priest makes, with the Host in his right hand, three signs of the Cross, over the Chalice, held in his left, in memory, some have thought, of Christ's three prayers on the Cross, namely, "Father, forgive them, for they know not what they do.[1] ... My God, My God, why hast Thou forsaken Me.[2] ... Father, into Thy hands I commend My spirit."[3] Again,

[1] Luke xxiii. 34.   [2] Matt. xxvii. 46.   [3] Luke xxiii. 46.

to remind us that our Saviour passed three hours on the Cross, the priest makes three signs of the Cross when saying, " Per ipsum, et cum ipso, et in ipso ; " and with the last words, " Est Tibi Deo Patri omnipotenti, in unitate Spiritus Sancti, omnis honor et gloria," two signs of the Cross are made outside the chalice, to represent the separation of the Soul and the Body of our Lord. These are pious, if not generally accepted, inferences. In terminating this prayer, the celebrant slightly elevates the chalice with the Host, offering in honour and glory of God the Body and Blood of our Saviour, in the two kinds, equally united in each part of each kind, by the miracle of Transubstantiation performed through the almighty power of God.

The priest breaks the silence with the words, " Per omnia saecula saeculorum," to which the assistants answer, " Amen," The " Pater Noster." in token of assent to all those demands he has just made to God the Father, in the name of the Son who lives and reigns for ever and ever. As preparation for Communion, and in accordance with the Apostles' habit of reciting the Lord's Prayer before the breaking of the Eucharistic bread, the celebrant says the " Pater," which in its simplicity and brevity, expresses all that we need ask of our Creator. After this he kisses the paten on which the Sacred Host has reposed, and breaks the Host, in imitation of our Saviour's act at the Last Supper. He divides it into three portions, to honour the mystery of the Blessed Trinity, and to signify the Communion of Saints in the three divisions of the Church : in Heaven, in Purgatory, and on earth. When the priest has broken the Holy Host in two equal halves, the part in his right hand represents the blessed of Heaven, who, after struggling victoriously to the end, are rewarded with peace and glory of which no power can deprive them. This is why the celebrant places it first upon the consecrated stone of the altar. With his right hand he breaks off a small portion from the lower end of the other half, and the part then remaining in his left hand represents those suffering for a time who have not yet attained to celestial happiness. As the term of expiation in Purgatory leaves no doubt of ultimate union in Heaven, the priest deposes it with the former, on the paten. With the third part, which is symbolical of the faithful on earth, he makes three signs of the Cross over the chalice, in remembrance of the three days our Saviour passed in the heart of the earth before His Resurrection. So pious authors have explained this matter. The priest meanwhile prays that the gift of Divine peace which our Lord's death gave to the world may descend upon the people: "Pax Domini sit semper vobiscum," and the people respond, begging this favour to be granted also to himself. The celebrant then drops this remaining portion of the Host into the chalice, signifying that they who have still to battle against evil, can triumph only by virtue of the Body and Blood of our Blessed Lord. Then he covers the chalice, as the Jews covered the entrance to our Redeemer's tomb.

"Pax Domini."

After the words, "Haec commixtio," the priest recites the "Agnus Dei," striking his breast three times, at the words, "miserere nobis," "miserere nobis," and "dona nobis pacem," asking mercy of the Lamb of God, who took upon Himself the sins of the world. But in Masses for the dead, the concluding words are changed to, "Dona eis requiem," and "Dona eis requiem sempiternam." The

"Agnus Dei."

repetition of the "Agnus Dei" is, according to some, in honour of the three conditions of our Lord's humanity, and of the triple object for which He descended from Heaven, lived on earth, reposed in the tomb, and reigned in celestial glory; namely, to preserve us from sin, to deliver us from eternal punishment, and to afford us a means of participating in Divine grace.

In solemn High Mass, the kiss of peace, with the words "Pax tecum," is given by the officiating priest to the deacon, who answers, "Et cum spiritu tuo;" and in the same manner it is passed from deacon to subdeacon, and successively to the rest of the clergy, as a sign of the charity that should unite the hearts of all Christians in communion with each other. In Masses for the dead this kiss of peace is omitted, as likewise the first of the three prayers that follow the "Agnus Dei," which essentially concerns the Church militant. These three prayers are addressed directly to our Saviour, the Victim of propitiation on the altar, to whom the priest appeals for the three graces demanded immediately before Communion, namely, that he may be freed from all sinfulness, adhere to the law of God, and receive from it not cause of condemnation, but rather a help to the salvation of body and soul.

The kiss of peace.

The celebrant takes both parts of the Sacred Host between the thumb and forefinger of his left hand, and the paten between the first and second finger of the same hand, saying the "Domine non sum dignus" three times, significant, as some will have it, of the three ways in which man may sin; through spiritual, intellectual, and physical means: by thoughts, words, and actions. The bell is rung at each repetition of the words.

"Domine non sum dignus."

316 CATHOLIC DOCTRINE AND DISCIPLINE.

The priest's
communion. Then, taking the Host in his right hand, and making with it a sign of the Cross over the paten and in front of his breast, in token of his faith in the Divine Presence, the celebrant says, " Corpus Domini nostri Jesu Christi custodiat animam meam in vitam æternam. Amen." Inclining profoundly, he receives the Sacred Host, places the paten on the corporal, and remains a short time with joined hands in adoration and thanksgiving. Then, having collected with the paten whatever particles of the Host may have been left on the corporal, he conveys them to the chalice, saying, " Quid retribuam Domino pro omnibus, quæ retribuit mihi ? " Afterwards the celebrant takes the chalice in his right hand, and with it makes the sign of the Cross over himself, saying, "Sanguis Domini nostri Jesu Christi custodiat animam meam in vitam æternam. Amen." He receives the Communion of the chalice in three separate draughts, representing thus, as explained by some, the mystery of the Holy Trinity, and belief in our Saviour's being equal in Godhead with the Father and the Holy Spirit.

If there are intending communicants among the faithful present, it is at this time that the Holy Sacrament is administered.

The first
ablution. For the first ablution a little wine is poured into the chalice, which the priest takes, praying that what we have received with our mouth may be received also with a pure mind, that it may become to us an eternal remedy : " Quod ore sumpsimus Domine, pura mente capiamus ; " and that no stain of sin may remain in him after this reception of the Blessed Sacrament. Then wine and water being poured over the priest's fingers, he drinks this second ablution, and
The second
ablution.

replaces the paten, chalice, and corporal, covering them with the veil, as at the commencement of the Mass.

Returning to the right-hand side of the altar, the celebrant reads the "Communion" of the day, followed by the "Post Communion." *The "Communion" and the "Post Communion."*

After turning towards the people and pronouncing the last "Dominus Vobiscum," the priest says the "Ite, Missa est," which at High Mass the deacon intones, as sentence *"Ite, missa est."* of dismissal, showing that the Sacrifice is accomplished, and signifying his belief that our prayers have been favourably entertained by the all-powerful Advocate, who will plead for us and defend our interests, interceding with our Heavenly Father for all the sinners of the world; to which a response of thanksgiving is uttered in the words, "Deo gratias." During Advent and Lent, and at all times when the "Gloria in excelsis" is not said, the "Ite, Missa est" is also omitted, the "Benedicamus Domino" being substituted as an exhortation to continue in praise and thanksgiving to the Lord. In Masses for the dead these words are changed for a supplication for the repose of their souls: "Requiescant in pace."

Bowing before the altar, the priest says the prayer, "Placeat Tibi, sancta Trinitas," imploring the acceptance *The Benediction.* of the Sacrifice he has just offered. Then, kissing the altar, —a figure of our Lord Jesus Christ, from whom all blessings come—he raises his eyes towards Heaven, extends his hands as if to grasp the heavenly gift he craves, bows to the Crucifix, and says, "Benedicat vos omnipotens Deus, Pater, et Filius, et Spiritus Sanctus," turning to the people after the word "Deus," and making the sign of the Cross over them, the assistants answering, "Amen." This benediction is omitted in Masses for the dead, because they can no longer be present to receive it.

"The last Gospel." Tracing the sign of the Cross on the altar, and on his forehead, lips, and heart, the priest reads the opening portion of the Gospel of St. John, kneeling at the words, "Et Verbum caro factum est." This Gospel is changed only under exceptional circumstances, when a special one for some feast has to be read in its place.

"Deo gratias." The holy Sacrifice of the Mass is terminated by the words "Deo gratias," expressive of thanksgiving to the Father, who gave His Son for us; to the Son, who took the form of man for our salvation: to the Holy Spirit, by whom we are sanctified in Christ Jesus; thus to the three persons of the Holy Trinity, for all the gifts and infinite mercies bestowed upon us.

CHAPTER LII.

THE ADMINISTRATION OF BAPTISM.

THE ceremony of Baptism is preceded by the priest going to meet the child at the Church door, signifying its unworthiness to enter the house of God before the Covenant of Baptism has been concluded. Then he inquires what the child demands of the Church, which is done because the Sacrament of Baptism can only be conferred on those who ask it. The priest forthwith proceeds with a short exhortation on the principal truths of the Christian doctrine, the knowledge of such being obligatory for those capable of understanding, and in default of this, for those standing as sponsors for an infant. After which he breathes lightly three times on the face of the child, indicating the near approach of the Holy Spirit in its soul, and that the grace of sanctification is the work of the three Persons of the Holy Trinity. The priest then makes the sign of the Cross on the forehead and on the breast of the child, as betokening the expulsion of the devil from its mind and heart. He then places his hand on the child, signifying the consecration of its body and soul to God, and in memory of our Lord having laid His hands upon children as a sign of affection and protection, and on the sick for their cure. The priest also puts into the child's mouth

Ceremonies preceding the administration of Baptism.

a little salt, emblematic of wisdom that should preserve its soul from the corruption of sin. Then, after certain prayers and signs of the Cross, he holds the end of his stole over the child, to show that he places it under the authority of the Church, and straightway conducts it to the baptistery, where the ceremony accompanying the Baptism is commenced.

Ceremonies accompanying the administration of Baptism.   The godparents, in the name of the infant, recite the Apostles' Creed and Lord's Prayer as a testimony of Faith and Hope, making also the solemn promises already explained on the subject of Baptism as a Sacrament. After which the priest moistens his finger with saliva and touches the ears of the child, saying, " Ephpheta," meaning, " Be thou opened ; " and adds, when touching its nostrils, " In odorem suavitatis," in remembrance of our Saviour doing this when healing the deaf and dumb. The person to be baptized, or the sponsors, if an infant, are interrogated as to the renounce-ment of Satan and all his works. Then the priest anoints the child on the breast and between the shoulders, with holy oil blessed by a bishop on Holy Thursday, signifying the gentleness and strength of the divine grace of our Lord, given in the Sacrament of Baptism. The profession of faith is most solemnly renewed in answer to three questions put successively by the priest, after he has changed the violet stole for a white one. This ceremony is indicative of a soul born in sin being purified and sanctified by this holy Sacrament; and, in the name of the child, the desire for receiving Baptism being again expressed, it is immedi-ately administered, with water blessed on Holy Saturday or on the eve of Pentecost. The priest pours the water on the child's head three times in the form of a Cross, saying

at the moment of each pouring, " N—, Ego te baptizo in
nomine Patris, et Filii, et Spiritus Sancti.   Amen." ·
The child is then anointed on its head in the form of
a cross, with the holy Chrism blessed on Holy Thursday,
signifying that it has been made a Christian by the gift
of justifying grace. The priest places on the head of the
child a white cloth, emblematic of the baptismal purity
and innocence it should treasure through life, and as a
sign of the beauty and glory of the life of sanctifying
grace given to the soul in this Sacrament.   Afterwards
the priest gives the godparents a lighted taper, which
they hold in the name of the child, signifying that the
newly made Christian should give forth the light of truth
and good works in the world, in readiness to meet the
heavenly Bridegroom at the Supper of the Lamb.   In
termination of the ceremony, the priest says, "Go in
peace, and the Lord be with you," as a blessing called
down upon the child. This is confirmed by the godparents, who answer, "Amen."

In the baptism of adults, the questions put by the priest
are answered by the adults themselves, not by the godparents.

Y

CHAPTER LIII.

THE ADMINISTRATION OF CONFIRMATION.

Ceremonies in the administration of Confirmation.

THE Sacrament of Confirmation is administered by a bishop, of right, exclusively. It is preceded by the chanting or recital of the hymn " Veni Creator." After various prayers said by the bishop, during which he extends his hands over the persons to be confirmed, invoking on them the seven gifts of the Holy Ghost, and making the sign of the Cross over them, he traces the sign of the Cross on the forehead of each person with the holy Chrism, calling them by the name they choose in Confirmation, saying, " N—, signo te signo Crucis, et confirmo te Chrismate salutis." The imposition of the bishop's hands signifies the abundant graces and gifts that descend on us through reception of the Holy Spirit in our souls. The act of anointing is expressive of the chief effect of this Sacrament, to strengthen us and give us courage to fight the great battle of life, that we may prove ourselves worthy to be called perfect Christians, and true disciples and warriors of the Cross. The oil, which forms part of the holy Chrism, denotes the strengthening and softening effect of the Holy Spirit in us. The balm signifies preservation from the corruption of sin, and its sweet perfume is emblematic of the good example we ought to give in following our Saviour by adhering to the practice of virtuous actions. The sign of the Cross made with the Holy Chrism, means that the virtue of the Sacrament comes through the merits of our Lord's death on the Cross, and that we should never be ashamed of confessing our loyal attachment to Christ crucified, and of proclaiming ourselves true Christians by word and deed. This sign is made on the forehead as being the most noble part of the body, and the seat of reason whence springs the choice between good and evil. The bishop gives a slight blow with his hand on the cheek of each person confirmed, to teach them that they should fear nothing in the service of God, but bear with patience and courage any contemptuous scoffing or persecution in the name of the Church and for love of our Saviour. While thus touching the face of the person, the bishop says, " Pax tecum," to show us that patience is the best means to obtain peace with God, our neighbour, and ourselves. The antiphon, "Confirma hoc Deus," is chanted, and after certain other prayers, the bishop, turning to the persons confirmed, makes the sign of the Cross over them, saying, "Benedicat vos Dominus ex Sion, ut videatis bona Jerusalem omnibus diebus vitæ vestræ, et habeatis vitam æternam." " May the Lord bless you out of Sion, that you may see the good things of Jerusalem all the days that you do live, and possess eternal life." The " Credo " and " Pater " are then recited by the bishop and by the persons confirmed.

CHAPTER LIV.

THE ADMINISTRATION OF HOLY COMMUNION.

Ceremonies in the administration of Communion.

THE administration of Holy Communion is commenced by the assistants reciting the "Confiteor" in the name of the communicants, as a public confession of sins, to which the priest responds by a general absolution, saying, "Misereatur vestri omnipotens Deus et dimissis peccatis vestris, perducat vos ad vitam æternam;" and, making a sign of the Cross over the people, he adds: "Indulgentiam, absolutionem, et remissionem peccatorum vestrorum tribuat vobis omnipotens et misericors Dominus." Then, taking the ciborium and elevating one of the Sacred Hosts, the priest says, "Ecce Agnus Dei, ecce qui tollit peccata mundi;" and repeats three times the "Domine non sum dignus;" then, descending the steps of the altar, he administers the holy Communion, saying to each person, "Corpus Domini nostri Jesu Christi custodiat animam tuam in vitam æternam. Amen." When Communion is administered out of Mass, the priest concludes by giving a blessing in these words: "Benedictio Dei omnipotentis, Patris, et Filii, et Spiritus Sancti descendat super vos et maneat semper. Amen." "May the blessing of Almighty God, Father, Son, and Holy Ghost, descend upon you, and remain with you for ever. Amen."

CHAPTER LV.

THE ADMINISTRATION OF PENANCE.

THE administration of the Sacrament of Penance is accompanied with but little ceremonial, because the Confession of sins, though no longer made in public, as it was in cases of public scandal in the early times of the Church, is a sacred rite of humiliation and contrition, in which all signs of outward show would be out of place. *Ceremonies in the administration of Penance.*

The confessional is the tribunal of justice founded by the authority of our Lord Jesus Christ, wherein He is represented by His ministers, who have power, from Himself, to remit or to retain sins, in the judgment they pronounce in His name.

The penitent begs the blessing of the priest, saying, "Pray, Father, give me your blessing, for I have sinned." And the priest answers, "Dominus sit in corde tuo et in labiis tuis ut rite et humiliter confitearis peccata tua, in nomine Patris, et Filii, et Spiritus Sancti. Amen." Which is translated: "May the Lord be in thy heart and on thy lips, that thou mayest truly and humbly confess thy sins, in the name of the Father, and of the Son, and of the Holy Ghost. Amen." Then the penitent, having recited the first part of the "Confiteor," avouches his sins, adding in conclusion: "For these and all my other sins which I cannot now remember, I am heartily sorry ; I purpose amendment for the future, and most humbly ask pardon of God, and penance and absolution of you my ghostly Father." After which, the penitent listens with respect and attention to the admonition, counsel, and penance enjoined by the confessor, who prays that our Lord may absolve him from all sins, as he does by virtue of Christ's authority, making the sign of the Cross while pronouncing the words of Absolution: "Deinde ego te absolvo a peccatis tuis, in nomine Patris, et Filii, et Spiritus Sancti. Amen." "Therefore I absolve thee from thy sins, in the name of the Father, and of the Son, and of the Holy Ghost. Amen." After which the priest prays that the Passion of our Lord, the merits of the Blessed Virgin and all the Saints, the penitent's good works, and his patience in trials, may be productive of the remission of his sins, giving increase of grace and promoting the attainment of everlasting life. Then, adding, not unfrequently, a request that the penitent would pray for him, the confessor dismisses him, with the words, "Go in peace," or some equivalent blessing.

CHAPTER LVI.

THE ADMINISTRATION OF EXTREME UNCTION.

AT the administration of Extreme Unction the priest, vested in a surplice and purple stole, gives the blessing with holy water, saying the " Asperges " and certain other prayers ; then the " Confiteor " is said, and a special benediction invoked on the sick person. If possible, the Penitential Psalms, or Litanies, or other prayers given in the Roman Ritual are recited while the priest is anointing the person sick unto death with holy oil, consecrated for this purpose by the bishop on Holy Thursday. The unction is applied to the eyes, ears, nostrils, mouth, hands, and feet, with a prayer at each anointing, that by this holy anointing and the most sweet mercy of God all sins committed, by means of these various senses and members of the body, may be pardoned. For these, being the principal organs of human activity, are as it were the doors by which sin may enter the soul. Then follow the " Kyrie eleison," " Pater," and prayers for the health of the body and soul of the sick person.

CHAPTER LVII.

THE ADMINISTRATION OF HOLY ORDER.

THE Sacrament of Ordination is administered by a bishop in a Church or Chapel. According to the ordinary law of the Church, the tonsure may be conferred on any day; the minor orders may be conferred on Sundays, on days of obligation, and on days formerly of obligation, but now of devotion, and on Ember Wednesdays and Fridays. The sacred Orders may be conferred only on Ember Saturdays, on the day before Passion Sunday, and on Holy Saturday. This is the general rule for all countries; but, by special privilege of the Holy See, the bishops of England and of other missionary countries may confer the sacred Orders on any Sunday, or holy day of obligation, or day of devotion.

Ceremonies preceding the administration of Holy Order.
The ceremony preceding the reception of Holy Order consists in the giving of the surplice and tonsure, which latter signifies detachment from the world, and represents our Saviour's crown of thorns. He who is to receive Holy Order, prostrates himself, in the sanctuary of the Church, with his face to the ground, during the recitation of the Litanies, to imitate our Lord in the garden of olives, and to intimate that he gives up the world and consecrates himself to the service of God.

For the ordination of a subdeacon, the aspirant touches the empty chalice and paten, held by the bishop, who places the amice on his shoulders, the maniple on his arm, and finally clothes him with the tunic; at each investment, pronouncing a formula of prayer, in connection with the objects he is bestowing. Ordination of a subdeacon.

The ceremony for elevating a subdeacon to the grade of deacon differs only in this, that the bishop commences by the imposition of hands, and invests the deacon with the stole, and dalmatic, then places the book of the Gospel in his hands, saying a special prayer at each separate occasion. Ordination of a deacon.

When a deacon is ordained priest, he must be accompanied by an ecclesiastical dignitary, who bears witness to his worthiness for elevation to the priesthood. The bishop explains the sacerdotal duties and functions, recites a prayer, and invests the newly made priest with the vestments peculiar to his order. Then, while the "Veni Creator" is sung, the bishop anoints the priest's hands with holy oil, on the inner side of the thumb and index finger, which have to come in contact with the Holy Eucharist; and the priest, touching the chalice containing wine and the paten with an unconsecrated host upon it, the bishop pronounces his right to celebrate the holy Sacrifice of the Mass. The newly ordained priest says Mass conjointly with the bishop, from the Offertory to the conclusion. After Communion, the priest recites the Apostles' Creed, as being a summary of the truths he is henceforth to preach. The priest's Ordination is terminated with a prayer to the Holy Spirit, and the imposition of hands from the bishop, giving him power to remit sins Ordination of a priest.

in the Sacrament of Penance. Then the kiss of peace is given and a special benediction.

Consecration of a bishop.   For the elevation of a priest to the dignity of the episcopate, a nomination must be obtained from the Pope, to whom the bishop designate makes a vow of fidelity. The book of the Gospel is placed upon his shoulders, to show that he must bear with strength and perseverance the burden of responsibility brought by his new appointment in the Church Catholic. The newly made bishop celebrates Mass with the three consecrating bishops, to symbolize the unity of the episcopacy that is one in spirit with the head of the Church ; and he forthwith commences his solemn functions by giving a blessing to the assembly, wearing his mitre, and holding his crozier in his left hand.

CHAPTER LVIII.

THE ADMINISTRATION OF MARRIAGE.

THE Sacrament of Matrimony should take place before the parents of the contracting parties, as evidence of their acquiescence; and always in presence of at least two witnesses besides the officiating priest.

The priest, vested in surplice and white stole, asks the man—who must stand before him at his right—his consent to the alliance, and puts the same question to the woman. Each in turn having answered in the affirmative, the Sacramental contract exists through the mutual consent of the parties. The woman is given away by a relative or friend, and the man, with his right hand, takes her right hand—which should be uncovered if she has not been married before—and repeats after the priest the words by which he plights his troth; the woman afterwards doing likewise. Their right hands being again joined, the priest pronounces the words of benediction, ratifying the conjugal alliance in God's name, and making the sign of the Cross over them while saying, "Ego conjungo vos in matrimonium, in nomine Patris, et Filii, et Spiritus Sancti. Amen." "I join you in matrimony, in the name of the Father, and of the Son, and of the Holy Ghost. Amen." He then sprinkles them with holy water, and blesses, in God's name, the ring and the pieces of gold or silver money which the man gives to the woman, as a pledge that he will maintain her according to his means in a Christian manner, and he then places the ring on the third finger of her left hand. The priest adds certain prayers, beginning: "Confirma hoc, Deus, quod operatus es in nobis," "Confirm, O God, what Thou hast worked in us," to which the assistants respond; and if Mass is to be said "pro sponso et sponsa" ("for the bridegroom and bride"), the celebrant turns towards them, immediately after the "Pater," saying two other prayers over them, and after his Communion and theirs—if they communicate—he gives them the nuptial benediction according to the form prescribed in the Missal, after the "Pater Noster," and again after the "Ite Missa est."

The nuptial benediction is not given in cases of second marriages, when the woman is a widow, nor in cases of mixed marriages.

INDEX.

PRINTED BY WILLIAM CLOWES AND SONS, LIMITED, LONDON AND BECCLES.

www.ingramcontent.com/pod-product-compliance
Lightning Source LLC
Chambersburg PA
CBHW021755110726
47902CB00006B/1530